In Memoriam

Jake Adam York
(1972 - 2012)

and

Jayne Cortez
(1934 - 2012)

PLOUGHSHARES
LITERARY MAGAZINE

Did you know that we have a regularly updated blog with posts about writing, reading, and publishing, from guest bloggers, plus book reviews and news?

Join us online:
Blog: blog.pshares.org
Website: www.pshares.org

Stay connected:
Tweet @Pshares
Facebook.com/Ploughshares

Also available on
nook by Barnes & Noble
amazon kindle

PLOUGHSHARES

Spring 2013 • Vol. 39, No. 1

GUEST EDITOR
Major Jackson

EDITOR-IN-CHIEF
Ladette Randolph

MANAGING EDITOR
Andrea Martucci

FICTION EDITOR
Margot Livesey

POETRY EDITOR
John Skoyles

PRODUCTION MANAGER
Akshay Ahuja

EDITORIAL ASSISTANTS
Alexandra Artiano & Abby Travis

SENIOR READERS
Sarah Banse, David Goldstein,
Wesley Rothman & Abby Travis

INTERNS
Ellen Duffer, Jordan Koluch
& Jon Simmons

COPY EDITOR
Carol Farash

BLOG EDITOR
Andrew Ladd

MARKETING ASSISTANT
Miriam Cook

ePUBLISHING CONSULTANT
John Rodzvilla

DIGITAL PUBL. ASSISTANTS
Jessica Arnold & Kathryn Deschamps

READERS
Jana Lee Balish | Mary Kovaleski Byrnes | Doug Paul Case
Anne Champion | Elizabeth Christensen | Marlena Clark | Susannah Clark
Lindsay D'Andrea | Elisabeth Denison | Nicole DiCello | Jennifer Feinberg
Diana Filar | Colleen Fullin | Joshua Garstka | Bethany Gordon | Kristine Greive
Adam Hanover | Amanda Hartzell | Mark Hengsteller | Rachel Inciarte
Ethan Joella | Eson Kim | Jordan Koluch | Aaron Krol | Renee Lamine
Karen Lonzo | Catherine Martin | LuzJennifer Martinez | Jean Mattes
Autumn McClintock | Caitlin McGill | Leslie McIntyre | Stephanie Mendoza
Marisela Navarro | Miranda Roberson | June Rockefeller | M. Austen Roe
Erin Salada | Mallory Schwan | Charlotte Seley | Stephen Shane
Alessandra Siraco | Matt Socia | Sarah Stetson | Katherine Sticca
Kristen Sund | Lauren Sypniewski | Sonja Vitow | Angela Voras-Hills
Ross Wagenhofer | Charles Walker | Caitlin Walls | Leah Welch | Caitlin White

ADVISORY BOARD
William H. Berman | DeWitt Henry | Alice Hoffman | Ann Leary
Tom Martin | Pam Painter | Janet Silver | Daniel Tobin | Marillyn Zacharis

FOUNDERS DeWitt Henry & Peter O'Malley

Ploughshares, a journal of new writing, is guest-edited serially by prominent writers who explore different personal visions, aesthetics, and literary circles. *Ploughshares* is published in April, August, and December at Emerson College 120 Boylston Street, Boston, MA 02116-4624. Telephone: (617) 824-3757. Web address: pshares.org. E-mail: pshares@pshares.org.

Advisory Editors: Sherman Alexie, Russell Banks, Andrea Barrett, Charles Baxter, Ann Beattie, Madison Smartt Bell, Anne Bernays, Frank Bidart, Amy Bloom, Robert Boswell, Henry Bromell, Rosellen Brown, Ron Carlson, James Carroll, David Daniel, Madeline DeFrees, Mark Doty, Rita Dove, Stuart Dybek, Cornelius Eady, Martín Espada, B. H. Fairchild, Nick Flynn, Carolyn Forché, Richard Ford, George Garrett, Lorrie Goldsohn, Mary Gordon, Jorie Graham, David Gullette, Marilyn Hacker, Donald Hall, Patricia Hampl, Joy Harjo, Kathryn Harrison, Stratis Haviaras, Terrance Hayes, DeWitt Henry, Edward Hirsch, Jane Hirshfield, Tony Hoagland, Alice Hoffman, Fanny Howe, Marie Howe, Gish Jen, Justin Kaplan, Bill Knott, Yusef Komunyakaa, Maxine Kumin, Don Lee, Philip Levine, Margot Livesey, Thomas Lux, Gail Mazur, Campbell McGrath, Heather McHugh, James Alan McPherson, Sue Miller, Lorrie Moore, Paul Muldoon, Antonya Nelson, Jay Neugeboren, Howard Norman, Tim O'Brien, Joyce Peseroff, Carl Phillips, Jayne Anne Phillips, Robert Pinsky, Alberto Ríos, Lloyd Schwartz, Jim Shepard, Jane Shore, Charles Simic, Gary Soto, Elizabeth Spires, David St. John, Maura Stanton, Gerald Stern, Mark Strand, Elizabeth Strout, Christopher Tilghman, Richard Tillinghast, Colm Tóibín, Chase Twichell, Jean Valentine, Fred Viebahn, Ellen Bryant Voigt, Dan Wakefield, Derek Walcott, Rosanna Warren, Alan Williamson, Eleanor Wilner, Tobias Wolff, C. D. Wright, Al Young, Kevin Young

Subscriptions (ISSN 0048-4474): $30 for one year (3 issues), $50 for two years (6 issues); $39 a year for institutions. Add $30 a year for international ($10 for Canada).

Upcoming: Fall 2013, a fiction issue edited by Peter Ho Davies, will be published in August 2013. Winter 2013-14, a staff-edited poetry and prose issue, will be published in December 2013.

Submissions: Ploughshares has an updated reading period, as of June 1, 2010. The new reading period is from June 1 to January 15 (postmark and online dates). All submissions sent from January 16 to May 31 will be returned unread. Please see page 229 for editorial and submission policies, or visit our website: pshares.org/submit.

Back-issue, classroom-adoption, and bulk orders may be placed directly through *Ploughshares*. *Ploughshares* is also available as full-text products from EBSCO, H. W. Wilson, JSTOR, ProQuest, and the Gale Group. Indexed in M.L.A. Bibliography, Humanities International Index, Book Review Index. Full publishers' index is online at pshares.org. The views and opinions expressed in this journal are solely those of the authors. All rights for individual works revert to the authors upon publication. *Ploughshares* receives support from the National Endowment for the Arts and the Massachusetts Cultural Council.

Retail distribution by Ingram Periodicals, Media Solutions, and Ubiquity. Printed in the U.S.A. by The Sheridan Press.

Major Jackson photo by Erin Patrice O'Brien.

© 2013 by Emerson College   ISBN 978-1-933058-99-3
                             ISSN 0048-4474

CONTENTS
Spring 2013

INTRODUCTION
Major Jackson   7

FICTION
Emily Bernard, *What Happens Next*   15
David Huddle, *Brief Encounter with the Household Gods*   46
Elise Juska, *Transfer Station*   53
Szidónia Molnár, *Andorra*   83
Sherri Phillips, *The Rubber Game*   109
David James Poissant, *Monkey See*   130
Anna Solomon, *Alan at the Kirschbergs'*   150
Kimberly Swayze, *Church*   168

POETRY
Peter Balakian, *Pueblo I, New Mexico*   9
Sandra Beasley, *Ukulele*   12
Erin Belieu, *The Body Is a Big Sagacity*   13
Traci Brimhall, *What We Lost in the Flood—*   32
Jericho Brown, *Another Elegy*   33
Stephen Browning, *Knowledge*   34
Maggie Dietz, *Demolition Derby*   35
Mark Doty, *Deep Lane*   37
Jaclyn Dwyer, *Praise Poem for American Girls*   39
Martín Espada, *Of the Threads That Connect the Stars*   41
Didi Gibbs, *The Florida Sandhill Crane*   42
Nathalie Handal, *Salt on the Tongue*   44
Tony Hoagland, *Crossing Water*   50
    The Complex Sentence   52
Laura Kasischke, *The Martyr's Motel*   68
    You tell me   70
Joanna Klink, *The Graves*   71
Rebecca Lehmann, *Swan Road*   72
Alex Lemon, *Dance Dance Dance*   74
Jamaal May, *Masticated Light*   76

Jeffrey McDaniel, *The Birds and the Bees*	78
Beware of the Dark Sedan Idling Inside You	79
Erika Meitner, *Porto, Portare, Portavi, Portatus*	80
Fred Moten, *test*	95
Harryette Mullen, *Tanka Diary*	100
Vi Khi Nao, *The Room in Five Moods of Cannots*	101
Jay Nebel, *Men*	102
Sharon Olds, *Douche-Bag Ode*	104
Meeting a Stranger	105
Yaddyra Peralta, *Ode to Piranha*	107
Carl Phillips, *The Length of the Field*	126
Chromatic Black	127
Catherine Pierce, *In Which I Am Famous*	128
Bethany Pray, *The Boss Who Fired Me During the Recession*	142
Nicole Sealey, *Even the Gods*	143
Maureen Seaton, *The Visions of Sane Persons*	144
Lisa Sewell, *Grusamericana (Whooper)*	146
John Warner Smith, *Zydeco on Dog Hill*	148
Tracy K. Smith, *Logos*	149
Pimone Triplett, *Because There Is No Ending*	166
My Dear Ego, Be	167
Anne Pierson Wiese, *Middle Distance*	181
Bruce Willard, *The Calling*	182
Jake Adam York, *Letter Written in Black Water and Pearl*	183
Javier Zamora, *Dancing in Buses*	186
ABOUT MAJOR JACKSON	187
A Profile by Gregory Pardlo	
THE GREAT DREAM	194
A Plan B Essay by Floyd Skloot	
PATRON SAINT OF QUIET LIVES	198
A Look2 Essay on Barbara Pym by Raina Lipsitz	
A CONVERSATION WITH GAIL MAZUR	212
An Interview by Sarah Ehrich	
POSTSCRIPTS	220
Alice Hoffman Prize for Fiction	

EDITORS' SHELF	221
EDITORS' CORNER	221
CONTRIBUTORS' NOTES	222

Cover: R. Gregory Christie, *Above the Floodplain*, 1997, acrylic on paper, 11" x 8 3/4". Used by permission of the artist.

PLOUGHSHARES PATRONS

This nonprofit publication would not be possible without the support of our readers and the generosity of the following individuals and organizations.

CO-PUBLISHERS
 Robert E. Courtemanche
 The Green Angel Foundation
 Marillyn Zacharis, in memory of Robert E. Courtemanche

COUNCIL
 Denis and Ann Leary
 Jacqueline Liebergott

PATRONS
 Carol Davis
 Drs. Jay A. and Mary Anne Jackson
 Thomas E. Martin and Alice S. Hoffman
 Eugenia Gladstone Vogel

FRIENDS
 William H. Berman
 James Carroll and Alexandra Marshall
 Gregory Maguire
 Elizabeth R. Rea of the Dungannon Foundation
 James Tilley

ORGANIZATIONS
 Emerson College
 Massachusetts Cultural Council
 National Endowment for the Arts

Co-Publisher: $10,000 for two lifetime subscriptions and acknowledgment in the journal for five years.

Council: $3,500 for two lifetime subscriptions and acknowledgment in the journal for three years.

Patron: $1,000 for a lifetime subscription and acknowledgment in the journal for two years.

Friend: $500 for acknowledgment in the journal for one year.

MAJOR JACKSON
Radios

Of late, I have been collecting vintage radios, a distracting hobby that I am mostly ambivalent about in comparison with sincere radio enthusiasts, which explains why I only own a handful. They are scattered throughout my house. The Fisher Model 100 sits regally aged in the living room between the fireplace and my bay window where I listen to VPR's morning news, watching early light stretch into day as a svelte neighbor makes her seemingly heroic, winter morning jog through our quaint neighborhood. A beacon of health choices, she never fails to secure my envy. A monochromatic powder blue Zenith from the 1950s matches my bedroom's midcentury decor. I purchased it from Anjou & the Little Pear, a consignment shop in downtown Burlington, Vermont, that specializes in high-end designer Danish and American home furnishings. Its presence feels delicate and slight until I turn its knob and a sharp crackling gives way to a gradual rising of voices or classical music. In my upstairs office, among the columns of magazines, literature, and art books that populate my floor, is a teakwood 1970s Panasonic Solid State AM/FM radio. It has a coffee stain on top, and I normally keep it playing even when I'm not home.

Despite their utilitarian and decorative functions, I cannot help but experience an occasional twinge of sadness when I look at them. Given the advances in online music services and all manner of available podcasts as well as iPhone apps that can stream radio stations from around the world, the radio at the beginning of the twentieth century, once a paragon of human achievement and engineering is, it is safe to say, approaching obsolescence. A few notable companies are working diligently to keep the radio relevant in our times, but its current incarnation will inevitably and eventually give way to other means and modes of communication.

I heard a prominent editor of an American literary journal once describe poetry as a "dead technology." I was startled by the invocation of poetry as though it were an outdated appliance or piece of equipment, but more that here was one of our most celebrated arbiters of literary taste, charged with the task of stewarding and curating works of contemporary literature into existence, joining the "poetry-is-dead" pack. He made his pronouncement, no less, before a group of writers, among them aspiring poets, some of whom I thought I needed to approach with a box of Kleenex. I instantly knew what plagued this editor was his inability to hear. This virus has spread widely, regrettably too, and also infects most critics of poetry. This accounts for our current crisis in poetry criticism, where *The New York Times* only reviews about three books of poetry per year; the omnibus reviews feel wretchedly obligatory and lackadaisical. Contemporary poetry requires radical listening and demands that we modulate our beings to its signals, if we are to enjoy its broadcasts and news updates. "Wait wait... Don't tell me!"

To pronounce poetry as dead is to also implicate other literary art forms as possibly lifeless. Genres are not islands unto themselves. In our age, a conversation happens between the latest bestseller and the independent, small-press volume of poetry; most of this conversation concerns the nature and force of a democracy that values each citizen's lone voice.

In his poem "Sporting Life," Jack Spicer famously states, "The poet is a radio. The poet is a liar. The poet is a counterpunching radio." Ever since I started collecting vintage radios, I have had a recurring dream of finding myself in a junkyard, atop a mountain of radios of all kinds. They all miraculously work, and if I strain and order my hearing, which requires stout concentration, I can discern what emerges from that cacophony of transmissions. This is the age we find ourselves with all the media before us.

The honor of editing *Ploughshares* has been of that same work; I have found it restorative and personally nurturing. The authors in this issue entertain, bring the news, and elegantly sing the underlying complexities of our existence. However, maybe even more notably, as Spicer suggests: against all that alienates us from each other, these authors, with their counterpunching visions and imaginative uses of language, render us more a community—flawed beyond belief, yet whose humanity is all the more striking because of our joyous nature to find redemption, to grasp and render all that is sublime, beautiful, and truthful. In the spirit of radical, attentive listening, I hope you enjoy what is heard and felt here.

PETER BALAKIAN
Pueblo I, New Mexico

Between mud walls and the kiva
wind off the mesa broke his phrases,
as we walked with Billy of the Parrot Clan

and with others. The windows
melting into blowing snow and the ripped-
off split-level doors jammed on the adobes.

Out of fleeting blue, then white,
we caught bites
about the time of killing Spaniards

under the full moon,
after the medicine men were hanged
by Hernando de Ugarte y la Concha

and everyone was smashed between the mesa
and the hardened lava of the caldera,
and the Spaniards ate dogs

and roasted cowhides
till they died of black blood.

Through loud wind we heard how
a ventriloquist convinced the natives
the cross of the mission was speaking:

walk into the bullets—
and they walked into the fanatical air
where the cruzobs ate wood

until the Virgin was cursed and let go—
and that was the beginning, and the beginning
was 1680 in the year of the friars

the year the squash grew
out of the trellised sanctuary
where a dozen Christs were bleeding

and the after-stink of heads
rotted into the ground.

Billy said parrots were smuggled
across the Rio Grande
and then froze on the plateau

and the clan kept the name
because of the spirit-brother
of the blazing eyes.

A kid in a Broncos T-shirt
wanted a picture taken
in front of his iced-over window;

the blue-corn girls kept coming
and going as we stood there

in the snow that obscured the Mission wall
and the Christmas lights

winding around the sagging turquoise
mullions of the dented windows
where the men left their marks.

The snow blanked the straw-mud walls
as we slid down the molten cliff-steps

to the street where the Christmas luminarias
burned into the fissures of tumbleweed.

Nothing is written down in our culture
Billy said. Even if imagination
is a shard of history, am I defiling it

the way the polymorphism of those birds
mimicked us with their thick tongues.
Greek soldiers carried them to war,

their wings rimed Tang pots
the rococo ceilings of Dresden
bore their manic green.

If the parrots followed Geronimo
from Guadaloupe in a dream
could we imagine that frantic air now

where Route 66 Casino rises on
red pylons that hold up the skittering dice
and the breeze of the shuffle

as we drive into the wager and stakes
of High Limits, the wheels of fortune
spinning, the cash-out buttons popping,

simulacra of feathers,
silver, beads, the blur of pots
in the rearview mirror.

SANDRA BEASLEY
Ukulele

The vessel is simple, a rowboat among yachts.
No one hides a Tommy gun in its case.
No bluesman runs over his uke in a whiskey rage.

The last of the Hawai'ian queens translated the name
gift that came here, while Portuguese historians translate
jumping flea, the way a player's fingers pick and fly.

If you have a cigar box, it'll do. If you have fishing line,
it'll sing. If there is to be one instrument of love—
not love vanished or imagined, but love—it's this one.
Fit a melody in the crook of your arm, and strum.

ERIN BELIEU
The Body Is a Big Sagacity

is another thing Nietzsche said
that hits me as pretty specious,
if not entirely untrue,
while sitting in my car in the Costco
parking lot, listening to the *Ballet
Mécanique* of metal buggies shrieking
as each super, singular, and self-contained
wisdom of this Monday morning rumbles
its jumbo packs of toilet paper and Diet Coke
up the sidewalk. So count me a Despiser
of the Body, though I didn't generate this
woe any more than the little man parked
next to me, now attempting the descent from
his giant truck, behemoth whose Hemi roars
like a melting reactor, and stands
as the ego's corrective to the base methods
by which the body lets the spirit down.

Buzz-clipped, tidy as an otter, he's high and
tight in his riding heels. Pearl snaps on
the little man's shirt throw tiny lasers
when he passes. But who isn't more war
than peace? And how ridiculous to suffer
this: to be a little man, with itty hands and
bitty feet, to know yourself lethal, but
crazy-glued for life to the most laughable
engine. Recycled, rebooted, product of
genes and whatever our mamas thought
to smoke, the spirit gets no vote, Fred.

My body once was whole, symmetrical, was
actually beautiful for three consecutive years,
expensive as a rented palace, and yet I blew

that measly era watching my clock hands move,
as if I were a trigger rigged to homemade
dynamite. But if you would look inside me,
into all the lonely-seeming folks here loading
their heavy bags, you'd hope we're something
more than a sack of impulses, of soul defined
by random gristle. Which is why the little man

pauses on the sidewalk, why he stops to look at
me looking at him, this pocket-size person
whose gaze unkinks a low, hairy voltage from
my coccyx. And thus speaks Zarathustra,

> *You Great Star,*
> *what would your happiness be*
> *had you not those for whom*
> *you shine?...*

Ask the little man, neither ghost nor plant,
his boot heels ringing down the concrete.

EMILY BERNARD
What Happens Next

"What's wrong with Vanderbilt? Not that she'd get in necessarily," Mrs. Holtzmann said to no one in particular. "There are plenty of good schools in the South." She stood in the doorway of her classroom with her arms crossed.

"Heil Holtzmann," Audrey said under her breath. It was Monday. She was kneeling at her locker a few feet away, collecting books and papers for her next class, Trigonometry. Mrs. Holtzmann was her European History teacher, a petite woman with the faint beginnings of a mustache. Her hairstyle was modeled after Jaclyn Smith's in *Charlie's Angels.*

"Mrs. Holtzmann hates me," Audrey said to Gordy when she went to see him at lunchtime.

"Now that is simply not possible." His accent made two syllables out of "that." "Teachers are simply not capable of expressing something so primitive as hatred for their students."

"You mean they don't feel it?" Audrey asked. She was sixteen, a junior.

"No, my dear. Because it's against the rules, the unwritten code of conduct among pedagogues. It's like the Hippocratic oath among doctors. We pledge to educate, but more importantly to preserve your fragile, childish vanities."

"So even if they don't express it they can still feel it."

Gordy was the kind of person who would never use the word *teacher* when there was a word like *pedagogue* to use instead.

"Gordy" was a nickname for Mr. Gordon, the Honors English teacher at Lyndon Johnson High School. His first name was Henry, but no one, not even the other teachers, called him that. To everyone he was "Gordy," and the simplicity and uniformity of the nickname seemed to please him. If every high school has one teacher who must assume the role of the beloved eccentric, then Gordy played the part at Lyndon Johnson with the precision of a method actor. He was an orderly man; his dark blond hair was always scrupulously parted and firmly in place.

He was whimsical. "What can we say about your case?" is what he said to every student who came to his classroom when they were supposed to be in the cafeteria, at gym, or in study hall. Even the students who didn't understand what he meant were cheered by the words.

Audrey always went to hear about her case at lunchtime. She sat on a chair next to his desk while he wandered the room, his hands behind his back. The room was a standard issue high-school classroom: a laminated map of the world, an aging chalkboard, an anachronistic set of encyclopedias, and plants in green plastic pots on a stand near charmless, institutional windows. Every stripe of high-school student was present at these lunchtime caucuses. There were athletes who towered over Gordy and clapped him on the back; anxious cheerleaders who described to him their romantic dilemmas while they made eyes at the athletes; nerds who bunched in the corners and mocked the jocks in a silent, elaborate vocabulary of facial expressions; losers who skulked at the threshold and muttered under their breath. Gordy was fluent in the language of each tribe, and moved between them without prejudice, dispensing his singular wisdom to all in need.

"I must tell you in confidence that Mrs. Holtzmann did ask me the other day what it is that you and I talk about when you come in here," Gordy said as he landed on the chair behind his desk. One leg floated across the other; he held his face in his hand.

"See?! She's obsessed with me. She won't leave me alone."

"Have you considered the possibility that it's me she's obsessed with? Or even better, perhaps she imagines that something untoward is going on between us." Gordy stared at her and raised an eyebrow.

Audrey felt her face get hot. She made up a taunting sing-song and played it in her head, You have a crush on Go-r-dy.

Henry Gordon was thirty-five years old and neither handsome nor stylish. He was thin in an eerie, ageless way; no one ever knew him to gain an ounce. His narrow frame was filled out exactly, so that his body itself looked like a suit that was snug but not tight. His rigid, military bearing accentuated the lack of give in his build. He wore brown plastic glasses that were decidedly out of fashion. He stood in the doorway of his classroom between classes with his hands behind his back, one upturned palm on top of the other. The collar of a bright white T-shirt always peeked out from under a crisp white shirt. He stood perfectly still, smiled a thin-lipped smile, and watched teenagers glide up and down the hallway. Other teachers passed by him, or stood beside him, and sometimes said things to him. Gordy would answer without moving his eyes away from the river of boy and girl bodies undulating in front of him.

Maybe the teachers and administrators at Lyndon Johnson would have been troubled by the rapt attention Gordy paid his students if the gym teacher did not present a relatively more significant cause for concern. His name was Jeffrey Childs, but he was called "The Child Molester." Whenever the bell rang to signal the end of a class period, inevitably someone somewhere in the school would announce, "Time to get molested!" The Molester had a flaccid, droopy body that made everyone, even other teachers, wonder why he had been hired to teach gym in the first place. He claimed the devotion of only one student, a flat, plain girl who slinked along the hallways, always looking as if something bad had just happened to her. Audrey watched the girl in the hall and wondered what would compel even someone like her to bestow affections on a man who looked like The Molester, and had such a nickname, to boot.

"I'm not interested in Vanderbilt," Audrey said to Gordy. "I didn't apply to any schools in the South."
"You may well rue the day." He seemed fascinated by her determination to leave the South forever after graduation. "The South has her fair share of noble sons and daughters. Take Jimmy Carter, for instance." He sighed. "Far too humane for the presidency."
"My mother says people up North are much more broad-minded." Audrey, like her mother, meant white people.
Gordy considered this. "The Southern black is in a curious position, by necessity married to Southern customs and rhythms, yet forced to seek, in the words of Mr. Langston Hughes, 'a colder mistress.'" The bell rang; it was the end of lunch period. He sat on his desk and looked at Audrey, and then turned his head to observe students as they filed in. His hands were laced over one knee, his right leg crossed tidily over his left.
Audrey shifted her weight from one foot to the other as she stood in front of him. "Yeah, I guess so," she said. "Time for gym." She excused herself, and left to face The Molester.

The gymnasium was all the way across campus. Audrey knew a shortcut, but today the heavy metal doors of the music wing were chained shut. She turned around and followed the flow of traffic down the stairs.

The trellis that covered the walkway cast an intricate shadow on the concrete. Audrey marched forward, not to let the continuous whirl of students bump her into the mud. When she saw Marshall, she stopped, forcing the kid behind her to stop short, grumble, and then ease himself around her. Greasy stains decorated Marshall's Guns N' Roses T-shirt. His hair was in a series of disorganized clumps; it seemed to be a look he was going for. Marshall was one of Gordy's special cases.

"Hey," she said.

"Hey. Last weekend was cool." They had met in the park to drink grain alcohol punch with a bunch of other kids. Marshall got drunk and asked Audrey if he could kiss her. Audrey said yes because he was her friend and because he was black.

"Do you want to hang out this weekend?" As she spoke, three black girls in cheerleader uniforms walked past them. She could feel them not look at her. And then one of them pivoted and smiled a good-manners smile. Audrey's heart sank.

"Nah. I'm getting some new parts for my car."

Not long ago, Mrs. Holtzmann had stood in her doorway with Mrs. Abernathy, the Social Studies teacher, and said in Audrey's direction: "I hope she's not going to the prom with that boy. She'd be better off with one of the retarded kids." That boy was Marshall; he was "different," like Audrey. They were the only black students in the honors classes, but Marshall's grades were plummeting. Maybe it had to do with the fact that he had interest in little else besides his car. Sometimes Audrey went to Marshall's house after school and sat on the back porch while he lay underneath his rusty blue Camaro and talked to her. Sometimes, they talked about Mrs. Holtzmann and why she hated them.

"Well, call me if the parts don't come in, or if you get bored, or something."

Mrs. Holtzmann didn't have to worry. Marshall was not allowed to go to the prom after he was fingered as the ringleader in a plot to sabotage the senior float. Audrey's escort was a proper black boy from a nearby private school. On prom night, he brought her to his house before the dance, where his mother took pictures and fantasized out loud about her future as Audrey's mother-in-law. "Oh brother," Audrey's mother said when she heard about the photography session. Later that night, Audrey ditched the boy and joined Marshall and his friends in the park to drink grain alcohol punch. When Marshall got into trouble for the scheme involving the senior float, Audrey wrote an impassioned letter in his defense and sent it to the principal, who called her mother. Audrey's mother told her not to waste her energies on a boy so intent on going nowhere.

Audrey bounced her leg as she waited for The Molester to get off the phone.

"How many times do we have to go over the rules? No. Street. Shoes. Get it?"

Despite his obvious annoyance, the timbre of his voice felt like a jovial pat on the shoulder.

"I'm sorry. I forgot." She examined his bushy mustache. He had big, straight teeth. He looked like a nice enough guy.

The door swung open. "I have to talk to you." It was the girl in the hall. She stood just inside the room with her hands on her hips. The ridge of her hipbone was visible between her fingers. Her dingy white socks came all the way up to her knees.

"There's a line outside," said The Molester, and gestured with his head. Unkind laughter sounded behind the girl.

The girl in the hall didn't move. She stared at him as if she could burn her thoughts into his brain.

"Here." The Molester put a wooden hall pass on the desk in front of Audrey. "Get dressed and go to study hall. Five extra laps on Wednesday."

Audrey took the pass and left the room. Students were lined up like dominoes outside. They stood on their toes to see the girl in the hall and The Molester, who watched her impassively from his desk. "Freak," one of the boys sang in an opera singer's baritone. The Molester got up and closed the door. Before Audrey turned the corner to the locker room, she heard a female voice near the back of the line whisper, "Disgusting."

Gordy was overwhelmed with cases the next day at lunch, so he invited her to come to his house that night for her "assessment." Audrey lied and told her parents she was babysitting. She pulled out of the chilly suburbs in her mother's car, and found her way to Gordy's house by inching along the narrow roads of his neighborhood, looking for his pale yellow VW Beetle. She found it, and then saw him sitting on the porch. He talked to her as she grabbed her backpack from the car, and she thought about how easy this was: car to curb to Gordy.

They held glasses of iced tea. Gordy talked about his youth. "In West Kentucky, dating a girl from across the tracks was just like being in an interracial relationship," Gordy said.

"What side of the tracks was Mrs. Gordon on?"

"She was on the right side, my side," Gordy laughed. "My mother was delighted—until she went and got herself pregnant." He looked sharply at Audrey. "That's a dirty trick to play on a man, my dear. Remember my words."

In the window behind him, she could see the duplicitous Mrs. Gordon herd their three sons up to bed.

"My mother said that rearing children is what brings meaning to an adult life," Audrey said. Gordy laughed out loud, and she was pleased the way she always was when she managed to amuse him.

Audrey sipped at her iced tea and surveyed the street. It was the sort of day her mother would call "balmy." A man in a green sweatsuit walked a compact, slow-moving dog. Before Gordy, Audrey had thought of marriage as something constant, something that just was. Your parents just were your parents, whether you wanted it that way or not. Other kids talked about liking and disliking their parents, but to Audrey such discussions were pointless because they implied choices that kids did not have. When she was younger, like many children, she dreamed of more romantic beginnings, but after she accepted the disappointment that she was not adopted, she stopped looking to her parents for revelations. Gordy taught her that parents weren't a given but sometimes tricked into the role, and that married people actually had feelings about each other that had nothing to do with kids, or family, or even love.

Mrs. Gordon was short and had frizzy hair. Her glasses were even less fashionable than her husband's. She taught Computer Science at another school.

"Does Mrs. Gordon mind my coming over here?"

"Well, you're hardly the only student who seeks my counsel after hours. Doug Mitchell was over here yesterday. And Cherise Walker usually stops by after cheerleading practice on Fridays."

Audrey dropped her shoulders at the mention of the pretty black cheerleader. "Cherise Walker hates me," she said gravely.

Cherise Walker was a senior. She wore makeup and carried handbags. Audrey wore glasses and sometimes the same kind of shirt, in different colors, for a whole week. Instead of a handbag, she carried a dingy blue backpack everywhere, even to the movies. She was neither experienced nor imaginative in the arts of self-adornment. Still, the next day after school, she gamely made two laps up and down the cosmetics row at CVS before she gave up. Gordy wasn't the kind of teacher girls competed for; Audrey knew that, even if Gordy didn't. She bought a *Seventeen* magazine and some jawbreakers.

That evening, Gordy talked about his fate. He had three sons. Stuart was ten, and Daniel and Michael were four and six, respectively. The younger two were wiry, boisterous boys who teased Stuart cruelly about his weight. Audrey felt bad for Stuart. She knew from her own experience that being the oldest boy should be something like having a championship belt, a guaranteed badge of entitlement to lord over younger siblings. It was as if his weight had stripped Stuart of his title. Sometimes he wore the flabby, exhausted look of an ex-prize fighter.

On the porch, in the darkness, Gordy talked about the unjust hand of destiny while his children fought, lounged, and enacted dance routines in the living room window behind him. He rarely turned the porch lights on. He said the darkness created a sense of elegance and intimacy, but Audrey suspected it was because he liked the fact that he could see but not be seen. What he saw there on the porch with the lights out were his memories and fantasies come alive, so that he wasn't as much remembering but narrating what he saw in front of him. Audrey sometimes wondered if her presence was even necessary. Sometimes when the boys were making a lot of noise, Gordy would turn to watch, and then it was as if the animation inside the house, too, was a fantasy, a movie, and he was just a spectator, his obligation to the scene no different from any random viewer's.

He had concerns about her love life.

"What's wrong with Marshall?"

"I like him. I just don't like him, like him."

"You like him but you don't like him."

"I mean, I like him as a friend, but not the other way."

"You mean not in a sexual way."

"I'm not talking about that, I'm just talking about liking him."

"You don't like him enough to have sex with him."

"I don't want to talk about that."

"I see."

Gordy had been unambiguously disappointed when he found out Audrey was still a virgin. He declared her "a closet Victorian," which was not necessarily an insult in his vocabulary. The book he considered an autobiography of sorts, at least in emotional terms, was *Clarissa*. Now Audrey sat on Gordy's porch in perturbed silence as he lectured her on the value of sexual experience, the hypocrisies of female chastity, and the failure of the "free love" movement to liberate women and men from their antiquated illusions about sexual innocence.

"Marshall is an interesting case," Gordy persisted, "a boy far too sensitive for the crudeness of his environment. He can only hope that whatever life has in store for him next will be more conducive for his intellectual growth. You could do worse, you know."

Just because he's black, Audrey thought.

"How do your parents feel about you dating white boys?" Gordy asked.

"Absolutely out of the question," Audrey said.

"Alas, Dr. King is rolling in his grave."

Audrey thought this was a pretty stupid thing to say. She knew that Martin Luther King didn't march on Washington so that she could date white boys. Still, she imagined that Gordy had some kind of point, just because he usually did.

"I think interracial love affairs are crucial to the country's moral health. It's high time I myself contributed to the struggle for harmony between the races."

"You're going to—. You mean dating?" Audrey said.

Gordy looked at her. "Remember that I grew up during segregation. I was deprived of the pleasure of black companions. I'm putting an ad in the newspaper. Let's see." He cleared his throat. "'Have we really overcome? WM seeks BF. Let's realize the dream.'"

Audrey sipped her tea and looked at the street. One streetlight illuminated a piece of sidewalk that an hour earlier had been crowded with children bumping plastic cars into each other. It was bedtime. In the window, Mrs. Gordon could be seen rounding up toys and boys and books.

"You shouldn't cut class to come here," Gordy said the next day when Audrey was supposed to be at gym. There was an assembly, but she was supposed to be at gym, running punishment laps. "In fact, I may have to close down my lunchtime operation," he said. "Holtzmann appears to be on the warpath." Gordy had his feet on his desk, his ankles crossed. His arms were folded behind his head. "She must have said something to the principal. She'll probably squeal on me for skipping assembly too."

"She's just jealous because everyone likes you."

"Perhaps. At any rate, I don't want to excite her ire."

"But I can't go back to gym. I forgot my shoes again, and The Molester will kill me."

"If you are not careful, you are going to wear out that ruse. And please, stop calling him that awful name, at least when you're in here."

"He's gross. He's a weirdo. He's going to fail me," Audrey groused. "I'm going to fail gym."

"He's lonely and misunderstood," Gordy said, his voice a tender reprimand. "Speaking of lonely and misunderstood, are you free to babysit on Friday? Mrs. Gordon has insisted I join her at one of her school functions."

"I thought you saw Cherise on Fridays. Why don't you ask her?"

"Ah, Cherise." Gordy leaned his head back until Audrey saw the point of his Adam's apple. He snapped his head forward. "She has a date. A ball player." He smiled at her. "Now go back to gym and throw yourself at the mercy at Mr. Jeffrey Childs."

The walkway was empty of people as Audrey made her way to the gym. She slapped her feet on the pavement. Friday was only two days away. "If you get a ride to my house, I will drive you home," Gordy had told her.

Audrey tried to formulate a new excuse as she walked up the steps leading to The Molester's office. But as she approached the door, she stopped. She tiptoed forward and leaned her ear against the door. It was unmistakable; the girl in the hall and The Molester were laughing together inside.

*

Audrey asked Marshall to drop her off at Gordy's on Friday. He roared up in his blue tin can and popped the steering wheel on and off to impress her. She told her mother that they were going to a play rehearsal at school. Audrey walked out of the house stunned that she bought it.

"Should I come over after the kids are in bed?" Marshall twisted one of his hair clumps as his engine gurgled in Gordy's driveway.

"Maybe. I'll call you."

Inside, the house was unpleasantly aflutter with tears, stern warnings, and fretful dartings back and forth. Audrey sat on the couch and waited. Finally, the Gordons were leaving the house in an irritated hurry. The boys wrapped their arms around their mother's legs and she leaned down to shush them and stroke their hair. Gordy marched through the living room and out of the door without turning his head.

"Goodnight, Audrey. I'm in the car!" Mrs. Gordon straightened up on cue, reminded Audrey of the basic instructions for bedtime, and followed her husband out the door. By the time Audrey had locked the door behind her, the two younger boys were already on the floor with their toys, deeply absorbed in an ominous-sounding drama involving a soldier, a dog, a spaceship, and a derailed train. Stuart sat in his chair above them, holding a tattered peach-colored animal in a loose embrace. He was wearing a red-and-yellow striped shirt that looked like a failed attempt at whimsicality. He looked dumpy and sad and tired. He regarded Audrey who smiled back at him guiltily as she walked past the boys to the den.

She found the remote and was settling into the couch when suddenly Stuart was beside her.

"My dad says prime time is the barometer of the nation's anxieties."

Audrey laughed because that was exactly the kind of thing Gordy would say. Stuart brightened.

"Can I sit with you for a while?"

"OK," Audrey said, and made room for him. For several minutes, Stuart sat perfectly still on the edge of the couch with his animal close to his chest. Finally, he relaxed and they became engrossed in a television show about rich but miserable teenagers.

*

Audrey woke to Stuart patting her knee. "It's past the boys' bedtime," he whispered to her. She bolted upright, momentarily confused. Then she looked at Stuart in his unhappy happy shirt and remembered where she was and what she was supposed to be doing. The boys grumbled perfunctorily about the unfairness of bedtime as she followed them up the stairs. She stood in the hallway as Stuart helped the younger ones brush their teeth. Once they were in bed, she read to them from an adventure story while Stuart read a book about insects, with his flashlight, his body turned to the wall. When she said goodnight, the younger two were satisfied with "sweet dreams." Stuart asked for a hug.

Audrey went downstairs to the kitchen and rummaged through the Gordons' bar until she found some triple sec. She mixed it with some pulpy orange juice she found in the fridge, and brought both ingredients with her into the den. She flipped through cable channels, looking for something her parents would disapprove of. Finally, she found a movie about a high-class prostitute with a drug problem. She watched for a while. Then she found a movie about a corrupt police officer with a drug problem. She replenished her drink and watched until she heard floorboards creak, and then a child's voice.

"Audrey, are you there?" His whisper was full of fear and excitement, as if he were addressing a ghost during a séance.

"I'm in the den, Stuart. What's the problem?"

"I can't sleep. I'm having bad dreams. You said you would come if I did."

Audrey remembered making no such promise, but she said, "Just a minute." Before she could hide the liquor bottle or change the channel, Stuart was in the room.

"What are you doing?" He stared in confusion. The obnoxious kingpin begged for his life while the police officer dangled him over a bridge by his ankles.

"Nothing, Stuart. Just watching TV." As far as Audrey was concerned, the kingpin was a cruel braggart who deserved to be dropped into the river after he begged for his life. But she understood that between his sadism and his drug problem, the police officer was hardly a saint himself. Audrey turned off the television.

"You're letting oxygen into the orange juice," Stuart said.

He was wearing a two-piece pajama set that was too young for him; it had feet. His outfit had faded to a soft, creamy yellow, and featured washed-out images of imaginary creatures all over it in blue and pink. Audrey recognized the creatures from a book-turned-movie that had been wildly popular some years back. She wasn't surprised when he held out his hand. She took it.

"Let's go back up," she said.

She followed Stuart upstairs. On the way to his room, Stuart said, "Wait. I want to show you something." He pulled her into his parents' bedroom. "Sit there." He pointed to the bed and then made for the closet. He stuck his bedraggled animal between his knees as he moved around the detritus on the floor of the jam-packed closet. Audrey knew that Gordy considered Mrs. Gordon's "hoarding" to be one of her larger sins. "Freud would see a natural connection between her indiscriminate saving and her inability to stay faithful to a weight-loss regimen," he once sniffed.

Stuart joined her on the bed with a magazine in his hand, and when she saw the busty girl on the cover, she understood what this was all about.

"It's my dad's," he said. Audrey started to respond sarcastically, but was stopped by the memory of a stack of dirty cartoons she once discovered at a friend's house. She returned to them again and again every time she went there to visit, until they one day disappeared. She had the same sped-up feeling in her heart and stomach then as she did now.

Audrey flipped through a few pages of the magazine. She knew she should probably take this moment to lecture Stuart about privacy, and how-would-you-like-it-if-someone-went-through-your-things, but she couldn't stop her hands from turning the pages as she stared, hypnotized by the girls in front of her. Stuart observed Audrey's hands and then looked up at her face.

"That's totally gross," he said.

"Uh-huh," Audrey said as she continued to turn page after totally gross page.

A few years ago, Audrey had accompanied her father on a visit to Mr. Covington, his mechanic and partner in a small business venture. She was reading a book in the waiting room when she was startled by the sound of the male laughter. She wandered down the hallway to Mr. Covington's office with plans to whine until her father agreed to take her home. When she looked through the door, she saw girls everywhere. There were pictures of them leaning against cars with their skirts hiked up, straddling motorcycles in bustiers and dark glasses, wet and laughing at a car wash, buckets in mid-fling. A calendar was pinned to the wall right behind Mr. Covington's head. It was December, and above the boxes and rows for the days and weeks was a picture of a woman in a Santa Claus outfit, only she wasn't the kind of Mrs. Claus you saw down at the mall. This Mrs. Claus had her head to one side, her lips puckered into a kiss and a long, blood red fingernail to her mouth. Her round brown breasts were ripe and shining against the white fur of her costume. Everything else was lost on Audrey as she stared at the breasts, whose nipples were halfway exposed, so that the breasts looked like a pair of round brown olives, their pimentos nearly spilling out.

"Audrey! Good to see you, honey!" Mr. Covington smiled broadly. She slid inside the circle of her father's arm sheepishly, afraid to look up. The big brown breasts shined and winked at her out of the corner of her eye. And when she closed her eyes, she could see nothing but long legs blooming out of hiked skirts, and big breasts nearly escaping from bustiers and wet and free under white T-shirts.

As they walked to the car, she asked her father about the pictures.

"Covington is crazy, you know, girl crazy." He laughed and twirled his finger around the side of his temple.

"But what does his wife think?"

Her father looked at her seriously, and misreading her curiosity as concern, said gently, "Don't worry about it, honey. It's nothing, just some bimbos on the wall. It's no big deal."

Stuart tapped her wrist. "Hey, what do you and my dad talk about out there on the porch?" Audrey closed the pages of the magazine.

"Nothing much," she told him.

"Does he ever talk about me?" He asked. Audrey looked at the shabby animal under the crook of one arm.

"Of course. Yeah. He talks about you all the time." She put her arm around his shoulders. The bosomy blonde on the cover of the magazine smoldered up at them.

"OK, Stuart, you really have to go to bed now."

"I know. But I gotta put the magazine back first."

"I'll put it back," Audrey volunteered.

Stuart narrowed his eyes at her. "OK. But you won't tell my dad, right?"

"And you don't tell about me in the den, you know." She poked his chest playfully.

"We have a deal," he said. His animal in one hand, he stuck out the pinky of the other one. She hooked hers around it. They smiled at each other. Stuart turned around and clomped down the hall on his padded feet.

Audrey made sure Stuart was asleep before she went back into the Gordons' bedroom and opened the magazine. Her hands quivered a bit, and she felt her heart beat in her stomach. For some reason, she made herself go through the magazine from beginning to end, not letting herself skip around like she wanted. She waded through reviews of garage door openers, razors, wristwatches, and speakers. Some of the cartoons were funny, but they were spoiled when she thought there must be a requirement that every woman in them had to have enormous breasts. The flowery writing in the "Confessions" column made her snicker and feel superior. When she got to the pictorials, she was surprised at how obvious the scenarios were—sexy secretaries menaced by vulgar bosses, housewives in lingerie caught unawares by well-endowed gardeners, etc. All of the women were white.

The pull-out featured the "Kitten of the Year." Her name was Elysian and she had no pubic hair. The baldness of Elysian's vagina surprised and repulsed Audrey so much that she lifted her head in embarrassment. When she looked back, she tried to concentrate on the little paragraphs about Elysian's life and ambitions, but she found them nearly too painful to read. As she turned the pages, she examined Elysian's body in various positions through the alternating lenses of pity and excitement. When she got to the end, she flipped back to the beginning and started again.

Some of their expressions looked fake, of course, but there was something almost unbearable in the hunger she also saw in the girls' eyes, the nakedness of the expectation on their faces. If a woman didn't have a penis in her mouth, then she held it open, gaping, waiting. Audrey heard the threatening sing-song of her mother's voice in her ear as she sat slack-jawed and spaced out in church: "Close that mouth or catch flies." The women in the magazine had legs that were open as wide as their mouths. This exhilarated Audrey, who had been instructed from a young age to keep her knees together always, even when she was at home. "I don't want you to get into the habit," her mother explained. The open mouths and gaping legs were trusting and daring, vulnerable and powerful too. They seemed to speak to her of endless possibilities, of desires that could be shown but not spoken, of voluptuous, elaborate stories without endings.

"Stuart wanted to show me some girlie magazine Gordy has in his closet." Audrey talked to Marshall on the phone in the kitchen.

"Gordy, all right!" Marshall said.

Audrey rolled her eyes into the receiver.

"My father has that stuff too." Marshall paused. "I think it's really unfair to women," he said confidently.

"But what if those women, like, want to do that? What if they get something from it too?"

"No way!" Marshall sounded shocked. "Then they bring it on themselves, I guess. Do you want me to come over?"

"I don't think so. I'm way too tired. And Stuart's on me like a hawk. I'll see you tomorrow."

Audrey went into the den and gathered the glass and bottles. She straightened the fuzzy green afghan that draped the back of the couch. What exactly were they bringing on themselves? Were the photographs like mug shots, a punishment for the crime of their gaping desires? Or did the women have yearnings that only the camera and the men who looked at their pictures could understand? Audrey thought about the secret world of women and men and the unmet hungers of Gordy while she washed her glass, sniffed it, then washed it again. What about Mrs. Gordon? What did she want? Audrey imagined that all Mrs. Gordon probably wanted was for Mr. Gordon to come in from off the porch and help her get the kids ready for bed. This thought depressed her.

Audrey was in front of the television when the Gordons arrived. She tried to make polite responses as Mrs. Gordon chattered about their evening and asked after the kids. Gordy came over to the couch and looked at her. "Let's go," he said.

In the car, Gordy talked about the recent developments in his romantic life. A few days ago, he received a positive response to his newspaper ad. The woman had agreed to meet him at a motel just out of town that afternoon. He had decorated the room with flowers and music, but the woman never showed up.

"I'm sorry about that, Gordy." Audrey felt genuine sympathy as she imagined Gordy sitting anxiously at the edge of a motel bed, his fingers laced around his knee as he waited for a mystery woman who would be the final piece in his puzzle. But then she saw Gordy sitting on the bed holding a dirty magazine in his lap, one hand down his pants. She pushed the image away, and recalled instead a time on the porch when he was talking to her about her future, and said, "Don't become a teacher. People never remember you, at least not for the reasons you want them to."

Instinctively, she had tried to comfort him. "But you're a great teacher, Gordy. Everybody loves you." Now she suspected that, in some way, this was exactly the problem he was talking about.

They were silent for a while and then Gordy cleared his throat. He tapped the steering wheel with his thumbs. "You know I was thinking of you being in my house while I was at that party…The thing is I rented that room for the whole weekend. We could meet there, say, tomorrow afternoon?"

Audrey sat up. "OK. That sounds like a plan," she said. She imagined standing in a hotel room in front of Gordy, thanking him for flowers she would soon ditch, complimenting him on music she didn't like. Maybe he would lecture her on the music. Or worse, maybe he wouldn't. Maybe he would lay her on the bed and tell her the things he wanted to tell Cherise Walker, or Elysian, or the woman who answered his ad. What were these things?

"I don't know, actually. You know my parents have all this stuff for me to do tomorrow, in the yard, and stuff."

She felt terrible when she saw Gordy clutch the steering wheel more tightly. "You could make up a story," he laughed. "You're good at that."

"So are you, Gordy," she said, but it came out much more sharply than she intended.

When he drove into her driveway, Audrey opened the door immediately. She had one foot on the pavement when Gordy put his hand on her arm and stopped her. "You know, Audrey," he said gravely, "there are some choices in life that are too obvious to make. They come to you, in fact, already made."

"Yeah." Audrey laughed lightly. Then she worried that he might think she was laughing at him. She remembered then the story he once told her of a boy who had graduated several years earlier, one of his favorite "cases." On a break from college, he had come to Lyndon Johnson to visit Gordy, as recent graduates often did. They talked for a while, and then the boy looked at him and said, "You know, I think I've outgrown you." When he told Audrey this story Gordy laughed like someone who took pride in the fact that he could laugh at a joke about himself. Audrey had laughed too, but she knew then, like Gordy must have too, that the boy had not been kidding.

She waited a minute, but Gordy looked ahead and didn't say anything else. "I don't know if I can meet you tomorrow, but I'll call you. Goodnight." Audrey got out of the car and went to the door.

When she looked back, Gordy was still there. She thought again of him in his hotel room, a naked need on his face, and she knew that he had wanted something more than just her, and that she had been the one to take it away.

Gordy and Audrey never discussed the fact that she never went back to his house during those last few weeks of school. They chatted amiably in the hallways, but Audrey no longer went to Gordy's classroom during lunchtime for a dose of his instruction and advice. "Somebody's not so special anymore," Mrs. Holtzmann said to the air as Audrey gathered her things for Trigonometry.

In the fall, when she was at college up North, Audrey heard that The Molester had been fired because of the rumors circulating about his "improper" relationship with the girl in the hall. And then she heard that he was filing a lawsuit because the rumors were proved false, his relationship with the girl turned out to be nothing other than a friendship. Gordy was right, Audrey thought, and wrote him a letter to that effect. He never wrote back.

TRACI BRIMHALL
What We Lost in the Flood—

the barber's best shears, Dona Rosa's toucan,
all the allamanda blossoms, the brown phantom

and his white shadow. The cuckold never came home,
but his pants basked on the courthouse roof for weeks.

Hippolyta sank. The cemetery swelled. The original Christ
above the church vanished along with the toothless nun.

We found the demi-virgin strangled in her hammock.
When the lupanar burned down, we wrote our names

in the fire. The fateful signature in our blood returned
to us as yellow fever, as the thin apostle of moonlight,

as the dwarf rooster in an albino caiman's stomach,
as the Pentecostal firing squad, as Senhor Lua's collection—

Divana diva, Papilio achilles, wings pricked by the too late,
the stay away, the not yet delight of tomorrow.

JERICHO BROWN
Another Elegy

I shouldn't be, but I'm thinking
About the woman who got shot
Fighting over that sweat-soaked
Headscarf Teddy Pendergrass threw
Into the crowd at one of those
Shows he put on for "Ladies
Only" the year I was born. How
Many women reached
Before the tallest two forgot
Their new fingernails matched
Purses and shoes? I'm no good.
I thought I'd be bored with men
And music by now, voices tender
As the wound Pendergrass could feel
When he heard what caused gunfire
Was a trick he rehearsed. Love
Is quick and murderous, bleeding
Proof of talent. He wanted to be
What we pay to see—Of course,
That's not special. I imagine
Someone who desires any
Worn piece of man must be
Willing to shoot and be shot.

STEPHEN BROWNING
Knowledge

I loved to walk down to the café where she worked
and stare at the menu with the Brains Beurre Noir
halfway down the page. She'd come to my table
with her order pad, pleasant and placid, dressed
all in white like a nurse, and her wonderful smell,
strong and female, would enter me like a sword.
When I used to brew beer in my basement a bottle
would sometimes burst, and I'd stand on the stairs
for a long time just breathing, breathing it in.
So I knew the virtue of accident as well as its sorrow
and, as I did about all the things I half wanted
but couldn't ask for, I thought of the brains beurre noir,
and how black butter with its vinegar and lemon
and chopped capers would bathe them in its rich darkness.
And I thought of the desert, and its sage, and how
the dead animals desiccated so quickly, leaking aromas
into the dry sand, and of hot loam steaming after rain,
and of the pungencies of this world and especially
of the ones that lovers knew, and it seemed to me
that this was a great gift of intimacy, as she stood there
waiting to take my order, waiting for the naming
of all those things we knew about but which just then
we couldn't speak about because we weren't sure how,
and about the problem of the brains beurre noir
and how we knew this also, and knew that we both knew.

MAGGIE DIETZ
Demolition Derby

Amped-up grid lights growl stars
onto the hay-baled dirt ring

onto blistered chrome and rust-lace,
car-shells taped and painted over

to resemble shapes of cars. We're
bleachered, gum-shoed, bleached

by glare, laughing at ourselves
for being here, spilling beer

and sponging powdered sugar
from our rumpled shirt-fronts,

smiling. Rumbles in the air,
our guts, the gears chunking

and purring, the stands gnashing,
owling Os. At the flag, the cornered

cars spring almost sprightly
for an instant, then hunch-buckle

into each other, crumple in smoke.
I am in love. With Todd and Jill

and Bob I bash myself through
minutes booing besters, leaning

into lurchers seeking comebacks.
Rev-engined mish-mash, mosh

pit of metal, brand-emblazoned
junk-car smash-'em-up, trash

rodeo, trough pigs brawling over
scraps and swill. O plastic tumblers

of shwag-brew in Topsfield under
an October moon. O America.

Wrestling angels, hum and bash your
hymn of destruction, breach and belch

your tailpipe spit and prayer. We're
happy here where nothing doesn't hurt.

MARK DOTY
Deep Lane

I'm resting on a bench in the cemetery
while Ned scrawls his self-delighted wild-boy trace
over the slopes of grass, but we can't stay long,

since it's a day I need to go into the city,
and when I stand up suddenly my left leg's half a foot
lower than my right, because I've stepped into the sunken,

newly filled grave of one Herbert Meyer.
I don't know it then, but that's when the wind
blows up from beneath; I think I'm just off balance,

and make a joke of it later, telling people my day began
with falling into a grave, and where can you go from there?
Later a storm blows down the moraine,

crisp and charged with ozone and exhilaration,
blows on my face and arms a wind I've already met,
one that winds up the lanes and rattles the cups in the cabinets,

and bends the beautybush and Joe Pye weed down
in the direction of beautiful supplication;
the maple and walnut sway in the highest regions of themselves,

leaves circling in the air like the great curtain of bubbles
blown by the humpback to encircle the delicious schools.
Blows in my sleep and blows while I'm cooking,

blows while I read and when I kiss, does it ever
blow then, the wind not particular to Mr. Meyer,
nor anyone else, and thus the nervy thrill

of its invitation: to be unbound, not at all
what you thought, to rush up from the sinking earth
on a gust of investigation: now go be the crooked little house,

and the cracks in the shingles, tunnel your hour as the mouse
in the stale loaf, fly back to the strong hands of the baker,
spring backwards into the wheat,

forward into the belly of the mousechild,
what reason to ever end? I know one:
if you don't hold still, you can have joy after joy,

but you can't stay anywhere to love. That's the price,
that rib-rattling wind waiting to sweep you up,

that's the price the wind pays.

JACLYN DWYER
Praise Poem for American Girls

Praise scissors that clip split ends easily as ex-
    boyfriends. The one who died in college, the refugee
who crossed a blood-soaked Nile, but never could
    get over you. Praise coffee and Kentucky bourbon.

Daughters pulled deep into Ohioan corn,
    romances banished to backseats and barstools,
and newlyweds two-stepping to the second line
    waving paper napkins with names printed in gold.

Praise helicopters hovering over frozen lakes in Madison.
    Wide blades break the ice, a thick fog of ozone trapping
brides and wives. Boys toppled out of boats, girls pushed in,
    the surfacing bodies of all the kids who couldn't swim.

Praise black loops, lazy coils etched down 80 like pubic hairs
    roping down a long white leg. Praise snow clotting
fat cataracts over the road. There is nothing for miles, only
    your hot breath unraveling a memory of wet wool.

Blond girls in hoop skirts getting hitched in a barn,
    yellow hair glowing brighter than a burnished brass sax
in Memphis. Praise grandmothers who still pin laundry
    outside, their long fingers the brittle wax of weeping candles.

Fruit flies that fill the kitchen and keep you company
    nights he is away, his skin clapping against
the sweet country ribs of his ex. Praise the end of an
    excuse with an interrogative. Who? Honey, praise you.

Long legs. High arches. The body you never used for ballet.
    Dinners you wasted and drinks you couldn't finish.
Praise your revolving hips: Hula hoop champ, flip flops
    shaken loose in the grass. Your heady lip gloss shines

a Montana moon. Denim laced to fringe over a fence
    during crowning for the Milk-Can Dinner Queen.
The silkscreened tee puckered across your chest:
    Not All Tetons Are Grand Tetons But Mine Are.

Praise scrapyards and salvation. Briny bodies,
    burrowing deep in flannel sheets. Bayou critters
boiled apple red and spread across announcements.
    You can't help but suck each fatty head

like a river lusting after oars. That great bully!
    Praise forgiveness. The mean girls, badass bitches
who stare you down and try to cut you with envy.
    Praise Jesus. Praise Jehovah, and baby, praise them too.

MARTÍN ESPADA
Of the Threads That Connect the Stars

Did you ever see stars? asked my father with a cackle. He was not
speaking of the heavens, but the white flash in his head when a fist burst
between his eyes. In Brooklyn, this would cause men and boys to slap
the table with glee; this might be the only heavenly light we'd ever see.

I never saw stars. The sky in Brooklyn was a tide of smoke rolling over us
from the factory across the avenue, the mattresses burning in the junkyard,
the ruins where squatters would sleep, the riots of 1966 that kept me
locked in my room like a suspect. My father talked truce on the streets.

My son can see the stars through the tall barrel of a telescope.
He names the galaxies with the numbers and letters of astronomy.
I cannot see what he sees in the telescope, no matter how many eyes I shut.
I understand a smoking mattress better than the language of galaxies.

My father saw stars. My son sees stars. The earth spins beneath
our feet. We lurch ahead, and one day we have walked this far.

DIDI GIBBS
The Florida Sandhill Crane

By wings whose shapes
are but half a heart?
    Feathers oiled with
    country clubs and
gasps of delight? Not for these
the sandhill crane
shakes her beaded voice.

Gauche and gangrene,
she is the gatekeeper of gibe,
    a cement-gray song
    edged and pocked in grassy
fields, a frock of scarlet
over her eye, her own letter
to time and her maker;

a bow, a leap, all a dance
to the heavens and the blue
    plastic tarps mapping
    the devil in a state
of wind and rain,
a crucifix in her throat
to scratch the itch of her fable.

Fruit flies darn the citrus fallen
and rotten in the late spring
    she sidesteps and heads
    for the wetlands, to a river
that flows north pierced with blossoms
and the song of Marsyas,
a Supremacist's White on White, blossom on flesh,

small Corinthian dreams gargle in her throat,
her voice of leaves and muck
    folded up in an awkward flight,
      a frieze of battles and victories
lining the sky as if in a couplet
of straight lines, as if she could know she would wed
the palette of one into a mural of two.

NATHALIE HANDAL
Salt on the Tongue

Thierry

I am here because it's too crowded on the other side of this sentence. Take this page—where do I place myself? At the beginning or the end, or in the middle? Or maybe in the corner. I can't be everywhere, that's what I've been told my entire life. They say we have a choice, but where do you find that truth? What I know to be true are the lives of rooftops. I've been careless. Have woken up without a shirt, with bras left close by. What's making love if not the practice of forgetfulness? Around me forgetting is a way of surviving. I think we keep preparing to begin, as you do when you see a woman for the first time, a flower on her breast. And in a blink, you realize you saw her at a bar once. She was serving you rum while you were trying to find the moon. It's all in the emptiness. The bare branches. The room without a window. The sky without a cloud. The whisper about to break in half. And suddenly, the tree decides to blossom, the woman dresses, the room and the sky decide to keep the whisper from collapsing. In other words, we decide to tolerate. As for me, I never drowned, never found a place either. I did, however, see another woman. She wasn't wearing shoes.

Jean-Baptiste

Sak pase man? Leon asked, scratching his hair before opening a button of his red shirt. He always greeted with his head down when he got some love the night before and I didn't. Mine was bigger than his. So he felt he needed to prove something. I never told him anything 'til the day he said I'd only been with one woman. I said, *The blan has a bigger one than you.* Course, I didn't think a white man could be bigger. Hell grew in his eyes. He said, *you can't crucify me 'cause we both black men. Shut the fuck up and kill the cockroach by your feet, then give me a piece of sugar cane.* That was my worst moment. He handled it well. I think we grew up that day. What would he tell me now if he saw me lying here, stiff? Last thing I remember him saying to me: *Frè m, Bro, they kill us, say they can't see us when they drive in the dark. But they lie. Our black skin glows in the dark, lights up the night and the road—even ghost knows that. At our center is a blue flame. Those were the good days.*

Pascal

The smell of *cleren* lingers on his breath. His face is numb. His memory backwards. He took me to Jérémie once. But he was from Gonaïves. He said, *les artistes sont ici*. In those days, there was hope. He could have painted the country but instead he bruised the language in his hand. He crossed borders to find new prayer, worshipped bones, tip to tip. Then he forgot he did that. He measured the silver surface of light, the corners holding secrets. One blackout at a time, he counted his ribs. On his sleeves a last light reflecting as if he'd never seen one before, or was it his reflection that startled him? The mirror recorded every motion. But smoke rose to his mouth. He thought this was my curse. But smoke was also my gift. Also my country. Also my end. Why do we need roots when an island broken apart for air still has more space in the sea?

DAVID HUDDLE
Brief Encounter with the Household Gods

My mom says my dad had to work so hard he didn't really notice how angry it made him. Nowadays he can't watch the news without losing his temper. He comes from country people who hated the government going all the way back to the revolution. My mom says my dad's grandfather used to talk about assassinating Roosevelt. I don't ask her who's Roosevelt. She knows those old names are just so much blah-blah to me. She says my dad's always had this anger, but it's never come out in the open like it is now. On payday he comes home early & rips open the envelope to see what they withheld. Then his face heats up & he starts shouting. My dad is not a big man, but when he's mad, he fills up our whole house.

My mom takes it as a good sign when I listen to her. She better not get her hopes up. Yes, I'm her daughter, but there's no law that says I have to be her pal. Or start helping her cope with my dad's new ways. It's the political woman who's responsible for his new phase. I see him watching her on her TV show. With her husband & her kids, she's traveling around her totally backward state. My dad loves that show. He gets all excited because sometimes she climbs out of their obnoxious vehicle & somebody hands her a rifle & she shoots a dog or a moose. "This woman's real, Juby," my dad says. "You've got to sit down and watch this. This is how women used to be in this country."

This is my cue to leave the room. He wants me to be interested in her, like a role model, but it's fruitcake dad I'm studying. I need to start learning how not to turn out like him. He can sit for hours in front of the TV watching that one channel like it's beaming down the truth from heaven. & for him, the truth is that sharp-faced woman with bank-teller glasses & nonstop blah-blah. I've started calling her Ms. This-Great-Nation. Her show is like reality TV for the brain-dead. I mean any fool could see how somewhere along the line this woman's family got shocked into submission by aliens.

That could be what worries me the most. Most of my friends have issues with their families & sometimes it goes beyond just issues. My mom & my dad don't do drugs, & they make an effort to be nice to me. My mom & I fight, but we both know how far to go, & most of the time it's just bickering. This thing with my dad & Ms. This-Great-Nation could go just about anywhere. She's transported him into Delusion City. & my mom won't admit it, but she's worried. We don't say so, but we both think he'd be a lot better off if he just hooked up with his secretary at the office & then came home & watched sports on TV. The Green Bay Packers might bring my dad back to his right mind.

Used to be my dad was a fanatic for family dinner. No matter what went down during the day, he wanted my mom & me in the dining room with him for family dinner. We could all three be screaming at each other from different rooms in the house, but come dinnertime, he wanted us at the table, stretching out our arms to hold hands with each other while he said grace. Our heavenly father whatever us to Thy loving service Amen. Now he wants us in the TV room with trays set up in front of us & keeping quiet to hear Ms. This-Great-Nation give us the news. Our food doesn't need to be blessed anymore. "Juby, you need to listen to what she's telling you," he says. "Neither you nor your mother gets it about—"

We've all adjusted to the new family TV hour, until one evening I make the mistake of glancing at my cell to see who just sent me a text, & my dad jumps up & knocks over his tray. Then my mom's scrabbling around on the floor trying to clean up his mess, but he doesn't even see her; he's standing in front of me frothing at the mouth, swelling himself up & snorting into my face.

For like half a minute I'm sure he's going to slap me. He's red & sweating, his mouth is moving, his hands are flapping around like injured birds. I sneak my cell down under the sofa cushion, because I know if my dad sees it, he'll grab it & fling it against wall. Meanwhile, behind him my mom's down there scooping the spilled pork roast and green beans onto the tray while Ms. This-Great-Nation stares at us through the TV screen. She's got this fake-sincere smile pasted on her face & she's talking the way she does. That's when it comes to me she might be able to help us out. & I know my mom is still down there on the floor madly trying to think of what to do to guide my dad back to earth. I take a chance & whisper just loud enough for him to hear me. "Dad, listen. Listen to what she's telling us."

All my life he's never listened to me, but right now in his craziness, he turns away from me & faces Ms. This-Great-Nation.

The camera's moving her closer to us. It's eerie. We're getting so intimate with her it's creeping me out, but my dad actually steps around my mom to be nearer the TV. It's like he wants to sit in the woman's lap.

She's telling us about her family & her son who's got Down Syndrome & how she sometimes thinks this child is an angel sent down to them. A pure soul whose sweet face gives her & her husband counsel when the world seems to be turning against them. My dad's paying so much attention he's forgotten me & my cell. He's blind to my mom crawling on the floor right beside him, picking up his food scraps.

"A child whose only skill is to love everybody he sees. I'll be frank," Ms. This-Great-Nation says. "If it weren't for Greg"—she pauses & kind of swallows & her voice goes half squeaky—"If it weren't for Greg, we'd have a lot of hate in our house."

My dad takes another step toward the TV. He's so close now he could touch her face. She's just blinking at the screen now & it's awkward. It takes me a few seconds to process what's going on with her. Either she's really choking up, or she's pretending to be choked up. & you know what? To me it doesn't make any difference which it is. It's a TV show. I'm just embarrassed. But when my dad's arms drop to his sides, & his shoulders start shaking, it hits me how it's a whole other thing for my dad. Ms. This-Great-Nation isn't quite letting herself cry, but my dad is doing it for her.

Girl or not, I'm a tough kid—anybody at our school will tell you that. & I feel like minus zero empathy for this woman on the TV. But I do feel something for my crazy dad. I can't help it, I've never seen him even close to crying. My mom's still on her knees on the floor, but she's straightened up into a kind of kneeling position. & like me she's got her eyes on my dad. She's got her back to the TV, so I know she's not thinking about Ms. This-Great-Nation either.

Then my mom gives me this look that's like the whole history of our family. Or at least the part of it that began when she gave birth to me. I can't read all of her expression, but I get enough of what she's telling me to know that we need to just clear out of this room. Let my dad have his moment with Ms. This-Great-Nation. Whatever happens between him & her, he's not going to be the same loony dude he was when he made us sit down in this room to eat our dinner & listen to her.

My mom & I act out her wordless plan. We ghost-step around my dad—even ducking to keep from getting between him & the TV. We gather up every little item & crumb onto our dinner trays. Quiet as shadows, we're even picking up the salt & pepper shakers. She and I don't have to say that we don't want to have to make another trip into the TV room. I hold my breath to make myself invisible & rescue my cell from under the sofa cushion. Then she & I glide out of the room & pull the door shut behind us & step into the kitchen.

It's like we just escaped from prison. That's when my mom snatches a couple of Kleenexes out of the box on the counter & hands them over to me. At first I don't understand. But then I feel it scalding up behind my face & I let it out & start bawling. & I let my mom put her arms around me. But not for long because we've got to get busy with the cleanup.

TONY HOAGLAND
Crossing Water

In late summer I swim across the lake to the stand of reeds
which grows calmly in the foot-deep water on the other side.

It is like going to a florist's shop
you have to take your clothes off to get to,

where nothing is for sale and nothing on display
but some tall, vertical green spears,

and the small, already half-shriveled pale-purple blossoms
sprouted halfway up the sides of them.

Squatting softly in the cool, tea-colored water,
hearing my own breath move in and out

leaning close to see the tattered, soft-edged
             purses of the flowers,
with their downward hanging cones and coppery antennae

—This is more tenderness than I had reason to expect
from this rude life in which I built

a wall around myself, in which I couldn't manage to repair
my cracked-up little heart.

Each time I make this trip,
I get the queer idea that this

is what is waiting at the end of time:

long stalks slanting in the breeze, then straightening,—
flowers loose-petaled as memory, blue

as the aftertaste of sorrow.

Tonight, I'll lie in bed and feel the day exhaling me
as part of its long sigh into the dark,

knowing that I have no plan.

I will remember how those flowers swayed and then held still
for me to look at them.

TONY HOAGLAND
The Complex Sentence

The kind Italian driver of the bus to Rome
invited her to his house—she was obviously
hungry—and gave her sandwiches
and raped her.

All those years ago—she smiles
while telling it—contemptuous,
somehow
of her younger self,

who drags behind her like a can.
Grammar is great
but who will write the sentence that includes
the story of the damage to her soul

and how she thought her bad Italian
was at fault, and
how it took a month for her to say
the word for what had happened
                             in her head?

But that's why
we invented the complex sentence,
so we could stand at a distance,

making slight adjustments
of the harness,
while following the twisty, ever-turning plot:

the loneliness of what we did;
the loneliness
of what was done to us.

ELISE JUSKA
Transfer Station

After the death of his wife, Loring began giving away things for free. His sister-in-law worried it was some kind of "suicide thing," as his brother Bill put it, which only showed how little they knew him. Loring wasn't suicidal. If anything, in the four months since Gloria died, there was a new kind of calmness about him, a welcome flatness, an absence of things.

For as long as Gloria had been sick they hadn't talked much about what Loring would do after, which struck him as kind of funny now; they'd had the time. But they'd never been planners. They weren't organizers either, which left Loring with a cramped, tired Northeast Philadelphia row house jammed with stuff—old cameras and workbenches, sewing machines and candles, canning jars, camping lanterns, dozens of colored glass bottles and stoneware bowls, hundreds of books and records. At first, he didn't notice. Gloria died in June. Loring could barely account for the weeks since, most of them spent in the dark cave of the living room. Then one day he tripped and fell down the basement stairs, splitting his head open and spilling his beer down his shirt. As he pulled himself onto his elbows, touched the blood above his eye, he felt a spasm of fury—clean and bright and fleeting, but enough for him to see how his life looked. Some of the stuff was sentimental, but most of it junk. Giving it away was not symbolic of anything. He had too much in his house.

He wrote the sign on a piece of corrugated cardboard from the bottom of a case of Pabst: FREE STUFF. Then he found a pair of rusty shears in the garage and cut back the blunt, mossy hedges by the front door, the dull blade chewing slowly through the thick stems. When he was finished, the bushes looked sloppy, but he'd managed to clear away the porch, a gray concrete square. The living-room windows let more light in, he noticed. Gloria would have liked this; he wished he'd done it before.

He and Gloria had lived here thirty-three years, and she'd been sick for most of the last ten. They had neglected things. The lawn was overgrown and weedy. A long crack wandered crookedly down a kitchen window, patched with duct tape—Loring couldn't remember how it got there. A corner of the bedroom ceiling dripped when it rained. Bill, his brother, wanted Loring to move. This section of Philly wasn't "good" anymore, Bill said. He didn't know the half of it—the car windows smashed for loose change in the cup holders, the ten-year-old shot just blocks away. When Loring and Gloria first moved here, there was still a sense of community, people sitting on stoops and kids playing ball in the street. But over the years the neighborhood grew sunken, wary. People moved away. Still, Loring felt immune to serious danger; this was his house. His home. The week after Gloria died, Bill and his wife, Sharon, made a rare visit, Sharon grimacing as she stepped over the threshold, pulling on a pair of rubber gloves and briskly taking charge—bagging up Gloria's pills and supplements, scrubbing dishes, sifting through the flowers the school had sent and picking out the dead ones. When she found Gloria's weed, Sharon gave a pointed sigh but tucked it back in the utensil drawer.

While Sharon was jabbing a vacuum into the dark corners of the living room, Bill took Loring outside and suggested he think about moving. "The memories," Bill said, awkward, hands in pockets, change jingling, peering down the street toward the store that sold lottery tickets and cigarettes. "Plus, you know…" he added, and waved one hand, as if to indicate all of it—the sagging row houses, the graffiti-smattered bus shelter, the eviction notice pinned to a neighbor's door. A car drove by, radio blasting. Loring smiled. He enjoyed seeing his brother squirm. "I mean, you could afford to, right?" Bill said, but the money wasn't the point. When had Loring ever cared about something so material? His brother knew at least this much about him, unless his rich wife had brainwashed him completely. Bill looked at him and said, "Don't stay just to make a point."

Loring gazed over his brother's shoulder. "You wouldn't understand," he said, but stopped himself there. Bill had accused him of acting superior before. What Loring might have added was that he'd rather die tomorrow than live in a neighborhood like Bill and Sharon's, one of those cookie-cutter developments where people looked at you sideways if your backyard wasn't pruned. Here no one judged. No one cared. Gloria had strung their backyard with white lights, crammed it with wicker chairs, shaggy plants, and cedar mulch, a tangle of clotheslines.

"Fine," Bill said. "Stay. But at least don't be idle. Do something. Get out of the house." He glanced at the recycling barrels, three of them brimming with cans, and some bags besides. "You could teach again. They'd bring you back, in some capacity, right?"

Two years before, Loring took early retirement; the school district offered him a generous package and it allowed him to take care of Gloria full-time. There had been a goodbye dinner, speeches, presents. Loring had taught high-school history for thirty-two years. The low track, the "bad" kids, though he never once referred to them that way. He prided himself on his ability to connect with his students, to find the good in kids whose lives were far worse than his own. At Christmas, he always received gifts—a watch, a book of stamps, a bottle of cologne. Loring thanked them, meaning it, hoping the stuff wasn't stolen. He kept it all. He still remembered his favorite present—1989, little fat-faced Maurice Morris, who made a replica of Vet Stadium out of half a milk jug, each tiny paper seat stuck on with a wad of chewing gum. The kid was a genius.

It was all here, Loring thought, somewhere. On a Sunday in September, after assuring his brother he wasn't suicidal, Loring hung up the phone and scanned the packed basement. He felt a single beat of excitement, the first he'd felt in a long while, contemplating what to give away first.

The first day it was a coffee table, only slightly scuffed. Cheap cherry wood, a single cloudy water ring on top. Loring had decided he wouldn't put out anything in truly bad condition. Standards were low around here, but still, it wasn't right. In smaller letters across the bottom of the cardboard sign, he added: GENTLY USED. Then he propped his sign against the leg of the coffee table, opened up a frayed lawn chair and carried it to his porch. He would give away just one thing each day. He liked the prospect of stretching out the process—maybe into October. Maybe it was his old teacher's instinct kicking in, equating the fall with a new project. Each afternoon, he could sit and wait for takers, see whose hands his stuff ended up in, like watching birds alight on the feeders Gloria had hung all over the backyard.

He sat down, cracked open a beer, and watched the people. He saw only a few faces he recognized. Most shot a wary glance at the table, as if suspicious of anything free. It was over an hour before someone stopped, a heavyset woman with a wide, shiny face. She smoothed a palm over the surface of the table, glanced at Loring. "My son just went away to college."

"Good for him," Loring said. In this neighborhood, it was not a small thing.

"Might be nice for him. For his room. You know?"

Loring agreed.

"I'll send my husband back," the woman said. As he waited, Loring envisioned the coffee table's new life in a dorm room, propping up a boy's shoes, piled with textbooks and beer cans. Fifteen minutes later, a rotting Chevy pulled up. The husband strode to the table and, without a glance at Loring, tossed it in the back and drove off.

The next day, a pair of speakers. These went quick. "They work?" said the guy who paused. He was twenty-five maybe, in a jumpsuit and black Phillies cap.

"Guaranteed," said Loring. "Two hundred watts."

"Free, huh?"

"That's right."

The man inspected them, looking for the catch, and it occurred to Loring that wariness had become the norm—nobody trusted anything anymore. Loring sipped his beer, feeling magnanimous, wanting the guy to take the speakers. Finally he said, "All right, man," and tucked the speakers like two footballs under his arms.

"Enjoy," said Loring.

It was the third afternoon, Wednesday, that the kids came. Two boys and a girl—sophomores, Loring guessed—all of them carrying backpacks, walking home from school. They were making their way slowly down the other side of the street when one shouted, "Yo! Free!" and they all ran over and crowded onto Loring's uncut lawn.

"Check it out," one of the boys said, the bigger of the two. He was wearing enormous, drooping mesh shorts and a green Eagles jersey that strained across his soft gut. His cheeks were flushed red, topped with a white-blond crew cut and a cap turned backwards, the stained bill turned up. The boy picked up the ottoman in two hands and pumped it over his head, as if it weighed nothing. It was dark green velvet, one small tear.

"What is it?" asked the girl. She was leaning over the boy's shoulder, sipping at a can of Sunkist. Tall and angular, her eyelids coated with makeup and her thin brown hair streaked with blond.

"What do you think?" said the boy. "A footrest. You know, for resting my tired fucking feet on." He dropped the ottoman and flopped backwards on the lawn, propping his huge puffy red sneakers on it, his chubby calves. Loring smiled. There was something he loved about these kids—their easy bravado, their playful lack of caution. This one, he thought, was the clown.

"Yo, look," said the girl. She was pointing at Loring.

"Good afternoon," Loring said, which made them all laugh.

"What's up with him?" said the boy, as if Loring wasn't standing there.

"He's a hippie," the girl said knowingly, which caused Loring to reflect for a moment on what he looked like. His ragged gray beard, his bald freckled head. He wore old paint-stained shorts and his feet were bare. It had been a long time since he'd thought about his physical appearance; as Gloria grew sicker, she didn't like mirrors.

"What's a hippie?" said the boy on the ground, hands locked behind his head.

"Were you at Woodstock?" the girl said, squinting at Loring over her soda can.

"What's Woodstock?" said the boy.

"Shut up, Eddie."

"What?"

"Tell him," Loring said, nodding at the girl. "Go ahead. Tell him what a hippie is."

She regarded him suspiciously, as if this might be some kind of trick, carefully pushing a lock of hair out of one eye. "It's like a freaky person," she said. Both boys laughed. "A freaky person who smokes drugs." The chubby boy—Eddie—looked at Loring with new interest, raising his eyebrows and lifting his head. "You smoke drugs?"

"Not anymore," Loring shrugged. "Sorry." He thought of the bag of weed his sister-in-law had unearthed in June. Gloria had smoked it at the end, to escape the excruciating pain; at some point this summer, Loring must have finished it.

Bored, Eddie and the girl turned back to the ottoman. The other boy, the quiet one, hung back. He was small, swimming in a giant striped polo shirt and baggy jeans. A fake diamond stud anchored each ear, but with his smattering of freckles and long lashes, his face was almost pretty. The boy was looking closely at Loring, probably weighing this information—Woodstock and hippies, how Loring had gotten from there to here. A thoughtful kid, shy, hanging on the sidelines. A kid who could be reached.

"This a footrest, right?" Eddie was saying. He was standing on the ottoman now, bouncing slightly, hands cupped around his mouth, and bellowed, "Hey, hippie, this a footrest?"

"It's an ottoman," said Loring.

"What?"

"Ottoman. That's what it's called."

Loring sipped his beer. He had gotten through to kids like these before. Just a few years ago a former student, Charles Rush—now in his thirties, a husband and father, a bus driver—looked him up in the White Pages and called him on the phone. He was calling to thank him. They talked for a half-hour, and Loring and Gloria ended up going over to their house in Fishtown. When Charles answered the door, he broke into a grin. *Damn, Mr. Walsh, you got old!*

"Free, huh?" the quiet boy said.

Loring nodded at him. "That's right."

"We can just, like, walk off with it?" Eddie demanded, almost as if he wanted some resistance to make it worthwhile.

"It's yours," Loring said, and added, "I'll have something else tomorrow."

"Yeah?" They glanced at each other. "See you tomorrow then."

The next day, as Loring surveyed his basement, he had the three kids in mind. Finally he settled on his old turntable, even picked out a few albums in their soft, furred jackets. He waited until mid-afternoon, about the time school would get out. And there they came.

"Hey, hippie!" they called, crowding his lawn.

"Welcome back," said Loring.

"What's this?"

"That's a record player." He smiled. "We hippies used to listen to records."

The other boy, the quiet one, lifted the lid.

"What are we supposed to do with it?" said Eddie, shoving the sleeves of his jersey up to his elbows. Loring saw the cheap tattoos blurring the insides of both arms. "We don't got any records."

Don't have, Loring thought, a reflex he fortunately checked.

"There are some—right there." Loring nodded at the pile and Eddie scooped it up. "Bob Dylan," he said. "The Band." He screwed up his face. "What kind of name is The Band?"

"Dumb," the girl breathed. She was wearing a necklace that said TRISHA in glittery gold script.

"Cream," Eddie read, and burst out laughing. "*Cream?*"

"That's Eric Clapton," Loring told him. "The best guitarist there ever was."

"Hey, I know him," the girl said, grabbing at the album.

"Like hell you do, Trish," Eddie said. He flipped quickly through the rest, uninterested, but the other boy, Loring noticed, was inspecting the turntable, lifting up the needle and placing it gently back in its groove. "Man, we don't listen to no hippie music," Eddie whined.

"It's classic rock," said Loring, sipping his beer. "Vintage."

"What's vintage?" Eddie said.

"Old," said the girl—Trisha—looking pointedly at Loring. She was smart, perceptive, he thought, probably funny; but she had a bite. "It means *old*, right?"

Loring shrugged. He understood this balance of power, how fragile it was. Best to pretend indifference. "You don't have to take it," he said. "Just leave it."

The kids exchanged a look. "How much is it worth?" the quiet one said.

Loring looked at him. It hadn't occurred to him that these kids might be taking the stuff to sell it—a pawn shop or eBay or something. Did it matter? But it did; for some reason, Loring wanted them to keep it. Either way, he wasn't about to tell them the value of that turntable. A Pioneer—his parents had splurged on it for his eighteenth birthday.

"Why don't you tell me your names," he said instead. He scratched his beard. "You're Eddie. And you're Trisha."

"The hippie pays attention," she said, but her voice was wary.

"What about you?" he said, addressing the smaller boy.

"You first."

"My name's Loring."

At this, they all cracked up, as he'd known they would. He drained his beer and let them get it out. "*Loring?*" they cried. He imagined what would happen if he told them he was a teacher—a bad idea either way it went. If they had bad associations with teachers, they would hate him by proxy; if they respected teachers, they would think he was pathetic. "*Loring?* What kind of name is that?"

"It was my father's name," he said, then addressed the quiet boy. "And yours?"

"Calvin," he said, proudly. "You know, a *normal* name." He picked up the turntable and Eddie grabbed the albums and they took off down the sidewalk, the long cord trailing behind them. "See you tomorrow, Lorrrrring."

The mirror required some searching, but Loring was certain Trisha would like it. Red mosaic tile, shaped like a sunburst; Gloria had found it at a flea market out in Bucks County, and it hung above their mantel when they first moved in. Eventually he found it, wedged under a wine rack and covered in dust a quarter-inch thick. Loring rubbed it with some of the Windex that Sharon had tucked under his kitchen sink. When he picked up the mirror, he caught his reflection in the glass— the craggy red contours of his nose, his wiry beard, completely gray. There was a healing cut above his eye, from his fall, the skin around it still green.

It was a cloudy day, and the air smelled like rain. Loring dug around in the shed and found an old blue camping tarp that he slung across the branches of his Japanese maple. He put the mirror and his sign under the tarp. Under FREE, he wrote DRY. Then he sat down on the porch, under the corrugated lip of roof. It started raining. A young woman pushing a stroller paused, and Loring willed her to keep going. She tried once to lift the mirror, then glanced at the weather and put it back down.

Hard drops began pelting the tarp. Raining, and a Friday—Loring hoped the kids would show. Then he heard a fast smattering of footsteps and breathy laughter and they crowded under the tarp, Trisha shouting, "Ooh, that's mine!"

Calvin lifted his chin in Loring's direction. Loring nodded back.

"What you mean, yours?" Eddie said, hiking up his giant shorts. His round face hung, dripping, over the glass.

"It's a *girl* mirror, dumbass," Trisha said, laughing. "You a girl or something?" They jounced and joked, and Loring felt an opening in his chest. Happiness.

Trisha picked it up. "Damn, it's heavy!"

"It's an antique," Loring explained.

"See, Trish," said Eddie. "An *antique*. Because you're so fancy."

"Like you would know, fat boy," Trisha said, but the humor was gone. Her voice was sharp, probably wounded. Loring had seen it a million times—how quickly vulnerability could turn into meanness. She shoved the mirror into Eddie's gut. "Carry that," she told him. Her eyes flicked toward Loring, and though she didn't say anything, he imagined her look said thank you.

"See you Monday," Loring told them as they walked off, like a teacher on a Friday afternoon.

Loring put away his sign for the weekend. He would set up shop again on Monday, a school day, when he knew the kids would be coming. To have something to look forward to—he had forgotten the feeling. On Saturday he wandered into the backyard and noticed things he'd been neglecting. The unfilled bird feeders, the plants gone brown at the tips. What had he been doing for the past four months? Looking back, one empty day blurred indistinguishably into the next. He bent to finger the dead leaves, wishing suddenly they'd had children. He and Gloria had talked about it years ago, but like many things, it never felt urgent. They were happy; they had each other. Besides, Loring's days had been populated by kids, hundreds and thousands of kids—to think there was once a time when life felt almost too full to contain. Loring sank onto his knees. He could not have anticipated this loneliness; to anticipate it would have meant admitting it would one day come. As he stared at the ruined garden, a warm spring night returned to him—he and Gloria sitting in this very spot, under the knotty clotheslines and the pale sky, paper lanterns and Carole King and a bottle of Clos du Bois, a stubborn universe of their own making. His arms felt heavy. He was aware of his solitude; he could feel it. He stood up and went back inside, opened a beer. When the phone rang, he saw it was his brother, and ignored it.

"It's a telescope," said Loring.

Calvin had picked it up immediately, and Loring tried to conceal his pride; he'd known Calvin would like it. He'd chosen it with him in mind.

Elise Juska

"You can look at things in the distance and they look closer," Loring told him.

"I know what a telescope is," Calvin breathed, and Trisha's head snapped around. "You think he's stupid or something?"

"No," Loring said. "I don't. Not at all." He was standing on his porch, surveying the scene, rocking slowly from toes to heels. "In fact, I think he's a very smart young man."

"Ooh, hear that?" Trisha said. "The hippie thinks you're smart."

Loring ignored her. Calvin was holding the telescope in both hands, examining it. Brass and snakeskin leather—a beauty.

"Give it a try," Loring said.

Calvin raised the telescope to his eye, aiming it across the street. "What the fuck?" he said. "Thing's busted."

He was holding the wrong end up. "Other side," Loring said. He came down off the porch and moved toward him, felt the old teacher in him returning. "Just turn it—"

"He's got it backward!" Eddie exploded. "He's looking down the wrong side!"

Trisha chimed in laughing and Calvin instantly dropped the telescope on the lawn, caught feeling stupid or caught caring about something—maybe both. Loring's heart sank. "Forget them," he tried again. "Point it at the sky." But he'd already lost him. Calvin looked down, picked something off his baggy sleeve. "Nah," he said. "What else you got?"

Loring rubbed a palm over his bald head. All three were watching him, waiting. It was a cold day, but Eddie still wore shorts, his fleshy calves blotched with pink. Trisha's eyes were so thick with makeup they looked sunken, her temples traced with pale blue veins.

"Well, that's it for today," Loring said.

They glanced at one another. Eddie scratched hard at his cheek. A bus stopped on the corner, brakes squealing, exhaling a sour plume of exhaust. "We got to come back tomorrow?" Calvin said.

"That's how it works," said Loring.

"How come?" Trisha demanded.

Loring shrugged. He didn't have an answer, not one that he could admit. "That's the way it is," he said. "Take it or leave it."

"Leave it," Trisha said, folding her skinny arms across her chest. "We don't want your stupid hippie shit anyway."

"That's fine," Loring bluffed.

The bus pulled away. Calvin was studying him carefully, hands in his deep pockets. "Why are you giving all this stuff away anyway, Loring?"

If there was a note of derision in his name, Loring couldn't hear it. He looked the boy in the eye and said: "My wife died."

"How?"

"Sick," Loring said. "Sick for a very long time."

Calvin held his gaze. Behind him, the other two were still now, listening.

"How long?"

"Ten years."

"With what?"

"Cancer," he said. "Breast cancer."

At this, Eddie laughed, which Loring should have seen coming. He was angry at himself, angry at the boy—the disrespect, the superficial toughness. He thought of Gloria parting with her breasts, electing to lose both, thinking it might save her. Loring had seen true toughness. What he had seen—these kids could not imagine.

He cracked open a new beer, dropping the empty on the grass. "Hey," Trisha pointed. "That's littering. Hippies ain't supposed to litter."

For a moment, Loring felt a bolt of pure dislike for her, but knew better than to let it show. He took a sip and said evenly, "I can do what I want, Trish. It's my house."

Eddie scratched his elbow. "Let's go. I'm hungry."

But Calvin was still looking at Loring, his face solemn and lean. "Why are you giving this shit away, though?" he asked again, and he was right; Loring hadn't answered the question. He considered it, staring down at the worn toes of his leather moccasins. He had always believed in taking young people's questions seriously.

"Because," he said, lifting his head. He squinted into the middle distance, squaring his shoulders. "None of it matters to me anymore, Calvin."

"Shit," said Eddie, and he started laughing again, but this was a laugh born of discomfort—Loring knew there were a million different reasons kids laughed.

"This is depressing," Trisha said. "Loring, you're the most depressing person I ever met in my life."

But Calvin was looking at him seriously. Something had gotten through to the boy; maybe there was something in this sentiment he recognized, something about hopelessness he already understood. Loring smiled down at him, trying to take the edge off. "Besides," he said, "there's just too damn much in my house."

Right away, he realized his mistake. Calvin's bearing seemed to change, an almost imperceptible shifting. "You got a house full of good stuff, huh?" he said.

It occurred to Loring then that they might rob him. They might have been playing him this whole time. They had seemed like decent kids, but maybe he'd been naïve to trust them. He thought of Eddie scratching, the loose laughter. If they were into drugs—they were capable of anything. But still, he trusted them; he wanted to trust them. He wasn't willing to give that up yet.

"I've lived here for a long time," Loring shrugged. "I'm old, remember?"

"So you're getting rid of all of it?" said Calvin.

"Not all," Loring said, rubbing at his beard. "Some." He was trying to find the place between guarded and friendly, but couldn't quite get his bearings. He wished he hadn't had so many beers, wished he were dressed differently—a tie, a pair of decent shoes.

"I know," said Calvin. The other two were hanging back now, and Loring realized he had been wrong about this group: Calvin wasn't on the sidelines. He was the leader. "Why don't you let us go pick out what we want? You know, then we don't got to keep coming back."

Loring lifted his beer and sipped it, squinting at the ground, trying to think of a good excuse. He couldn't admit how much he looked forward to their visits, how they filled his gaping, empty days—they would eat him alive. And he could think of no other reason to drag out this game. Still, to let them into his house—anybody knew this was unwise, but did he care? What was he protecting anymore? Maybe it was the beers, or the need to prove his brother wrong, or a career built on teaching kids like these. Whatever the reason, Loring let them inside.

In the basement, sunlight filtered through the two small dirty crescent windows above the oil burner. The dust hung thick in the dull shafts of light. In some places, paths were started where Loring had dug through the junk looking for the mirror, the telescope, but in many places the boxes piled all the way to ceiling.

"Holy shit," said Eddie. He sounded almost reverent.

"It smells," Trisha said, and it did. The smell was like mildew and damp earth.

Looking around, they all seemed at a loss for how to begin. "Well, have at it," Loring told them. They fanned out slowly. Trisha started by lifting up a stack of old quilts—Gloria's mother's quilts. She let them slump to the floor.

"Hey," Loring said. "Careful with those."

Calvin was inspecting a pair of carved wooden bookends, like a buyer in a store. Eddie ripped off the top of a large cardboard box. "Yo, hippie, what's this?"

He was holding a brass sundial that Gloria once had in the garden. "A sundial," Loring said. "It's a clock that tells time by the sun—" but Eddie had already let it fall with a loud clang. Loring began to feel uneasy. It was the carelessness.

"Look what I got!" Trisha announced.

She was wearing a floppy wide-brimmed hat, straw with a red flower, and all at once the day rushed back at Loring—long ago, after Gloria got that first clean diagnosis. They celebrated by driving to Barnegat Light; she'd bought the hat, and as they walked along the beach, the hat kept blowing in the water, Loring kept chasing it. He was filled with sudden clarity: this had been a mistake.

"Yo, look!" Eddie laughed. He was holding the long body pillow that Gloria sometimes slept with, rubbing it on his crotch. "It's a sex doll!"

"Stop that," Loring said. "Be respectful." But it was a line that hadn't worked on students either; discipline had never been his strong suit. The kids ignored him, tearing into more boxes and tossing things to the floor. "Oh, shit! Look!" they yelled, laughing. Eddie had opened up an old steamer trunk filled with Loring's teaching memorabilia—student projects and papers, the globe from his first classroom. He upended the trunk and poured it on the ground. Loring saw the milk-jug stadium hit the wall, made by Maurice Morris, little gum-backed paper chairs skittering all over the floor.

"Eddie," Loring said, trying to sound firm, but Eddie was throwing things in the empty trunk. Now that they had momentum, they were moving quickly, greedily. Trisha let out a shriek—she had found Gloria's jewelry box, a delicate stained-glass case that Gloria had stashed on a high shelf for safekeeping. The jewelry wasn't expensive, most of it, but it was Gloria's.

"You can't have that," Loring told her, taking a step forward.

Calvin looked up. "You said you were getting rid of it," he said.

"I said most of it—not all of it. That's sentimental," Loring said, then wondered if they'd know the meaning of the word. "It's meaningful to me," he said. "It's very important to me."

But Trisha had already begun piling bracelets on her arms and slinging beads around her neck. Loring saw a strand of blue freshwater pearls disappear over her head—Gloria had worn them at their wedding. "Please," Loring said, the beginnings of desperation. "Please. Leave that alone."

"Here, use this," Calvin told her, unbuckling a suitcase, and the memory was like a shot to his spine—the powder blue Samsonite Gloria had in college, the one she had been carrying the first time she came to visit and Loring picked her up at Thirtieth Street Station— Trisha poured in the rest of the jewelry, tossed the box on top. "That's enough," Loring said. There was a note of pleading in his voice. "You have enough now. I'd like you to leave."

Calvin paused then and gave him a measured look, assessing something—the possible ways to deal with the increasing obstacle that was the sad old man in the corner, the relative ease and difficulty of things. It was the first time it occurred to Loring that the kids might be dangerous. Not only might they take everything he owned, everything he thought he didn't want, they might hurt him. It also occurred to him that, a few weeks ago, he wouldn't have cared. He hadn't been suicidal, but he had been reckless in his passivity. Several nights he'd deliberately left his house unlocked. He hadn't cared about anything. Now he did.

"I want that," Loring said to the boy. "The suitcase." His voice broke. "It was my wife's."

Calvin studied him for a moment, then said, "But we need it," and returned to the task at hand.

Loring thought of going upstairs—but for what? He could call the cops but the kids would be gone by the time they got there. If he made for the stairs, they might try to stop him; he wasn't sure what they were capable of. And it wasn't like they were robbing him, exactly. He had invited them inside. He had given them things—his mirror, his turntable—at the memory of that Pioneer cord trailing them down the sidewalk, he felt a sickening plunge of loss. White spots snowed before his eyes. But when he moved to sit on the bottom step, Calvin glanced over sharply—Loring knew then he wouldn't get upstairs if he tried. He sank onto the stairs and watched them fill up Gloria's suitcase. "You miserable little fucks," he whispered, his eyes swimming with tears.

Eddie hoisted up one end of the steamer trunk. He was panting, his red face sweating. "Grab that side, Trish," he said, and she lifted the other. They came toward the stairs, trunk bumping between their knees, and Loring had to stand to let them pass.

"Shit, he's crying!" Eddie said.

Trisha brought up the rear, wrists jangling. Gloria's engagement ring flashed on her hand. Loring remembered, last spring, Gloria telling him she'd put her rings away for safekeeping. She'd lost so much weight they had started falling off her fingers. She was afraid she might lose them.

"Don't cry, hippie," Trisha said, as tears crawled down Loring's cheeks.

Calvin buckled the blue Samsonite and started for the stairs. At the bottom, the boy paused and placed one hand on the railing. He looked at Loring with something like pity. "See you around, Loring," he said, then hoisted the suitcase in both arms and bounded up the stairs.

Loring listened to the quick, jubilant thunder of footsteps across his living-room floor, the slam of the front screen door, then the silence. He sat on the bottom step and held his head in his hands. He willed the rest of the house to buckle and collapse around him, but it was oblivious to what had just happened, as oblivious as it had been on the morning Gloria stopped breathing. A morning in June, a morning like any other. Loring had sat for hours holding her hand, watching the sky turn from orange to pink to a diffuse, milky white. He hadn't cried then or since, but he did now. Hard, racking sobs that seemed to rise up from his core. He pictured his chest cracking open, guts spilling out. He cried for everything he lost, everything he loved. He loved so much.

When finally Loring stood up, head throbbing, the windows glowed softly with dusk. His limbs were light and hollow, though every nerve rang with pain. He climbed the stairs slowly, feeling humbled and strange. Upstairs, the front door was flung wide open but the first floor appeared untouched. Loring pushed the door shut and locked it. He looked out the living-room window. The tarp was still draped across the tree, the sign flattened on the grass. The telescope was gone. He pulled the shade down and retreated to the darkness of his couch, but with the hedges cut back from the windows, he couldn't keep the light from coming in the room.

LAURA KASISCHKE
The Martyr's Motel

They'd traveled one by one
on their knees beneath the earth
to be gathered at the station

to be given robes and haloes and official papers.

And a bus ticket each to the roadside motel
in Ohio that held
the reservations in their names, where

those who'd been slain before them were waiting.

Can these be the right martyrs? Can this be the place?

They rubbed their eyes as they pressed, to the bus
windows, their faces:

Everything
was the same.
The familiar children
splashing in the pool.
The barbecue.
The sound
of ice being dumped
into plastic buckets.
My God, we're
here again, out of all
the possible motels
in time and space?
Who

could have prepared them
for such homely terror? Even

after the eyes gouged out
and the necks severed, the hands
cut off and the racking
wheel, how

such a simple, happy memory
captured in a photo
could mortally wound a martyr
long after the slaughter was over.

LAURA KASISCHKE
You tell me

And every morning the sun comes up. And the pretty coffee in a cup.
And a bird meowing outside in a tree. And, on the ceiling, the water
stain of England made sadder by singing in a minor key.

The size of a coffin, and full of bees.
Shadow on a tractor, mowing the field.
The cat, awake now, my disheveled beast.

You tell me: Are these flowers in a vase on the table blind? And, if not,
what do they see? If it never budges, this turnstile between you and
me and the only train leaving? And the door to the stall—if the latch is
broken? And the misplaced subway token. And the change for the bus,
if I lost it all? Slipped it into the sewer grate as the officials hurried to
lock the gate?

The birds full of tree, and the shoulder bone beneath it. A glass shattered
into the sun's billion pieces. Holding that, thirsty, and trying to drink.
And never again to wake, or to sleep.

You tell me.
You tell me.

JOANNA KLINK
The Graves

So here are the strange feelings that flicker
in you or anchor like weights in your eyes.
Turn back and you might undo them,
the way trees seem to float
free of themselves as they root.
A swan can hold itself on the gray ice water
and not waver, an open note upon which minor chords
blur and rest. But she was born dark.
The shore of that lake is littered with glass.
How you came to be who you are
was all unwinding, the pedals of a bike in flight,
off to retrieve a parcel that could only be a gift,
or felt, as a child, the sea weed around my feet,
white light rushing in with the surf.
What lived there?

                    —joy, dispatched from nowhere,
and no need to think about your purpose,
and no fear that the sun gliding down
might burn the earth it feeds. Black habitat of now
in which decimation looks tender.
Sometimes the call of a bird is so clear
it bruises my hands. At night, behind glass,
light empties out then fills a room and the people in it,
hovering around a fire, gorgeous winds of shape
leaning close to each other in laughter.
From this distance, they are a grace,
an ache. The kingdom inside.

REBECCA LEHMANN
Swan Road

For every forest, there is a pig screaming
out like a child as the butcher's knife pops
open its throat. For every bucket of pig's blood,
a bucket of rainwater, saved to hydrate
a spring garden. For every Amish-horse-and-buggy
sign on a country road, a teenager exhales
pot smoke into a pillow in her parents' basement.
For every time I see you in a dream, friend
whose betrayal crystallized like spun sugar,
another dream where my grandfather speaks
to me in German and offers me candied ham,
the back of his white T-shirt blotched
with sweat stains. For every candied ham,
a stick insect blends into the trunk of an ironwood
tree in a Wisconsin forest. For every priest,
four plump nuns. For every stained-glass window
depicting a station of the cross, four atheists.
For every dark bathroom, a night-light.
For every despised work day, a tumbler glass
of whiskey, a joint, and a soak in a hot bath.
For every blockbuster set on Mars, my sister-
in-law gets a new dog. For every daffodil sprout
breaking thawed mud in March, a twelve-year-old
gets her first period in phys-ed class, during
the gymnastics unit. For every adolescent's
backbend, a squirrel on a high bough screeches
over her fallen nest. For every baby squirrel
salvaged from our driveway and taken
to the animal rescue center, a sentimental
movie starring Henry Fonda. For every twelve
angry men, twelve satisfied, preening swans.
For every swan, a river; in Anglo-Saxon, *swanrād*,
swan-road. For every swan-road, a broken

fingernail. For every hung-over morning,
an ecstatic, drunken night. For every proton, a neutron.
For every cat, a poem about ocean fish. For every
illegally parked car, a golden eagle's winter nest.
There will be time left to wander in the forest,
time to stroke the moss-covered side of each tree,
time to notice how the final patches of snow
clinging to the shaded bluffs resemble
stampedes of clouds on a buff-colored sky.

ALEX LEMON
Dance Dance Dance

Before it's too late—neck-
    Grope this life's most beautiful
Monsters until all of this disorder

Shapes sacred. Until flocks
    Of balloon animals—thousands
Of them—drop from the diamond-

Blue sky. Purple hippos & clownfish.
    Ticks like hubcaps & backpack-
Size wolves. A dancer will find

A carved-in-butter replica
    Of *The Garden of Earthly Delights*
Sprawling the Landing Strip's parking

Lot. Fingerprints will cloud
    The windows of the downtown
Storefronts. In them some will

See angels. Others will say, *Nope.*
    That there be Satan. Each sweltering
Morning, furred over the sidewalk

Like fresh snow, hibiscus. Explosions
    Will be seen in the sky & letter
After letter in the paper will attempt

To explain the taste of falling.
    First—the dancer, even when
Working the pole, will appear

To be wearing garments sewn
    From moonlight. A week later
& everyone will be splendor-

Garbed. From then on, without
    Fail, each passerby will see
Their own ghost in the glass

&, freighted with the neon glow
    Of blinking ads, feel an abundance
Of life opening like a fist in their chest.

JAMAAL MAY
Masticated Light

In a waiting room at the Kresge Eye Center,
my fingers trace the outline of money folded into pocket
and I know the two hundred fifty dollars there
is made up of two hundred forty-five I can't afford to spend
but will spend on a calm voice to tell me
how I am to be repaired. But *legally blind*
and *nothing can be done* means I'll spend
the rest of the week closing an eye to the world,
watching how easily this becomes that.
The lampposts lining the walk home
are the thinnest spears I've ever seen, a row of trashcans
become discarded war-drums, and the teeth
in the mouth of an oncoming truck
want to tear through me. Some of me
always wants to be swallowed.

The last thing my doctor said before I lost
my insurance was to see a vision specialist
to address the way light struggles and bends
through my deformed cornea.
Before the exam I never closed my right eye
and watched the world become a melting watercolor
with the left. Before a doctor shot light
into the twitching thing, before I realized
how little light I could handle, I never
thought much of the boy who clawed up at me
from beneath my punches, how a fingernail scraped
the eye, or how it closed shut
like a door to a room I could never leave.

Once, I swallowed the distance between
my fists and the boy running from my hunger.
I could see the reflective mesh of his shoes,

the liquor bottle tossed in an arc,
even before it shattered at my feet, and I am embarrassed
at how sharp my eyes were, how deft my body,
my limbs closing the distance—how easily
I owned his face, its fear, its fought-back tears—
all of it mine. I don't want to remember the eyes
that glanced over shoulder just before
I dragged him like a gazelle into the grass
that was a stretch of gravel and glass
outside a liquor store. How easily this becomes that.

When horns sprout from the head of my silhouette
rippling *dark, dark, dark* against the haze of water,
I try to squint that monster
into the shape of a man. How difficult for that
to become this. When I close my bad eye
it's like aiming through a gunsight;
even the good eye is only as good as whatever glass
an optometrist can shape. I'm told
it is worn down from the extra work of interpreting
what the broken eye leaves gnashed.
From a suspension bridge, my failing organ
watches a mouth opening out of the Detroit River,
broad and black-throated, devouring the skyline,
every reflection, a tattered bank of clouds,
and a clouded smear of orange and pink light.

JEFFREY McDANIEL
The Birds and the Bees

When I hit thirteen, the noun between my legs
turning into a verb, my father sat me down and said:

one day you will have a wife of your own. A man
will come—a helpful neighbor knocking

while you're at work perhaps, or a garlicky colleague
at an office party, or a lifeguard on a spit of sand—

and that man will have your beloved, perhaps
even in your sheets, but that won't mean you're weak.

Remember our great ancestor, Menelaus, biceps
the size of grapefruits, his chest far hairier

than that pretty boy who slipped in and swiped
his wife, like a calla lily from his lapel. Remember

Marcus Aurelius' words: *reject your sense of injury
and the injury itself disappears.* No need to launch

another Trojan just because some stallion
trotted into her. No need to perish like Pushkin

slumped in ice. Begin preparing now. When friends
sleep over, let them take your bed. Never yell

shotgun—the backseat will scrub you down,
so years later, when your wife returns home

with that glazed, seen-god look in her eyes, the sweat
of his trigger-happy fingers still greasing the white

napkin of her thighs, you can settle into that moment,
ask her how it was, if you can witness next time.

JEFFREY McDANIEL
Beware of the Dark Sedan Idling Inside You

I flick a switch—out flashes the light bulb,
like God snapping his fingers in my face:
Wake up, Pumpkinhead. I've been running around
half-naked, with the rest of America,
wearing only a credit card and a cashmere scarf.
Arf, arf. Yesterday, I went to Circuit City's
going-out-of-business sale to revel in the fall of capitalism,
but all I saw were the sad faces of underpaid workers.

Welcome to land of the freefall
and the freebaser, as well as the freelancer
and freeloader, and front-loading washing machine,
where you can empty your conscience and wash
all those illicit thoughts about illegal immigrants
out of your brain, where it's still OK
to dock your canoe at the racist joke island
at cocktail parties and chuckle. Two housewives
bang prescription medicine bottles together
and whisper *cheers.* An hour opens
its trench coat and shows you its stolen minutes.
A homeless man gets a boner while sleeping
on a steam grate. There's a dark car idling
inside you. The question is: do you get in?

ERIKA MEITNER

Porto, Portare, Portavi, Portatus

At the airport the conveyor bears small yachts shaped like luggage
into the distance, and I am headed, when they let me pass

through the X-ray arch, toward home. There is a distance
sometimes greater than this between us, since you are in

another state—gaseous, solid, liquid, light—and I admit
I am often absent lately from whatever is happening

in a given room. Portatus. Having been carried from one place
to another, I will be delayed in this terminal in Akron, Ohio

for the longest dusk, but I do not yet know this. I spend hours
trying to puzzle out the black script running a boy's entire right arm.

He is crew-cut Army, sits in the attached row across from me,
feet up on a digicam rucksack. It's probably bible, that tattoo,

John or Luke, maybe Timothy, and the boy is beautiful, the boy
is totally unmarred but for his tattoo. When he flips his cell phone

open & shut, open & shut, I want to reach out to stroke his
wheat-colored stubble, ask him what his black ink means.

Portare, to bear. *I still have many things to say to you,
but you cannot bear them now.* Portare bellum: to carry the war.

Before Thanksgiving, we will pull in to the Sunoco off I-78 in Jersey,
where one veteran in hunting camo carries another like a bride

over a threshold. They will be laughing when they chime
through the door of the Quik Mart. Every footstep and palm-press.

Every machine propelling us forward. Wrecked amen of beverage cases,
clicking gas pumps. Selah hallelujah. *And I will carry you away*

beyond Babylon, a passage, portare, to bear from one place to another,
on one's arms, head, or back. Our bodies bear witness (to the light

to the darkness), bear fruit (lucky lucky), bear the sins of many,
bear whatever it is into the distance. When our neighbor dies—

the pastor's wife—he calls over, asks me to go through her clothes,
take them home. She would want you to have them, he says.

*For we brought nothing into this world, and it is certain we can carry
nothing out* (except our stories). In this story, the door jingles hello.

The man being carried turns his head toward me,
over the shoulder of the man carrying him, and he is laughing.

The word I thought of was mirth: *and Sarah laughed
to herself, and God asked Abraham, Why did Sarah laugh?*

Porto. I bring my son inside by the hand, after them.
He has to pee. The bathroom is outside. There is no key,

says the cashier, and I see the laughing man balanced on a stool
at the counter, which is when I notice that he has no legs.

His buddy peruses the beef jerky aisle, and when he turns,
one side of his face is scarred and pitted. The bathroom

is fetid. My small son touches the graffitied tiles,
the toilet seat, asks about the condom machine

bolted to the wall, and I stumble through some answer
about adult things, about protection. He does not ask

about the soldier with no legs. Portant. They carry.
Outside, their pickup is filled with hunting gear,

Erika Meitner 81

camo tarps, a wheelchair, a USMC sticker. Portavi.
I have carried my son and I will not bear another one.

My neighbor's name was Ruth, and before she died I was often
tempted to ask her to pray for me, as if Jesus could cure

our secondary infertility. That story of him touching the bier.
Then the bearers stood still. And he said, "Young man, get up."

And he told the mother not to weep, and her only son sat up,
began to speak. Portamus. You & I, we carry the burden together

of not-exactly-barren. We were fruitful and now un-,
and some days we are so old that the gray in your hair

gleams like treasure, and others we are so young I get carded
for beer at the Food Lion. In this story, I put off visiting

the neighbor's to go through Ruth's clothes, and instead
get her back issues of *Good Housekeeping* from her husband.

In my story, your face is turned toward me, and we are laughing
at the ancient recipes, and in my story everyone is marked

and we all carry, have been carried, bear up under the weight
of our dead and our living and our injured and injured and injured.

Daily, we bear the weight of more weight forward;
portare is hardly ever said of a light load.

SZIDÓNIA MOLNÁR
Andorra

Sadie's lover, Marcus, called her every Thursday from Chicago as he drove to and from marriage counseling. (His wife drove separately, it goes without saying.) The end result of this was that it felt as if the three of them were in counseling together, but Sadie sort of liked that.

The reason Marcus had to go to marriage counseling was that three months ago, his wife had intercepted an e-mail from Sadie. Which meant, among other things, that Marcus had to agree to go to marriage counseling and promise never to speak to Sadie again, to banish her to the Ulan Bator of his heart, while in reality Sadie remained as central as Starbucks. Sadie liked that too.

Sadie was thirty-six. She had two little boys named Rufus and Leo, aged six and four, and a fifty-year-old husband named Roderick, who worked for the Council on Foreign Relations, and a big house in Washington, D.C., and a minivan full of dog hair. The fact that she had all this and a long-distance lover seemed to her like a sign of strength and character; not many people could manage it.

Of course, Sadie had help. She had a Filipino housekeeper named Nelda. When Sadie interviewed her two years ago, Nelda had said, "I'm slow."

"I don't mind slow," Sadie said, impressed by Nelda's candor. "I think IQ is...overrated." (The pause was while she looked for a simpler word for *overrated*.)

"Not slow like that," Nelda said, blinking behind her thick glasses. "Slow like not fast."

Nelda was indeed slow, and she had a disconcerting habit of going into a trance when asked questions, and it turned out that she was allergic to nearly all cleaning products. She also had a large, troubled family, many of whom came to work with her (some just hung out and made helpful suggestions, but some actually cleaned, so the house looked OK) and Sadie didn't fire her, because she had a vague idea that having so many people around the house gave her children a sense of family and community that might otherwise be lacking.

This was how Sadie's life ticked along, not like a finely tuned engine, but like some other thing that ticks: noisy pipes, or a bomb.

Marcus' wife said in counseling that she wanted to spend more time with him.

"She said that the only thing we ever do together is that one of us holds the dog still while the other one puts that anti-flea stuff on his neck," Marcus told Sadie afterward.

"Roderick and I do that sometimes," Sadie said thoughtfully. "It's nice."

Sadie had met Marcus a year ago when she sat next to him on a flight from Washington to Chicago. She was going to visit her parents in Wisconsin. He had asked her to name a small republic located in the Pyrenees on the French-Spanish border. (He was doing a crossword puzzle.)

It was ironic that he should ask her that because when she first started dating Roderick, her parents had offered to *pay* for her to take a geography course so she and Roderick would have something to talk about. Which was in itself ironic because Sadie was twenty-four at the time and didn't have any trouble getting men to talk to her, Roderick included.

So instead of telling Marcus the answer (she didn't know it anyway), Sadie told him the story of her parents' offer, and by the time the plane was over Ohio, he was already in love with her, or so he said later. And Sadie gave all the credit to the story about the geography lessons. It was everything a story should be, she felt. She was proud of it. Not everyone has a story that good.

Sadie and Roderick had to go to a dinner party at the Finnish Embassy. Sadie said she hated dinner parties, and Roderick said they weren't so bad if you got plastered as fast as possible. Sadie still thought the best part was probably picking out what to wear—a pink wool wraparound dress, which was new and came unwrapped if she made the slightest movement. Sadie discovered this when she walked downstairs, but Nelda was already there with five or six relatives to babysit. So Sadie just rewrapped her dress and asked Nelda if she could leave one of her nieces in charge of the boys and come pick them up at ten o'clock. They gave her the address, and off she and Roderick went.

At the dinner, Sadie sat between a man who told her that he was a world expert on the pistachio and another man who told her that he collected Early American documents as a hobby. Sadie concentrated on cutting her reindeer into very tiny pieces and drank so much red wine that her teeth turned purple. She held the thought of Marcus in her mind, like a Saint Christopher medal, or a dream catcher, or maybe just a hidden flask of whiskey in her purse—something that made survival possible.

After the dinner, they went outside to wait for Nelda to pick them up. They waited so long that Roderick said he was sober and then they waited even longer and Roderick said they could have walked home by now. Sadie said that Nelda had trouble with time, and Roderick asked if she meant that Nelda had trouble with time the way some people have trouble with money. Sadie said no, it was more that Nelda didn't believe in time, the way some people didn't believe in ESP or Bigfoot. Roderick said they really had to get some decent help, but he said that about twice a month anyway.

Finally an SUV with a bunch of Filipino people in it pulled up and Nelda rolled down the passenger window, her eyeglasses glinting opaquely in the moonlight. Sadie had a very bad moment where she was sure Nelda was going to say there wasn't room for them, but all Nelda said was, "Good evening."

So Sadie squeezed in the front next to Nelda and Roderick squeezed in the back with some of Nelda's relatives. Sadie could hear him discussing the Chinese claims in the South China Sea. He sounded fairly happy. She sighed and leaned her head back.

"How was your dinner?" Nelda asked. "You enjoy yourself?"

"I sat next to a man who was an expert on *nuts*," Sadie said.

Nelda didn't say anything. Sadie closed her eyes, the passing streetlamps flashing white oblongs against her lids. Finally Nelda seemed to come to life again. She patted Sadie's hand and said, "Well, soon you be in your own bed," and Sadie thought, not for the first time, that Nelda understood her on some deep and fundamental level no one else did.

Marcus had a rule against saying bad things about their spouses. Sadie broke the rule all the time; why have an affair if not to say bad things about your spouse? So she went ahead and told Marcus that when she tried to talk to Roderick about how terrific Leo's preschool teacher was, Roderick only told her a bunch of facts about Bosnia.

Szidónia Molnár

"I mean, Leo's teacher *is* from Bosnia," Sadie said, "but that wasn't what I wanted to discuss."

"What did Roderick say about Bosnia?" Marcus asked.

A small silence followed while Sadie wished that it were permissible to say bad things about your lover to your husband. But then she sighed and said, "Well, just that it's the twentieth anniversary of the siege of Sarajevo, and something about the Dayton Peace Agreement."

"What's fascinating about Bosnia—," Marcus said but Sadie had to hang up abruptly because Rufus came running into her bedroom to tell her he had a rash on his belly button.

Sadie looked at his belly button and told him it was nothing to worry about, although privately she wondered if maybe a mushroom was growing in there and resolved to give more thorough baths. She thought that was the essence of motherhood: acting like you knew what you were talking about when you didn't. That, and looking at people's rashes. It was probably why people had affairs.

"Who wants to go to the park?" Sadie asked.

Rufus and Leo scrambled up from the sofa and, too late, Sadie realized that Nelda's assorted relatives were showing their nearly imperceptible signs of preparation, as well. It would be a group outing.

They left in stages, like a military operation. First went Rufus and Leo on their little bikes with the training wheels and a couple of the spryer relatives to help them cross the streets. Next was the dog, panting and straining, the leash wrapped around the waist of one of Nelda's nephews, and the remaining relatives lending moral support. Last were Sadie and Nelda.

"Sorry," Nelda said to Sadie as she locked the front door. "I'm always last, like a caboose."

"That's OK," said Sadie, although she thought Nelda was more like an anchor than a caboose because at least a caboose went where the rest of the train went; she and Nelda might still be here when everyone else got back.

Sadie put the keys in her pocket and they began walking.

"You walk slow, you don't feel the heat," Nelda said.

It was October and they could have walked as fast as they wanted without feeling the heat, but Sadie didn't say so. Maybe it was still summer in Nelda's private world. Maybe it was *several* summers ago.

A jubilant shout and small burst of applause came from the relatives far ahead of them. Sadie knew that meant Rufus or Leo had done something praiseworthy, had pedaled up a small hill without stopping or bumped their bikes over a big crack in the sidewalk without falling over.

She was missing them grow up, she thought suddenly. They were passing all these milestones with strangers while she talked to Nelda and snuck away to call Marcus.

But that was foolishness. You couldn't have everything the way you wanted all the time. You were lucky if you got it occasionally. Leo had taken his first steps at Hooters when they'd gone there for an Australian diplomat's farewell lunch party, and Sadie had been unable to bring herself to record it in Leo's baby book. She gave up on baby books entirely after that.

The marriage counselor wanted Marcus to do something nice for his wife every day.

"So right away," he said to Sadie afterward, "I'm thinking: *how* nice?"

"You could give her flowers," Sadie said.

"I'm not buying flowers every day," Marcus said, sounding shocked.

"I didn't mean every day," Sadie said. "Just once, in the beginning."

"Also, I think it's sort of hilarious how much women like to get flowers," Marcus said.

"No more hilarious than how much men like to get blow jobs," said Sadie, who liked to get flowers herself.

"Flowers and blow jobs are *not* comparable," Marcus said, sounding even more shocked than he had about the idea of flowers every day.

"They are in how predictable it is that whoever's getting them will like it," Sadie said. "A lot."

"They're not even in the same *category*," Marcus said.

Sadie thought they were actually very similar except that after a few really excellent blow jobs, men often fell hopelessly in love with you, whereas women knew, no matter how beautiful the flowers, that it was all for show.

Sadie was chopping celery when Nelda arrived. Sadie hardly ever cooked, and Nelda gave her a big smile and squinted at her approvingly. "Ah," she said. "You making dinner for the man you love?"

"No," Sadie said. "I'm making dinner for the Health Minister of Togo."

Szidónia Molnár 87

Besides, Marcus was the man she loved. Or had Nelda meant Marcus? Sometimes Sadie wondered.

"Anyway," Sadie continued. "The Health Minister is coming here for dinner tonight at seven, so I need you, or someone, to clean the living room."

She realized as she said this, though, that Nelda was alone, a movie star without her entourage. Sadie was surprised she'd recognized her.

"Nobody come with me today," Nelda said. "They all go to vote at the embassy. Big election in the Philippines."

This seemed to happen every few weeks. And although most of the time, Sadie actively suppressed the part of her brain that dealt with politics and foreign policy (she feared becoming a female version of Roderick), she wondered exactly how many elections there could be. She was just as insecure as everyone else, and now suddenly she worried that all the relatives had found some other house to hang out in— someplace where the time went faster, the conversation was livelier, the atmosphere more relaxed, the hostess friendlier and funnier. Wasn't that what everyone ran around looking for, in some form or another?

"What about the living room?" she said to Nelda.

Nelda went off into a reverie, while Sadie began chopping the celery again. Finally Nelda shook her head and said no, she had to go pick up everyone else in an hour but that Sadie worried too much, she was so sweet and had such a pretty smile no one would notice the dog hair.

Sadie and Marcus had phone sex by the bushelful.

"You don't measure phone sex by the bushel," Marcus said.

"Well, then how *do* you measure it?" Sadie asked. Sometimes she thought she'd gone crazy; other times she thought she was the only sane person left in the world.

Marcus sounded thoughtful. "Maybe by the minute."

"But I have an unlimited calling plan," Sadie said doubtfully.

"I guess it can't be measured," Marcus said.

"But it can," Sadie said. "Because you can have a lot or a little."

"Or none," Marcus said. "Like right now."

"We will," Sadie said. "In a minute. Right now I'm all distracted by phone-sex units."

"It's unique," Marcus said. "Everything else can be measured except phone sex."

Everything except love, Sadie thought. Love can't be measured in units either, unless it's by phone sex.

"Anyway," Marcus said, his voice deepening. "What are you wearing?"

"What are you wearing?" Sadie said later to Rufus when he ran through the kitchen in his underpants, and she said, "Good…good…" to Leo when he helped her mix the cake batter, and "I'm coming," to Nelda when she called up that the UPS man was there, and "I wish you were here," to her mother on the phone, and "Oh, fuck me," when the dog threw up on the carpet. She didn't say "I want you in my mouth right now," to anyone, but it occurred to her that she could get through most days with only a limited number of phrases, that it was how you said them and who you were at that moment that mattered.

Marcus' wife said in counseling that she'd rather have a car accident than find out Marcus was still seeing Sadie.

"What kind of car accident?" Sadie asked.

"I don't know," Marcus said impatiently. He was always in a bad mood after counseling. "She might have meant a fatal car accident or she might have meant a disfiguring car accident or she might have meant a fender bender. I also don't know where she figures on it happening or whether our insurance premiums would go up."

This bothered Sadie all day, being compared to a car accident.

As she and Roderick lay in bed that night, it was still on Sadie's mind.

"What would be worse—," she began, but her nerve failed her.

"Worse than what?" Roderick asked. He was reading *The Economist*.

Sadie fingered the lace on the edge of her nightgown. "Just—what would—what is a very bad thing you could imagine happening?"

"Egypt electing a Muslim-brotherhood president," Roderick said without hesitating. "That would be a disaster."

It was actually just as reassuring as anything he might have said if he'd known what Sadie was talking about, and she rolled over suddenly and pressed herself against him.

The phrase "I want you in my mouth right now" began to worry Sadie. Or rather, the fact that she only said it during phone sex, that she could not say it innocently in some other part of her life.

No one said it at Leo's playgroup, although sometimes they said nearly the opposite—"Don't put that in your mouth!"—when a child picked something disgusting off the floor or sidewalk. No one said it at school drop-off or pick-up, and Sadie sometimes wished someone would say it, wished someone would say anything besides talking about how to get your kid to eat more fruits and vegetables. No one said it at Sadie's book club, no one said it at the pediatrician's, no one said it at the supermarket, or the pharmacy, or the post office, or the dry cleaners, or the bank, or story time at the library.

No one said it, it seemed, but Sadie.

Roderick joined a bicycling club for people over fifty. The club was going to cycle from Washington, D.C., to Portland, Maine, to raise money for the Arthritis Foundation and they trained three times a week.

The upside of this was that Roderick was out of the house more and would actually be gone for three whole weeks in May. Sadie thought surely she would be able to see Marcus then. Roderick was opposed to leaving Nelda in charge of the children overnight—he said he was afraid they'd come home and find that all the relatives had opened a bake stand in the front yard and were making empanadas in the kitchen. But Sadie trusted them. She would make it work.

The downside of the cycle club was that now on Monday, Wednesday, and Thursday evenings, Sadie's kitchen was filled with sweaty gray-haired men in cycling shorts, filling their water bottles and talking about freewheel cog removal. They all had a special biking app on their iPhones that recorded their times and distances, and reminded Sadie of when the children were babies and she used to talk about how many ounces of formula they'd drunk. Frequently Nelda and her relatives were still in the kitchen too, because although Nelda's workday officially ended at five o'clock, they took no more notice of that than they did of any other time.

This made a lot of people for Sadie to step around as she made pancakes for Leo and Rufus, a lot of voices to talk over when it was time to persuade the boys to go to bed. And although when Sadie was younger, she had hoped someday to have a house that was a place where people liked to gather, a hub of social activity, she had had something else in mind. She hadn't meant this.

Marcus' wife went on a business retreat for her company, so Sadie told Roderick she was going to visit an old school friend and flew to

Chicago for the weekend. She took a cab to Marcus' house and then there was the usual awkwardness of seeing him, of their standing in his front hall together.

Sadie felt like a school girl, because despite all their hundreds of hours of phone sex and conversation, she and Marcus had only spent a limited time in each other's physical presence. Sadie supposed that timewise, they were actually only on their fourth or fifth date. And she felt like a hooker because, let's not mess around, they were here to have sex and lots of it. (Always at this point Sadie secretly wanted to start discussing whether an hour was an hour or fifty minutes.) And because Sadie couldn't wait for the sex, she also felt like a man, or how she supposed a man went around feeling pretty much all the time.

And then she and Marcus were kissing, and his tongue was in her mouth and her hands were in his hair, and then for a little while, although not nearly long enough, Sadie felt like herself.

Marcus' wife called every few hours, apparently to reassure herself that if Marcus was home, then he wasn't out somewhere, up to no good. Of course, Marcus was in and up to no good, but his wife didn't know that. Sadie and Marcus were invariably in bed when she called (because they spent all their time together in bed) and sometimes while he talked to his wife, Marcus would run his hand absently over Sadie's naked hip, like an executive fiddling with a coffee cup.

The third time his wife called, Sadie slipped on a T-shirt and walked very quietly to the bathroom and sat on the edge of the bathtub, her bare feet on the cold tiles. She seldom thought about Marcus' wife, even while staying in her house, except for noticing that this house smelled like furniture polish and lavender while Sadie's own house always seemed to smell like a garlicky Labrador. But now, as the cold worked its way up Sadie's legs, she thought of Marcus' wife, warm and dry and snug in her hotel room, with no idea that the very air she moved through was swarming with hidden dangers, that she might as well be driving home after the bars closed on New Year's Eve in a car with broken headlights and balding tires.

Of course, Sadie called Roderick from Chicago too.

She called and he told her that he'd cycled seventy-four miles and could have gone a hundred but his bike threw its chain in Silver Spring.

"Oh," Sadie said. "Be sure to pay Nelda extra for working on the weekend."

"What about all these other people?" Roderick asked. "Do I pay them too?"

"No," Sadie said. "They just show up."

She asked if she could speak to Rufus and Roderick set the phone down, and in the background she could hear Rufus say, "I can't stop now!" Roderick came back and said that she couldn't speak to Rufus because he was in the middle of a tinker-toy construction. He said she couldn't speak to Leo because he was asleep with his head on the kitchen table next to a bowl of rice. He said she couldn't speak to the dog because the dog had escaped from the backyard and run away, but that some nice woman called to say she'd found him, and a bunch of Nelda's relatives had gone off to collect him an hour ago.

"But you can speak to me," Roderick said.

"Well, yes," Sadie said.

In the cab on the way to the airport on Sunday, Sadie suddenly caught her breath. She didn't know where her underpants were. Not the underpants she was *wearing*, obviously; she knew where those were. But the pair she'd been wearing when she arrived at Marcus' house. The ones he had pulled off as he pressed her against the kitchen counter. She could remember them dangling from her ankle briefly and then she'd kicked them off. But where had they gone from there? She had meant to pick them up—had reminded herself—but had she? Or were they now lying in Marcus' recycling bin or fruit bowl?

She called him as soon as the cab dropped her off. "Don't freak out," she said. "But it seems I may have left a pair of underpants at your house."

"Underpants?" Marcus said. It sounded like he'd never heard the word before, but Sadie knew it was just the early stages of shock.

"Yes," she said slowly. "In the kitchen somewhere, I think."

"Underpants?" Marcus said again.

They seemed to be stuck.

"Go look," she said. "And call me back if you find them."

Her mouth was dry and she could feel her pulse thudding in her ears. She checked all the pockets of her purse and stopped to open her suitcase and paw through it frantically on the sidewalk, but her underpants weren't there.

Marcus didn't call back, and the fact that Sadie checked her phone a hundred times—in line at security, rushing through the terminal, waiting at the gate—failed to summon him.

She boarded the plane and the flight attendant came through with little foil packets of peanuts. Sadie leaned down to put hers in her purse to give to Rufus later, and there in the outside pocket, completely flattened, were her black lace panties. She could see them now, in the harsh light of the plane.

Suddenly it was not blood flowing through Sadie's veins, but honey: slow and sweet and delicious.

She pulled out her phone and called Marcus.

"Guess what?" she said happily. "I found my underpants!"

The man sitting next to Sadie was about to eat a peanut and he appeared to inhale it when she spoke. He began coughing.

"Marcus?" she said. "Did you hear me?"

"Yes," he said. "I heard you."

"Well, isn't that great?" Sadie said. The man next to her was still coughing and she had to stifle the impulse to snap at him to be quiet.

"Look," Marcus said. "I don't think I can keep doing this. This last hour has been terrible. I thought I was going to have a heart attack."

"I know—," Sadie began but he cut her off.

"I can't go through my wife finding out again," Marcus said. "Even the therapist says we'd never come back from that."

The therapist! Sadie could not believe he was quoting the therapist, to her of all people. It felt like a small animal with sharp claws was digging at her chest.

"Marcus—," she began desperately, but suddenly the flight attendant was standing beside her.

"You have to turn your phone off now," she said, smiling an iron-hard smile.

Sadie was about to protest when she realized Marcus was no longer there.

She dropped the hand holding her phone to her lap. The screen was dark.

"You have to turn it off, not just stop talking on it," the flight attendant said. Then she looked past Sadie to the man next to her. "Are you OK, sir? You're not allergic to peanuts, are you?"

Sadie turned to look at him. He was a businessman in a rumpled blue suit, still coughing. He shook his head at the flight attendant and she moved on, but Sadie kept looking at him. His skin was flushed and his eyes were damp and the muscles of his face were spasming slightly, as though he were in pain.

Sadie was sure she looked exactly the same way.

Sadie got out of the taxi in front of her house and started up the walk. The front door banged open, and the dog burst out, with a smear of green paint along his side. Roderick came out too, in his cycling clothes, and the boys followed, with Nelda behind them, wiping her hands on a towel.

Sadie tried to smile, wishing she had time to catch her breath before they all demanded something from her.

Leo launched himself from the top porch step into Sadie's arms with a fervor usually reserved for military homecomings. He smelled like syrup and his hands were sticky in her hair.

Sadie staggered slightly under the weight of him and kissed the top of his head.

"I *missed* you," he said accusingly, not loosening his grip.

"I missed you too," she said.

"There was a military coup in Mali," Roderick said, and Rufus, who loved to be the bearer of bad news, almost shouted, "Nelda's going back to the Philippines for six months!"

She looked at Nelda, who nodded expressionlessly, like a prison guard, or a housekeeper.

Sadie was so tired her hands shook and tears trembled on the edge of her lower eyelids, like the row of glass beads on a shower curtain. She bowed her head over Leo's blond one. Not many more years before Leo would be embarrassed to declare his love for her like this. Nelda was leaving. The relatives would disperse, never to be seen again. Roderick was going away for three weeks, the first cycling trip of many, she was sure. The thought of Marcus was like a stone in her throat, making it hard to swallow. This is how it was going to be from here on out, she realized suddenly, nothing but a long string of partings, each one ripping at the fabric of her heart: goodbye, and goodbye, and goodbye.

FRED MOTEN
test

(A small, and still isolated, incident in New York shows what can happen if authentic authority in social relations has broken down to the point where it cannot work any longer even in its derivative, purely functional form. A minor mishap in the subway system—the doors on a train failed to operate—turned into a serious shutdown on the line lasting four hours and involving more than fifty thousand passengers, because when the transit authorities asked the passengers to leave the defective train, they simply refused.)

Hannah Arendt, *On Violence*

More than 50,000 subway riders were stranded in the tunnels of the IRT Seventh Avenue line last night after passengers on a defective train at 110th street refused to leave as instructed by Transit Authority employees.

According to the Transit Authority, the trouble began shortly after 5:30 p.m. when the doors on a northbound train failed to operate correctly at 110th Street and Lenox Avenue.

One man said he had stayed in the tunnel directing others to the exits at 103rd Street. "I acted as though I knew what I was doing," he said, "because people usually believe you when you do."

Robert D. McFadden, *The New York Times*, January 4, 1969

this is how we never arrive, infuse what we surround to not remember. every day we cross from slave state to slave state in the barrack cars. we pass by, to avoid examination, in the sun. we were dark to ourselves when that bird start whistling in the tunnel. making music we were made to follow, fail to legislate. refuse to get off got off so hard we got off everywhere. our breathing empties the air with fullness and we're in love in a state of constant sorrow. the outcome is another process, a way into no way. the refuge is open and can't be safe.

transport by the mobile engineer. here the alternate dutchman, johnny cash. the F train stand for fuck whoever won't ride this train. the private investor's inability to afford himself is more and more clear as a general costliness. m2 gone whenever they want to. people need to get to church and it's a bike tour. you can't drink that store-bought coffee from a flying saucer. the animachine is henry dumas stopping bullets, wide-intervalled woody shaw flying transfers, the newly born instrument as a whole bunch of differences.

your refusal ain't unsustainable it just can't sustain itself. you do what they say till you die like a dog. too much stress on the impossible one. we stress this past the point to bring the history of getting down. experimental slant can't help but hurt you. look how hard and sharp it makes you breathe. you have to refuse in real time with things that revise in real time when the wind is closed. there some ways not to love refreshment but they all fucked up. we quiver with work and revival. we carry ourselves till you ready to hear what that sound like.

across 110th street is a helluva tester. the blackness of the
witty partition, hand to mouth to hand, and the subway out of
breath is an airshaft under a rent party. the rent party is the
curriculum of the rent party department. the department was so
outlandish and groundless that she was arrogant for cause, stiff
up in the face of the unadmitted, as they exist on paper, in
donation, in contempt of their training, though a citizen of
riverside, just up from hamsterdam, might not want to try to
understand charisma. like kenneth warren, she didn't know what
african american literature was. soul courses in marburg were an
expense of spirit in a waste of shame. seelen were solo
unadmitted, anechology of the supplement department, the burnt
fringe of speakers, la coping strada, bottom and jug off
centering. everything, every good, every trumpet was deported by
her voice, which was never more than enough from holding her
breath on riverside, where you can still feel the burn of the
eastern question, eastern man alone in her caress, feenin rubbed
study in the desert, in the church of the unnaturals. there's a
riot going on and on for the making of black revolutionary stone
on stone.

HARRYETTE MULLEN
Tanka Diary

Along a familiar hiking trail I recognize
agave, sage, the summer-blooming yucca,
and sticky monkey flower.

*

As if they might be learning a new dance,
elders plant their feet on steady ground,
gathering wind in their arms to move cloud hands.

*

Returning home tonight I avoid crushing
a snail that casts a scant shadow
on the wide sidewalk in clear light of a full moon.

*

Whiff of just-cut green grass, notes of spring
with bracing citrus, distilled and bottled
to create the designer's signature fragrance.

*

Feeding on a single weed, its habitat
dwindling, can the caterpillar afford to be
so choosy with its appetite?

*

Several species of elegant butterflies
are known to be attracted to mountains
of dung and decomposing garbage.

*

Unseasonably warm, and in the background
of the afternoon press conference, you can hear
mockingbirds on the White House lawn.

*

Thin airmail envelope with indecipherable
handwriting; I tear it open
to release an inky blue butterfly.

VI KHI NAO
The Room in Five Moods of Cannots

The room cannot feel its arteries stuffed with animal fat from the insulation. Cannot hope to alter its mouth and eating is not a thing that it can do well. The room hasn't taken a bath since 1987, but there was a slight wash in 1992 bestowing the room its perforated body. The room cannot control the content of its character. Cannot control if happiness is a regular visitor of the closet. What can it control? The room can sit naked for a really long time until someone moves in. Sometimes at night, the room falls in love with the refrigerator near the sink. Cannot help but stare at the light and the carton of eggs and the miniskirts of green onions & the underpants of cilantro floating on the clothes hangers of the cilantric stem. The room doesn't want to be redundant, but how can it write a love letter to something that cannot even cross its legs?

JAY NEBEL
Men

We're in the middle of it, in the middle
of the backyard barbecuing steak
and chicken. Telling stories

with our wives and girlfriends away,
red and blue psychedelics, Coors Light
and breasts falling into our mouths again

like basalt cliffs into the sea.
Jeremy says, *I did CPR on a gorilla once.*
A girl gorilla, a big one.

I kept thinking, she's going to wake up
and she's going to fucking kill me.
But she just peed all over the floor

before dying on her back
in a room full of humans.
What do you think happens

to the male gorilla back in the cage
somewhere waiting for her?
Do they give him the news?

Slide her body into the cage
so he can smell her dead hand?
Zookeepers, Bill says. *We should grow*

mustaches. And we're gone,
the Apache helicopter of our middle
age flying out over the dunes.

It's not the gorilla that scares me.
It's waking up alone. And I'm not a man
anymore but a paper bag someone's blowing

into to keep from hyperventilating,
the camels long since sunk down
into their kneecaps, the sand everywhere.

SHARON OLDS
Douche-Bag Ode

When I hear the young refer to someone as a
douche bag, I want to say, You may have
never seen a douche bag. They were red
rubber bags, like hot water bottles, you'd
fill it and hang it high enough
so that gravity…I can't go on,
I see my mother's douche bag, my poor
douche-bag mom's pathetic douche bag with its
clamps, and its aorta tubes,
dangling over the bathtub, awesomely
shameful, and which reminded me
I'd been some kind of catsup Halloween
costume in her, almost before I was
human. And so to call someone a
saline sac—let's take some pity
on the creepiness of how women were treated
in the 1950s. It drove my mother
crazy, but she did the best she could—
she never turned, and said, I could have got
rid of you, my little valentine,
but I gave you the warm, rose-colored lunch-bag
of the placenta: I gave you my heart, to eat.
And now I remember it, not my mother's
but mine, like a dowry—lock the door, then
hang it from the shower rod like food hung over
a bough, out of wild animal reach,
slide the perforated wand inside you then un-
clasp the clamp, and Lo!, you are
a night clearing, in which a fountain
of Aphrodite leaps up, and cascades
down, making her music, her brine
sea chantey, her sparkling douche-bag song.

SHARON OLDS
Meeting a Stranger

When I meet you, it's not just the two of us meeting.
Your mother is there, and your father is there,
and my mother and father, and what they might have
thought of each other. And our people—back from our
folks, back—are there, and what they
might have had to do with each other;
if one of yours and one of mine
had met, what might have happened is there
in the room with us. They are shadowy,
compared to us, they are quivers of reflected
light on a wall, but they are there. And if I were a
German, and you a Jew, or I a
Jew and you a Palestinian,
or, as this morning, when you are an African
American woman, and I am a WASP,
one of your family might have been taken
from their home, and brought through murder to murder
by one of my family. It is there in the air
with us. And if you're a woman in the city
where you live, and I am staying at
the hotel where you work, and if you have brought me
my breakfast on a tray—though you and I have not
met, before, we are breathing in
our lineages, together. And whether
there is guilt in the room, or not, or blame,
there is the history of human evil,
and the shame, in me, that someone I am
related to, may have committed,
against someone you are related to, some
horror. And in the room, there is
a question, alive—what would I have risked
to try to protect you, as I hope I would risk

for a cousin, a niece, or would I have stood
aside, in the ordinary cowardice and self-
interest of my flesh now sharing your breath,
your flesh my breath.

YADDYRA PERALTA
Ode to Piranha

After Pablo Neruda

This piranha in your poem,
this river-missile drawn to flesh
I once dangled from a fishing line.
I know you won't believe me,
but when I held its flapping body to my ear,
it moaned.
The piranha moaned,
like the medicine man moans
of a river
he believes is an anaconda,
a sibilant serpent
swallower of men.

In turbid waters
the piranha sigh,
and baring jagged and prehistoric teeth,
they surface in the rainy season
searching for the flesh
of fallen fruit.
It must trouble them to know
that their name in Tupi means "tooth-fish"—
unfair when you think
of the dogfish, the knifefish
the spotted and buck-toothed tambaqui.

I remember all the bathers I've seen
swimming in those waters
the girls from Milan with their Rio G-strings,
submerging, emerging in one piece.
I consider flinging it back,

that maligned little omnivore,
but instead I watch it die and eat it.
I still hear its stories
whispering within me.
Very often, I write them down.

SHERRI PHILLIPS
The Rubber Game

So when the doctor pulls the camera tube out of my rectum, the old joke comes to mind.

"Wrecked 'em?" I say. "I slayed 'em!"

The nurse lets herself out, carrying a fresh cut of me between two little panes of glass. The doctor rewards me with a snort, but I can see he's only being polite. He doesn't even look up from his laptop. He's busy flipping through the photos that, like magic, bloom on the screen with each little twist of the tube.

"You rooting for the Mets tonight?" I shoulda thought to ask before he had me with my pants down.

"Not really my game," he says.

Figures.

I try another one while I buckle my belt. "My kid's graduating college next month."

"Oh?" he asks. He presses a button and the screen goes blue, then he pulls down the X-rays I brought with me. "Congratulations."

"Double major," I say. "Proctology, like what you do. And geology."

He looks at me. In the eyes, I mean. Finally.

"I don't got high hopes, though," I tell him. "After four years of college, he still can't tell his ass from a hole in the ground!"

"How old is your son?" he asks.

This guy's dry as burnt toast. "I don't really have one," I say.

"Well, Mr.—," he looks down at his clipboard, "Mr. Arbus."

"George. Everybody calls me George."

"George." The little pause after he says it puts me on alert. "George, you have a great sense of humor and a positive attitude, and that's going to be crucial—"

But I don't hear the rest. Because that's when I know I'm dying.

It's the times I'm leaving the chemo that I think most about the life I haven't lived. Why didn't I get married? Why haven't I ever traveled? At the bookstore, I look in the window and realize I haven't read a single book on display.

But I don't do anything about it. All my life I've put one foot in front of the other, and that's what I do now. The chemo's no stroll through Central Park, but it's not so bad I can't go to work. Thirty-five years and I've only missed three days: the strike in '91 and two funerals. Guess the next time will be when my own lights go out.

One Saturday, Ms. Nosybritches from 304 comes in from a late night grocery run. She gives me the once-over and announces in front of the guys and God that I sure have lost a lot of weight. Some nerve, but what am I gonna say? I'm the doorman.

"Just watching my girlish figure," I say, taking the bags from her. Trailing her to the elevators, I swing my hips for the guys, mimicking her. Ba dum! ba dum! ba dum!

She looks back over her shoulder and I give her a wink. She likes it when I flirt. Never serious-like, but enough to remind her she's got great tits and a nice smile. I set her groceries down in the elevator, press the button and step back, taking the fiver she slides me.

"Is everything OK, George?" she says, quiet-like.

I just look at her, surprised to be asked. "Fine," I manage to say, just before the doors slide shut.

Twenty-plus pounds in six weeks, and this is the first anybody's said a word.

When I turn around, they're looking everywhere but at me. "Mets," I say, picking up where we left off. "All the way."

"Not a chance," says Mr. Jasperovic, 407. He's a cold fish whose new dog loves me more than him. He yanks Tater by the leash and makes a beeline for the hall to the stairs, waving me off when I go to get the elevator for him. "Got to lose a few myself," he says. Tater has to scoot fast to make it into the stairwell before the fire door swings shut. Jasperovic tips me with joints for walking Tater. It was an easy deal to work. He and his connection meet right in the lobby, like I'm not even standing there hearing every word, seeing every deal. Up to a few weeks ago, worst drug I ever done was cigarettes, but now I count on my predawn toke. Until I started on the Oxaliplatin, I didn't know it was possible for bones, my actual bones, to hurt.

Larry from 512 says good night too, and heads up. He's a good man, Larry, the only one in the whole building who insists I call him by his first name. Gets home deliveries four or five times a week, but I still haven't figured out what he does for a living. Sometimes when I'm trying to fall asleep, I run through all the jobs I can think of, but nothing lines up with the hours he keeps. He's the only man in Manhattan who's never in a hurry.

"Like rats off a sinking ship," I say to Vin, our maintenance guy. He's the only one left in the lobby.

Vin leans back on the shelf of the open half-door to the utility closet and looks at me, waiting. Thirteen years we've known each other. Lots of mornings after clocking out we go grab a brew. Sometimes in the summer we take the 7 train over for a game and he tells me about whichever tenant he's shtupping. Most union guys won't cross the line like that, but Vin says it's the biggest bennie of the job. Never had a lonely day in his life. Every Christmas, we compare tips to see who's ripping us off and who we ought to start kissing up to.

I almost spill the beans about the cancer, but for what?

"Mets," I tell him, "and that's my final word."

He shrugs, picks up the brass cleaner, and goes outside to polish the banisters.

What can anybody do about it anyways?

Cloudy saline on the top hook, then pale blue, yellow, and a clear one at the bottom. "Like Christmas ornaments," I say. Bella double-checks the label on each one as she hangs them. The clear one is the roughest. Turns my stomach inside out every time.

"I think I'll put up a Christmas tree this year," I tell her. I haven't had one since I was a kid.

"That'll be nice," she says. She doesn't ask why I'm thinking about this in May. Maybe she thinks it's doubtful I'll make it that long.

Two rows of us patients are plugged into our stations, each with an IV, a nurse button, white headphones for music, black ones for the TV, and a little electric blanket. Must take a lot of juice to keep this place running. At my place in Astoria, there's not a single outlet in the bedroom or the bathroom. The living room makes up for it with five in a row beneath the wide window. When I first moved in, I got a kick coming up with how that came to be. Maybe the first tenant had a bunch of TVs so he could watch all the games at once. Who knows? Maybe the electrician who wired it got sight of some looker sunbathing on the roof next door and couldn't bear to leave the view. In sixty-one years I've lived in four apartments, and they all had some quirky something or other. Bathtub in the kitchen, front door in the bedroom. But five outlets suits me fine. I got my portable drill, the mini-vac, the rechargeable batteries, my cell phone, a lamp, the television, and a radio.

And Christmas lights this year. This month, maybe. Why wait?

Bella sets out two flavors of Juicy Juice on the tray.

"Make mine a double today. Shaken not stirred," I say to her.

She smiles while she sticks me. She's the ugliest, oldest nurse here, but when she gets the needle in on the first try, she's nothing but beautiful to me. My insurance won't cover the permanent shunt, so this is a pleasure I get to have every time.

"Full house today," I say to the guy next to me. He nods and slides on his headphones. Some units have privacy curtains and guest chairs, but they go fast, so people use headphones like walls. Me, I don't care so much for being alone. I prefer to look around, take things in. Like the thirty-something Korean lady leaning back on the recliner opposite me, working through her book of Jumble puzzles. I know she's Korean because her T-shirt says it in big red letters: *I'm Korean.* Under that, in letters that get smaller and smaller as they go down the list, it says *Not Chinese, Not Japanese, Not Thai, Not Vietnamese, Not Tibetan, Not Filipino, Not Hawaiian, Not Any Of Your Business,* then the letters get too little for me to read. She has a timer, a real timer with a black button on top that she punches before she turns the page and punches again the second she's done.

"Anything else I can get for you, George?" Bella flips the switch to start the drip and pulls off her latex gloves.

"You got kids, Bella?"

"Sure." She pulls out a slim plastic wallet insert from the front pocket of her uniform. "Three."

I take the pictures and flip through them. "Two boys and a girl, nice. And a tabby here."

"And a bird and a dog and a gerbil, at least as of this morning," she says, shaking her head, but I can see she doesn't mind. "You?"

"Dog," I lie. "Tater. Crazy little ball of white not much bigger'n a baseball."

"Funny name."

"Yeah, ain't that a kick?" My lie leaves me at a dead end. I can't think of anything else to say even though I wouldn't mind her company.

"You buzz if you need me," she says. "I'll be back in an hour to check on things."

A little girl maybe six or seven, what do I know?, comes up to the Korean lady and whispers something, then pulls a purse out of the locker beside the recliner. The lady fishes out a couple of dollars and hands them over, then watches the girl trot down the hall and around the corner. She catches me looking at her and just like that, big tears start rolling down her cheeks.

"I'm sorry," I say. She lays her head back on the recliner and puts the Jumbles book over her face.

My mother always had a crossword with her. She kept score in a little calendar, her against the *Times*. A hash mark meant a win with every clue filled in, a zero was a loss. There was no such thing as in-between for her.

She died on a Saturday, the day the *Times* runs its toughest puzzle. When I came to see her at the hospital that morning, she put her calendar down on the bedside table. "You beat 'em, Ma?" I asked. "You bet I did," she said. She handed the finished puzzle to me. Not twenty minutes passed before she was gone. I opened the calendar to give her a hash mark for the day, and she'd already put a zero there. I guess she was looking at the bigger picture. I cried like a baby.

I mailed her notebook and that last puzzle to the Times. Not two weeks later, I get a note handwritten from Mr. Shortz who makes up the puzzles. Said he was sorry for my loss, and that he does the same thing, keeping track and whatnot. Would've made my mother's day to see that.

The doc told me if the chemo doesn't knock out the cancer, there are other steps, like taking out my rectum. I couldn't believe my ears. What kind of life is that, collecting shit in a bag pinned to your pants? That's not for me, I told him.

Lately, I'm thinking I could make do, if it comes to that.

The guy next to me takes off his headphones and pulls a deck of Bicycles out of his knapsack. "You play Rummy?"

"You bet I do," I say. I drag my tray between us for a table. When he turns on his side to face me, I see what's printed down the side of his sweatpants. *Fear the Goat*. "You Navy boys did a helluva job yesterday."

He grins like he pulled the whole thing off hisself. "Fuckin' A, man. Yes, sir, fuckin' A!"

"You know how I heard about it?"

"No, sir." He starts shuffling the cards.

"You catch the Mets last night?"

That grin gets so big you'd think he wasn't plugged in right beside me getting pumped with three kinds of poison.

"So Murphy steps in the box," I say. "And the fans, they're—"

"They're going nuts. I know, I couldn't figure out what was up," he says.

"Right? Nice guy and all, but Murphy? So I turn up the volume."

"Yeah," he says. He's nodding.

I clench both my fists. "U-S-A!"

He joins. "U-S-A!"

We're both chanting now, pounding on the trays with our voices rising. "U-S-A! U-S-A! U-S-A!"

The Korean lady looks a little worried. Bella comes trotting down the hall. "Shhhhhhhh! What are you two fools doing?"

"Sorry," I say.

"We're sorry," my new friend echoes.

She shakes her head and does a U-turn back down the hall. He shuffles the deck and slides it over to me.

"Queens, born and bred," I tell him.

"Bay Ridge," he says. He shakes my hand.

"Wasn't it something, though?" I cut thin to win and slide the deck back. "Mr. Osama Bin Laden. Kaputski. May of took ten years, but did I mention kaputski?"

"Talk about ridding the earth of a fucking cancer." He looks down at his lap.

"Nothing short of a miracle. Your boys did good."

He deals out the hands. I rearrange mine backwards the way I like. "Mets turned it around last night," I say. "They got a real chance."

"Amen to that," he says.

I keep up the chemo, I don't call in sick a single time, and I put on five pounds in less than a month. What's my reward?

Jasperovic comes in after partying it up and tells me I won't be needing to walk Tater come August. Tater's sacked out on my stiff old shined-up shoes, like they're made of goose down.

"It's no problem at all," I say. I'd walk him for free if it came down to it. I lift my toe a little and he licks the leather with a tongue tiny as a gumdrop. "Me and Tater are buddies."

"I got recruited by *The Tonight Show*," Jasperovic says. "We're heading to LA."

We? Jasperovic and Tater don't even like each other.

"Big leagues," I say. "Congratulations. Bet Letterman would hire you too." Leno's no better than a thief for taking that show. And Letterman came back from a heart attack. I scratch Tater behind his floppy ears and his leg starts jigging. "The Sullivan's ten minutes down the tracks. Why bother moving?"

Jasperovic pulls Tater off my shoes. "If you want to keep getting the weed after we move, I'll give you a name," he says.

Big of you, I wanna say. But I'm the doorman. And the weed helps.

The same week, the elevator opens and there's Ms. Nosybritches, Tupperware in one hand and two folding chairs with nice padded seats in the other. She sets them up, sits down and pops open the container.

"Homemade cupcakes," she announces, like she and me been doing this for years.

I let myself pretend, just a little, that we have.

"Trying to fatten me up?" I ask.

She gives me that smile of hers and passes me a napkin. "Chocolate or vanilla?" She sees how I perk up on the chocolate and hands one over. "So what's new, George?"

I want to tell her the chemo kills my sense of taste. I want to tell her she's sexy as hell. I want to tell her I been thinking about Christmas.

So what do I say instead? "How about those cherry trees? Seems like the blossoms burst open overnight."

All I know how to talk about is weather and baseball, which up until recent was fine by me. Now I got a million things piling up in my head, but they all dry up before I can get them out of my mouth.

When she's packing up, I thank her for bringing me such a treat. "Do you know my first name, George?" she asks.

"Sure I do," I say. "Alice." Damned if I don't start blushing.

"Good," she says.

People surprise you.

When morning comes, Vin and me stop off at Tap a Keg, and I make a joke about Ms. Nosybritches giving me some sugar. He shakes his head and sets down his beer. "Ms. Nobrieski's a nice lady, George."

Sherri Phillips 115

"I guess *I* know that," I say. "I've known her longer'n you have."

"I don't think you know her at all," he says.

He looks upset, so I try to lighten things up. "Jeter'll get 3,000 come summer," I say. "Kills me, but at least he's keeping it local."

It's the cue for him to launch into his rant about the Yankees, how they waste money like it's water, what he'd do if he were the Mets manager to get some respect in this town.

"I don't want to talk about baseball," he says.

I almost fall off my barstool. "What *do* you want to talk about?"

He looks at the full beer I ordered but haven't drunk. Stares at it. "You gonna drink that?" he asks. Chemo and booze don't mix.

"Sure I'm going to drink it." I take a swallow. He shakes his head again, and now he looks mad.

"What?" I say. "You want to talk about something, spit it out." I'm talking to myself as much as him.

"Me?" He stands up. "Why would I wanna say anything? What the fuck *can* I say?" He chugs the rest of his beer, slams the mug on the counter, then grabs mine and drinks it down too. He drops a wad of singles on the bar and starts to walk out, then turns around. "George."

"What?" My throat feels scratchy, like I sucked in a mouth of pollen.

"You got friends in this world." He shoves through the door, out of the gloom and into the sunshine.

Near the end of May, the Mets melt down in the Bronx. You know the game.

Then the doctor tells me I have to take a break from the chemo because my whites are too low.

"Racist," I say. But it's not funny and I don't care when he doesn't laugh. I've given up. The man's a stone with moving parts.

When I ask how long before I can start up the chemo again, he says he doesn't know. "Your count has to move up to at least 1,000 before we can even think about it."

"So how do I make my numbers? What do we do if I don't get there?" I ask. He doesn't have an answer for that either.

I wonder what his win-loss is.

"It's the paradox of chemotherapy, George. It kills off the bad, but it inevitably kills off the good too. We're looking for the right balance."

Inevitably.

"So's I end up with some good left over."

"You got it." He says it like I finally understand, or maybe it's relief that I didn't end another sentence with a question mark.

"So I don't go to the clinic, then." I've gotten accustomed to it, seeing Bella, playing Rummy with Tom, checking in with the Korean lady on what her kid's up to.

"You always see the silver lining, don't you, George?"

Silver, my ass.

When I finally fall asleep later, I dream me and Alice are in bed together. Things get going. It's been so long that in no time flat, I let myself go, I can't help it. "I'm sorry," I say. "There's plenty of time," she says. "I'm sorry," I say again. I wake up and I've peed myself. It's wet and warm around me, and the stench of the urine makes me retch. I barely make it to the toilet in time to add puke to the mix.

Doc said this was a possibility down the road. Guess the road's a lot shorter than he estimated. I punch the wall. Take that, doc. I stomp on his head. And that. I stomp three or four times to drive the message home.

The downstairs neighbor gives me what-for with her broom.

"Fuck you," I yell at the floor. Words I thought a few times through the years with the tenants I've had to deal with, but I never yelled them at anybody. I don't think I've ever yelled outside of a Mets game. "Fuck you," I yell again.

She bangs on her ceiling again.

I clean up and put on my uniform even though I don't have to check in for another eight hours. All of us doormen gripe about the uniforms, how the synthetic material's hot in summer and cold in winter. Me maybe loudest of all, so as not to let on that I like mine. It gives me a direction to go every day.

Sitting on the front stoop, I flip my cell phone open, shut, open, shut. I pull up Vin's number. He's probably sound asleep. Not that he'd want to go do anything anyways. Alone on my concrete step, I pretend it's a mistake, a slip of the thumb, when I hit the dial key. At two rings there's the click of the line opening and I lose my nerve. I hang up and start walking.

He calls back before I've even made a block. "What's up, George?"

"Huh?"

"You just called me. What's up?"

"I did?"

"Thought I heard you say you're sorry," he says.

"Sorry for those limping Mets, that's who I'm sorry for."

"Sorry you're an ass, that's what I'm sorry for."

"Me too," I say. But still, I can't tell him. I haven't said it to anybody. Not even to myself after I've anchored the blackout shades and I'm lying wide awake in the dark of day.

"George? George!"

The voice is my mother's. I know right away that's nuts.

"George? Sweetie, are you asleep?"

I jerk awake. Third shift my whole career and I've never once nodded out on the job. Now here I am drooling on the front desk in the lobby.

Alice is setting up her chair, which means it must be round about midnight. The dream roars back in, a nightmare.

Sweetie, she said.

"Something smells good." I shake my head to loosen up the cobwebs. Smells like gardenias, I almost say, looking at her long dark hair, shining damp from a washing.

"I thought beef stew might be just the thing tonight." She pulls two stone bowls out of the wicker picnic basket she's taken to using each night, settles the little tablecloth over the footstool and starts ladling the soup. I pretend we're on a date. *Sweetie.*

"I went all over this city today." I wait to see if she'll remember to leave the carrots out of mine. "Name it. Everywhere. Nobody sells Christmas lights."

"It's barely summer, George," she says. "What do you expect?" She reaches back in and plops a carrot into my bowl like a challenge. She looks straight at me.

"Yes, Mother," I say, even though she's twenty years younger than me. Or more. Probably more.

"What are you smiling so big at?" she asks.

"Not a thing." It's going to hurt when the stew hits the sores in my mouth, but I don't mind.

"Hey, listen." She tilts her head at the doors I've left open to let in the air. "Is that a sax?"

"Piano teacher on three," I say. "Plays the horn a little too, I guess." The guy used to be the hottest sax in town until he canned his own career. But it's not my place to share.

"Wow. He's really good."

We listen to the music sliding in on the summer breeze. I could've sat there for another ten years or so, doing just that.

"I got my grades today." She unwraps some bread and rips off a hunk. "Butter?" She smears on a pat without waiting for me to answer and hands it to me.

"Straight As, right?" Turns out the reason Alice gets home late is she's working on getting a masters degree at night.

"One B." She reaches up and ties her wet hair into a knot. The pale skin on the underside of her arms looks tender as a baby's. "One more year."

"Tell me what you did today."

"Your turn," she says.

"You know what I did. Same's I did last week. I want to hear about you."

When she gets to the part about filming the dogs for the study she's doing at the pound, I make her slow down. "Any new ones?"

She stands and pushes her arms down, stiff, then leans forward and blows out her considerable chest to stagger around the lobby, turning her head this way and that. She does dog imitations like Rich Little used to do Nixon. I can almost smell those dogs, she's so good.

"Ernest," she says. "A mastiff, 220 pounds worth. He's going to be a tough one to place."

"That's double your size!" Last weigh-in, I was at 143. I picture a horse with a dog's head.

"Not true and you know it. Somebody found him tied up at a dog run, no collar, no nothing. Can you believe that?"

"He'd eat Tater for lunch."

"Lunch? One little treat maybe." She sits down. "What's up with these Christmas lights you're chasing?"

I take my last spoonful of stew. How do I say that maybe they'll get me to December? "I think it's strange is all," I finally say, "that in all of New York City nobody has any Christmas lights."

"The odds may be against it, George, but I'm laying my bet now you'll find some." She packs up her basket and looks at her watch.

Sherri Phillips

"How did it get so late?"

Vin sticks his head in through the front door. "I'm taking a break to go grab some chow," he says. "Hey there, Alice."

Since when is she Alice instead of Ms. Nobrieski to him?

"Hey, Vin," Alice says, and gives him that smile. I feel a pain in my stomach. "Why don't you come in and visit a little?"

I thought she had to get going.

"Next time, and looking forward," he says. "But the Halal guy shuts down his cart in five." He lifts his hand and is gone.

Alice brushes the crumbs from her lap. "How're those Mets of yours doing?"

"You know what? I been there for them for years. My whole entire life, for what it's worth."

"And?"

"And how do they repay me? With five losing seasons straight and a sixth one on the way. I'm done." And I mean it.

"You're not done, George."

I hear a whole other meaning, and it hits me so hard my eyes start to water. I go to the doors to pull them shut. "Say, Alice," I say, still with my back to her. "If Ernest doesn't get picked, how long will he have until—you know—"

"I don't know, George. I just don't know."

"C'mon, Doc," I say. "Chemo's my crazy girlfriend. I can't live with her, but I ain't gonna live without her. I don't care what my cell count is, I want it."

I've lost my hard-earned five plus another three on top. Eight pounds, same as 702's brand new bouncing baby boy.

"This is a girlfriend that will turn against you, George. You've got to have more white cells to take her on. We'll start up the chemo when your number comes up."

"When my number comes up? You wanna rephrase that, maybe?" I laugh at my own joke, and then I can't stop until he puts a hand on my shoulder.

I've started clearing out my place a little at a time, thinking I'll skinny it down to only what matters. You know, get a clearer look at things. It's easy, because I see pretty fast that nothing matters. Even the baseball my father left me, the one Clenendon signed in '69, has lost its magic. Ma used to say my father went off the high dive in the shallow end. Early Alzheimer's. I remember one time she and me come home and we go to put away our coats. There he is in the closet, standing there with a transistor radio at his ear, snapping away to it in the dark. "Now that's a beat," he says, and strolls out past us. When the time comes, I'll leave the baseball to Vin.

I give away my tools at work, some to the super, some to the guy, John, who lives in the basement apartment. He's a paralegal by day, but at night he's an artist. Pursuing the dream. He says it like an apology.

The books, the few I got, I drop off in front of the library one night. Every afternoon on my way to the subway, I leave a few pieces of clothing at the top of the stairs for the homeless guys to take. One Saturday morning after I get home, I load three boxes of plates and flatware and other kitchen odds and ends into a pull cart and head over to the thrift store. Right in the first crosswalk, one of the two wheels falls off. The sun's blazing and I'm tempted to leave the whole kit and caboodle in the intersection, but I keep yanking and dragging it till I get it there.

When I go in, it's so dark I have to stop inside the door to let my eyes adjust. The clerk's leaning on the register like it's holding her up.

"It's a scorcher out there," I say.

No hello, no smile, no nothing. She doesn't even stand. I step over to the counter, pulling the crippled cart with me.

"How are you today?" I ask. You're in a *service* industry, I want to tell her. To serve, to be of service. Something I know a lot about.

"Donations go in the back," she says. Her thin hair is shoe-polish black with gray roots. White plastic hoop earrings poke through it. Her eyebrows are inky crescents.

"I'll just leave it here. I don't need a receipt," I say.

"All donations gotta be logged in," she says, "or we don't take 'em."

I can't even give stuff away for free without a hassle.

"I dragged this here five blocks," I say. "There's a toaster oven in there."

"I don't make the rules," she says. "I just work here."

I oughta lay on her the litany of shit I got going on. If I can still smile every day at my place of work like the world is right, then she can be civil. "See, this kind of thing is why we're in the crapper," I say. "Here I am, trying to do something good, and here you are, making it hard for me."

Sherri Phillips   121

She blinks so slow it's like she's falling asleep and waking up again each time. "Suit yourself," she says. "If the cart doesn't go to the back, it's going out on the sidewalk." She lays her head down on her arms and shuts her eyes, like it's all too much to take.

That's when I see she's wearing false eyelashes. They're as long and thick and dark as a showgirl's. In the gloom of the store, something catches at me. There she probably was in her bathroom this morning, getting ready to head into a shitcan job she can't stand. She thinks *the orange hoops or the white ones?* and she chooses the white because for some reason that feels better today. Then she leans into the mirror to draw on her eyebrows and glue on her lashes and paint on orange lipstick to match her shirt.

For some reason only she knows, or maybe she doesn't, it mattered to her.

"OK," I say. I feel like I'm falling from a very great height, from a scaffolding maybe. "OK."

She nods, and her cheek makes a dry, whispering sound against her bare arm.

I start to head to the back then stop. "Any chance you got Christmas lights here?"

Damned if she doesn't sit up. A spark of life, look at that. "Christmas lights?" she asks. She starts laughing. Not mean-like, just surprised.

But the answer's no.

End of June, Vin comes strolling in with a little TV under one arm and a takeout bag from Papaya King in his other hand. My stomach growls for the first time in days. I can't eat it, but I don't want to tell him. I can't put most things down now because they won't come out, not the way they're supposed to anyway. It's disgusting.

I'm disgusting.

He sets the TV on the front desk. "They could use our help tonight, George. It's Detroit." Sliding the brim of his cap to the back, he unwinds the cord.

"They gave up," I say. "I told you already, I'm done with them."

"Like hell you are," he says. He plugs it in.

"You got a radio," I say. "Isn't hearing it painful enough? You gotta watch it too?"

"Who are you? Who kidnapped George?" Vin says. "I'm a believer because you're a believer."

"I'm a stone cold atheist, Vin. Help yourself to a chair." I unlock the utility closet. "I'm going to hose the sidewalk."

"Aren't you going to sit with me?"

"And after I'm done, I'm going up to feed Tater." Jasperovic's on his way to LA to make sure everything's set.

I roll the hose stand out the door and hook it up. Usually that scent of water on the concrete gives me a boost, reminds me of when I was a kid, but the drugs lately are killing off my sense of smell.

"One-oh," Vin calls out to me. "Two-oh," he says when I come back in. "See what I said?" He stands up and takes a few phantom swings. "I'm telling you, you should watch. At least eat your dog."

And God help me later, I do. I eat it like it's my last meal, gut be damned.

I look at the screen once and the Mets freeze up. "Maybe it's me," I say. "Can you keep an eye on the door while I run up?"

"I'm not going anywhere," Vin says. "Our boys need us."

I unlock the key cabinet behind the desk and slide 407 off the hook. The rows of keys jingle against each other. "I'm the doorman, correct?"

"Correct," says Vin.

"You'd think I'd have been in more of these places."

"Nothing special," says Vin. "I'm in and out of them all day and night."

I tick the occasions off on my fingers. "Mr. Petrie, 602, heart attack. 312, because they locked their baby inside by accident. 205, smoke coming out from under the door. And now, taking care of Tater for Jerkoffabunch. I've never even been to your place, come to think of it."

"Come next week," Vin says. "Now sit down, just for a little."

The teams are changing over. Mets laid an egg in the second.

"Fuck 'em," I say. I punch the elevator button, then I punch it again, harder.

"Geez, George, lighten up."

"Fuck you," I say.

"Fuck *me?*"

When I open Jasperovic's door, Tater's frantic, leaping up to my waist, running in circles, yapping.

"Shut up!" He goes dead silent. I feel like a monster. "At least somebody still listens to me. I'm sorry, buddy."

In the kitchen I pile up his bowl with food and get fresh water, then wander around the apartment while he eats. Out of habit I almost turn on the TV, but stop just in time. "Fuck 'em." I open the living-room window to let some fresh air in, and from across 106th I hear a cheer. Several of the apartments over there have televisions on.

I don't care.

On the shelves are some framed pictures of Jasperovic's kids, a boy who's maybe thirteen and a little girl. They live in Ohio with their mother. Jasperovic doesn't know shit about me, but I know what kind of toilet paper he buys. What's wrong with that picture? I pick up the photo of the boy and study it. He looks just like Jasperovic. "Don't grow up to be an asshole, kid."

The house phone buzzes. Vin. I cross over to pick it up but veer off into the bedroom instead. On the bureau are five trophies, all from Jasperovic's bowling league. My father used to take me bowling on Wednesday nights when I was little, before his mind got bad.

The house phone buzzes again. Can I not have five goddamned minutes? I yank the receiver from the wall. "What?"

"Alice is down here, George. Brought a little treat. And you ain't gonna believe—"

I hang up. It kills me to hear her name coming from him. Tater's sitting a few feet away, head cocked to one side, watching me. "You still love me, right, bud?" Scooping him up, I go over to the leather recliner. He climbs up my chest and nestles right there on my neck, a little white beard.

Another cheer goes up. The house phone buzzes. Mets must have put another one on the board. "You two are forgiving souls, you and Vin," I tell Tater. "Dying ain't no excuse for me to be a dick, is it?"

I lay my head back, look around the apartment and wonder what having this life would have been like. Kids, money, jet-setting around.

Wouldn't have mattered. I wouldn't have lived it any better than I lived my own. Tears start leaking out the sides of my eyes, and I use Tater's leg to wipe them off. I could've had my own doorman, maybe. My own dog.

I sit up and Tater slides down to my lap. "Some things it's too late for, Tater," I tell him. "But guess what?" He wags his tail. "Some things we still got a shot at." It's an idea so bad it's good. Jasperovic'll probably think I did him a favor.

I go to the kitchen and find a grocery bag under the sink, same place as I stash mine. I load it with Tater's food and his bowls and a couple of toys. Tater starts dancing around, running back and forth and making little dives at my feet.

"May not be for good," I tell him. "But it's good for now." As we go to the door, the house phone rings again. We walk right past. "Sorry, Vin," I say.

Tater runs to the elevator. "We gotta take the stairs, buddy, so's we can slip out the side door."

Tater skitters down the stairs so quick that I have to lean over the banister to keep an eye on him. With two flights on me, he looks like a little cloud riding a fast wind. He runs back up twice to make sure I'm still coming.

At the bottom, I leash him up, then open the door to the hall. The fire door's to the right, away from the lobby.

"Oh my god," I hear Vin scream. "Jason Bay, I love you!"

Tater's pulling to go see what all the commotion's about, so I scoop him up and plop him into the grocery bag with his things. "What do you say, buddy?" I whisper into his ear. "You ready?"

"George!" Vin yells. I jerk around, thinking we've been found out, but nobody's in the hall. Tater pokes his head out and licks me.

"Shhh, you're gonna wake up the neighborhood," says Alice.

"Where the hell is he? I can't believe he's missing this."

The TV's around the corner. A wavering reflection is playing across the elevator doors at the end of the hall.

The thing is, even if the Mets was to pull a '69, October's a long way off.

I look at the elevator doors again, the colors shimmering across it.

For the life of me, it looks like Christmas lights.

CARL PHILLIPS
The Length of the Field

In the stories it's different: grief,
like the dark, lifts eventually—
a tenderness inside which, with all
the clarity of bells when for once they
ring like nothing but the ringing bells
they are, it can seem that at last you've

gotten away with something, like
a horse you've stolen that, now, lighter
than ash on a sudden wind, or any wind
at all, takes the length of the field, but
as if bewildered almost, any man
for whom to have trusted too easily

has merely meant disappointment,
not disaster, and the long
longing-in-vain for that moment when
either one could have been the other
starts to stir a little, slowly it unfurls itself,
its languorous disease, inside him.

CARL PHILLIPS
Chromatic Black

Of the many things that he used to say to me, there are two
I'm certain of: *You taste like a last less-than-long summer afternoon
by the shore just before September;* and

*You're the kind of betrayal, understand, I've been waiting for,
all my life.* When did remembering stop meaning
to be lit from within—bodily—

and the mind, briefly flickering
again out—wasn't that forgetting? Somewhere
abandon's still just a word to be turned away from, as from a man

on fire. Remorse, I think,
is not regret. How new, as in full of chance, the nights here
still can seem to be,

if you keep your eyes closed. Here's a lullaby:
"No more bondage, no triumph either, no more the bluing waves
of shame…"

CATHERINE PIERCE
In Which I Am Famous

This endless room is deep blue, dark red.
I'm wearing my Valentino gown, vintage silhouette
but hand-stitched for me. It's the same purple
as my favorite twilight, just as I requested.

Everyone is here—I can see across the way
the black-rooted starlets and reality queens
drinking acai Cosmos. And I can see the disgraced
congressman studying his notes at the bar,

his tan tie loosened. Slow-dancing in the corner,
the large-haired, button-eyed parents of the dead
pageant girl. I ignore them all. I am leaning elegantly
against a banister. My drink is a gin martini (up, very dry,

with a twist). My lipstick is sunset-cruise red.
All night, handsome, craggy men have murmured
things like *Hello, cupcake* and *You will be responsible
for the resurgence of the marquee* and *Your nose*

is so legitimate, and I've blushed in my practiced
unpracticed way. My three gold bangles clink lightly
as I tell about Monte Carlo last May (the passport
mix-up, the boa constrictor). Everyone laughs,

and their teeth gleam like china. At dawn, I know,
we'll head to Zuma Beach. One of the starlets,
hoop-eyed on Percocet and vodka, will drown
in her faux-fur boots, and we'll all be questioned

at the station. The congressman will slip away.
The pageant-girl parents will weep large,
professional tears. Later, there will be a movie
about the incident. I will be played by a no-name

Australian actress with an exquisite doll-like nose.
It will be her big break. Soon, when she enters
the room, the dance floor crowd will part and she
will be the mirror ball, shining on us all.

DAVID JAMES POISSANT
Monkey See

Out back of the motel, a man and a boy feed alligators in the dark. I can see them past the curtains. Past the paisley curtains and through the cracked and dirty pane of glass, I see them, like shadows, see them and the slow, casting motions they make. I see things leave their hands, see these things caught, or, uncaught, hitting the water. Then, in the water, I see circling.

My wife stirs.

"They're back," I say, meaning the man and the boy, meaning the gators. Last night, I saw but didn't wake my wife, and this morning she didn't believe me.

I push the covers aside and sit up.

"Look," I say, but Lori keeps her back to me. She wants me to pretend she's asleep, and I do.

It's been weeks since she left the bed.

Orlando isn't what she expected when I took the job. Disney, she was thinking. Theme parks and beaches and maybe a few animated birds to fasten the loose strings of her apron. A pie cooling on every windowsill—that sort of thing. Except that Disney isn't in Orlando, not really. Orlando's a half-hour from Disney and an hour from the beach. Noisy and garish, it's a city on a grid, a city of stoplights and the cars that drive fast to get through them before they wink red. Think strip malls and strip clubs. Think suburbs ten miles out. As a shortcut, picture any other American city.

Lori and I live in the Crestview Motel, our $175-a-week *home away from home*. We're waiting to close on a house—have been waiting three months—since word came of the transfer that has me doing the same work I did in Atlanta, selling office supplies for a shrinking company in a digital world with a shrinking need for office supplies. The house we're waiting for is vacant, a short sale that's turned out to be anything but. We can cancel the contract any time, but with Lori out of work and the pay cut that came with my transfer, it's really all we can afford.

"Hang in there," our realtor says when I call. "Any day now," she says. But she doesn't have to live at the Crestview with its rattling window units and water-stained ceilings, its curling carpets and torpedo-headed cockroaches. Every surface—table, carpet, couch—is pocked by cigarette burns. Every pipe sweats. The refrigerator roars.

Outside, the figures are still chucking things into the pond. I pull on a T-shirt and slip on my sandals. The locks are so old they take keys, and I make sure mine's in my pocket before I pull the door shut and follow the tube lights' hum down the hall. The walls are thin, and from two rooms I hear the same TV show cutting to commercial, one a few seconds before the other. The hall smells like cigar smoke and wet dog.

At the front desk, Dora, the owner, white-haired and overweight, is asleep in her chair, a TV on and tuned to Letterman. Dora's been good to us, taken our rent late and seen that we get extra towels when we need them. I hate to wake her, but she locks up at midnight, and getting back in can be a hassle.

"I'm stepping outside," I say.

"You can prop it," she says, meaning the door and the tire-size elephant that lives in the shade of the lobby's lone potted plant. The statue is carved from some kind of porous, charcoal-colored rock that's too heavy to lift, so I push. The thing slides, trunk-first, over the lobby's buckling, sneaker-scuffed laminate, catching only once where a laceration opens like a pair of split lips in the floor. The door opens with a chime, and I prop it with my shoulder while I slide the elephant into place. He does the job, the door sticks, and Dora waves without looking, eyes already closed.

The man by the pond is young, early twenties, tall and shirtless with muscles that ripple his body's surface like smooth river stones. His head is shaved, but his face is goateed. The boy looks four or five. He has thick, black hair and a girl's lips, small and pursed and pink. Their skin is dark. They could be staying here or they could live nearby. I'd never noticed them before last night.

The man stands at the water's edge, the boy at a distance.

I can't tell what the man has in his hands, then I see: It's one of those plastic packs of baloney or turkey or ham, the kind where the meat's been punched into an O with a rind you can tug from each slice like a tan rubber band. It's off-brand, not even Oscar Mayer, a big pack of cheap deli meat.

The man's fingers riffle the meat-stack like playing cards, and a slice comes unstuck. He waves the meat over the water, and the water is interrupted by a snout. Then come the eyes, the jaws, a scaly throat the color of smokers' teeth.

"*¡Mire sea cabeza!*" the boy shouts.

The meat leaves the man's hand and the alligator bobs, head up, jaws opening and snapping shut. It catches the food exactly like a dog.

"*¡Cocodrilo!*" the boy shouts. "*¡Cocodrilo enorme!*"

The man steps back from the bank. Quickly, he flings a few slices to the pond's middle. The gator turns and cuts through the water where it's joined by three of its friends.

It's stupid, what they're doing, stupid and illegal. People feed alligators, then alligators see people and think: *food*. Signs at park lakes and ponds advertise thousand-dollar fines. It's a thing I'd never do. Still, seeing it, I can't help being a little impressed.

"You're brave," I say, not knowing whether they speak English, but hoping.

The boy jumps, then closes the distance between himself and the man. He runs a hand along the man's belt, hooks two fingers through a belt loop, presses his face to the man's hip, then plugs his mouth with the thumb of the belt-loop hand.

The man laughs, and I wonder whether he's the boy's father or brother. The boy's awfully young to be this man's brother, and the man's awfully young to be this kid's dad.

The man still holds the meat, and now he brings a slice to his mouth and bites it in half. He offers what's left to the boy who unplugs his mouth long enough to poke the meat in, then returns the thumb to his mouth and chews around it. In the pond, the alligators make figure eights.

I introduce myself, extend a hand.

"Roberto," the man says. "Rob."

He takes my hand, and we shake.

"This is Freddy," he says.

I offer my hand, but Freddy shakes his head, so I make like I'd only meant to wave.

"He's shy," Rob says, and the boy presses his face back into Rob's hip.

Me, I'm trying not to grow alarmed. I watch the pond where the gators draw near. They glide, fat and brown and prehistoric-looking, and two almost reach the bank before Rob machineguns a second round of meat to the middle of the pond. The gators turn and race.

"One oh eight?" Rob says.

"I'm sorry?"

"You're with the lady in Room 108?"

His English is perfect.

"Yes," I say, thinking: *How?* Thinking: *Lady?*

"She your wife?" he says.

"She is."

"She sick?"

It's not the kind of question you get from most people. Certainly, it isn't one you expect from a stranger. It's a question with *youth* wrapped around it. He doesn't mean to be rude. He's curious. And it hits me that Rob isn't in his twenties, he's in his teens. And, just as quickly, it hits me that he *lives* here, that, months now, he's watched us and wondered at our story, just as tonight I've wondered at his.

But I don't tell him about the move or the job. I don't say that if bad things come in threes, we're due for one more. The house was number one. Then, last month, Lori miscarried our kid. I say kid. Embryo is what it was. Embryo or fetus. I can't remember which you call it at ten weeks. Babies, pregnancy—I'd always called myself pro-choice. Funny, though, how when the person you love carries the thing inside her, it's a *life*. It just is. It's a life and already you love it. One minute you love it and the next the toilet bowl's a bloody, goddamn mess and your wife is crying and you're on your knees trying to fish the thing out with a slotted spoon.

"FEMA?" he says.

"Sorry?"

"Oh, just most people don't stay here long as you. I thought maybe you'd lost a house."

"Something like that," I say.

"We had a house," he says, "Freddy and Mom and me. Then the bank took it. This place is better, though. We get HBO."

The boy puts out his hand for more meat, and the man who's just a boy himself uncurls a slice from the pile and fills the boy's hand. The rest he Frisbees, slice by slice, into the pond. The alligators lunge.

I want to tell Rob to be careful. I want to say how quick accidents happen, how, in an instant, a curtain is drawn on the world you know and a new world rises, ugly and unfamiliar, from the orchestra pit.

How, onstage, it squats, red-eyed and ready to fuck you up.

I want to tell him that, when it comes to suffering, the thing they say about other people's shoes and how far you have to walk in them before you'll know turns out to be true.

I want to say many things, and, of course, I don't. I keep my mouth shut because he'll learn. Soon enough, and with no help from me, he'll figure it out. He's young, and who am I to teach him that this, this pond and this night and the boy at his side—the world and all that's in it—isn't here just for him? That it won't—it can't possibly—last.

I'm quiet coming in, but Lori's not asleep. She's not in bed. The crack beneath the bathroom door's lit up and the shower is on.

"Can I come in?" I say.

Lori doesn't answer, and I open the door. I lower the toilet's lid and sit. The bathroom fan's broken and the room's steamy. The mirror is fogged, and soon the walls will drool.

"Where were you?" Lori says. They're her first words since morning, her first shower in I don't know how long.

"Outside," I say. "The guys I told you about, they were back feeding the gators."

"That's dangerous," she says.

"Tell me about it," I say.

A magazine is open on the floor at my feet. The toothpaste tube lies uncapped by the sink. In the trash can, the core of an apple. All of this is progress.

"Did you tell them?" she says.

"Tell them what?"

"That it's *dangerous*."

"Lori, they're feeding alligators. I think they know the risks."

Lori's quiet a long time. I hear the fart of the shampoo bottle, then the lathering.

"They were being careful," I say. "They—"

"One's just a boy. Isn't that what you said? That one was a boy?"

"That's right," I say.

"Well, for your sake, I hope he doesn't get eaten."

"For *my* sake?"

I stand. I sit.

"Say something happened," she says.

"Say it did?"

"And you had a chance to say something. And you didn't. You wouldn't feel bad?"

"If something happened? To the boy? Of *course* I'd feel bad. But that wouldn't make it my fault."

There's more I'd like to say, like, *Lori, the fuck is this about?* More I'd like to say and more I'd like to do, like maybe storm out, slam the door.

Except that she's out of bed. The woman I love is up and eating and washing herself off. And so I say nothing, do nothing, because I don't know what I can't yet do, can't yet say, and because I don't want to be the one to send her back to bed.

And there's this: I know what this is about, or I think I do. Some people, your sadness doesn't look the same as theirs, and they don't understand.

I could explain. I could take my wife by the hand and lead her to the bed, look into her eyes and say what I feel, except that to say it wouldn't do any good, just like it wouldn't do any good to tell two boys not to do what they know full well no one should be doing—like scolding every smoker you see. The boys won't learn until one loses a hand.

Because, in the end, we don't trust our elders or our lovers or our ears. We trust our eyes.

And that's where Lori and I are at an impasse. Because what goes on inside *me* doesn't come with a show.

The water cuts off, and Lori pulls back the curtain. Her stomach, which didn't have time to get big, is as flat and smooth as it's been the ten years we've been together.

"Towel?" she says.

I open the door beneath the sink and see that we're out. "Back in a minute," I say.

At the front desk, Dora's asleep again. The towels, I know where they're kept, the cabinet and the shelf. I could unlatch the desk's waist-high door, scoot past the sleeping woman and grab one, but it feels wrong, self-important, somehow, and rude.

"I'm sorry to wake you," I say, and Dora shakes her head and stands. Her glasses are on a red cord around her neck, and she fits them to her face. She rises, opens the cabinet behind her, but the shelves are bare.

"I'll be back," she says, pulling an oversize key ring from a drawer and disappearing into the bowels of the hotel.

By the back door, the elephant watches me and, briefly, I consider returning him to his home beside the potted plant. But I'm feeling suddenly tired, like I'm not good for much, not cut out for pushing stone elephants over fake-tile floors.

Against one wall, a large wooden rack displays a hundred pamphlets from every corner of Florida, Disney and Sea World and Legoland. *Pick me,* they scream in garish colors, letters swollen like Mylar balloons.

"Towels," Dora says. I turn, and she's back behind the desk, towels in a neat, white square on the countertop.

"Thank you," I say, and then I have to grab the top towel quick and push my face into it. I'm shaking, and I can't catch my breath. I sit. Right there on the floor, I sit down.

My face is in the towel and Dora's hand is on my back, and I'd pull the towel away except that I don't want her to see me sob.

We stay like that awhile, me on the floor and Dora at my back.

And then I'm OK. The towel is snotty and wet, and I'm sure my face is swollen and red. And Dora, God bless her, Dora doesn't say a word, just takes the towel, folds it, and offers a hand to help me up.

I stand. I smooth the front of my shorts. One of my sandals has come off, and I slip my foot into it.

"I'm so sorry," I say.

"What are you sorry for?" Dora says.

It's a question I can't answer, but I get the sense I don't have to. I wait for her to ask what's wrong, and she doesn't, and so I don't have to answer that either.

"Thank you," I say. "For the towels."

"Always plenty of those," she says.

"The boys," I say. "The boys out back—"

"I know," she says. "But what are you going to do?"

She shrugs.

I shrug.

She laughs.

"Son," she says, "you look a fright."

And, right then, I remember the reason for the towels. "Shit," I say. "Lori's waiting."

She lifts the stack from the counter and drops it in my arms, and then I'm bounding, my thanks unspooling behind me.

*

The door's locked and, like an idiot, I've left my key. I can see it, the table by the bed where I dropped it when I came in.

I knock. I knock again.

Then Lori's at the door. Her hair is stringy and wet. She's in one of my shirts, a T-shirt cannon freebie with the Atlanta Falcons emblem embossed big and red and black on the front. The material hugs her skin in wet patches.

"I got back in the shower," she says, "but then the hot ran out."

"I'm sorry," I say, thinking how nice it would be to feel Lori's hand on my back, to hear her say *What are you sorry for?*

She pulls the top towel from the pile and pulls off her shirt. She dries herself, drops the towel on the floor, then sits on the bed.

Moonlight cuts through the window where the curtains don't meet and lights up her breasts. The way it does makes me think of this painting I saw in a museum once. *The naked lady painting,* we called it. I was nine or ten on a class field trip to the High. I can't imagine what pains our teachers took to steer us from every nude, but we managed to miss them all. All but one. Near the tour's end, we passed through a room of impressionists, all landscapes—gauzy flowers and polka-dotted fields—all but this one of a woman seated on the lip of her bed, skin white with moonlight coming through the window. The other kids were laughing, boys and girls both, so I laughed too. Except that I didn't get it. The woman looked so sad. I'd never seen sadness like that, not in a painting and never in real life, and just knowing that it existed, that such sadness was out there and real in the world, was enough to wreck my day.

I'd forgotten it, the painting and the day. But, seeing Lori, sad in the moonlight, it all comes avalanching back.

I set the towels at the foot of the bed and move behind her. I put an arm around my wife. She shivers, and I pull the bed sheets to us. But Lori doesn't lean back. A pocket of air runs between us, cold like a mountain stream.

Between the parentheses of curtains is the pond, and the boys are gone, back to their room or else wandering the night. Setting off fireworks maybe, or maybe juggling circular saws.

"It wouldn't be your fault," Lori says.

David James Poissant

"I'm sorry?"

"The boys," she says. "I was just...I only mean that, whatever happened, it wouldn't be your fault. I know that."

Lori leans back, and her spine is a lightning rod up and down my chest. I put my other arm around her.

"I thought," she says. She's quiet. "It was only for a second, but I thought maybe you weren't coming back."

I grip her shoulders, but still she faces the window.

"I thought I'd made you go."

"You could never do that," I say, and, when she turns, tears streak her face.

"Just be patient with me, OK?" she says. "I just need a little more time to be this way, and then I'll be all right. I can already see it, you know? Things coming back into focus. But, until then, I just need you to be OK."

She turns back to the window, and her shoulders tense.

"Can you be OK?" she says. "With me being this way? Just for a little bit longer?"

In a box in storage is a portrait of the babies we were on our wedding day, black tuxedo and white gown in place of the graduation robes of a week before. And I wonder where we'd be, Lori and me, if what happened last month had happened back then. Probably, it would have ended us. Probably, Lori would have spent her days on the couch with her mom. Probably I'd have confused pity with fury and taken out on my wife my frustrations with fate. *You're not the only one who lost a kid here, you know.* Crystal-clear, I hear the words leave my lips, see the dish leave my hands, the kitchen floor a minefield of china.

I think of the people on reality shows, on *Dr. Phil* and MTV. And I think maybe they aren't bad people. They aren't cartoons. They're just children, most of them, kids who never got to grow up before life dropped something gruesome in their laps. I consider this, then I consider Lori and me, and I thank God for the small kindness of timing.

"I can be OK," I say.

And I can. I don't like it, but no one's having fun here, and this is what it means, loving someone. It means facing the music. It means growing the fuck up.

I feel Lori relax. And then she slips from my arms and onto the bed. Her head finds the pillow, and she pulls the covers to her chin. I run a hand over her hair, and it's still damp.

At some point we'll have to have it, the talk about whether to try again and what that means for her, for us. But we don't have to have that talk tonight.

"I love you," I say.

Lori speaks, but her words are choked. More tears come, and I don't make her say it, what I already know.

Lori sleeps through the sunrise, and late morning finds her still in bed. I eat a banana for breakfast. I read the paper twice. Finally, I have to leave the room.

In the lobby, I hope to see Dora, but a man's in her place, someone I've met only once. He must not remember me, and I must be staring, because there's an edge to his voice when he asks, "Can I help you?"

"I'm good," I say.

I look for the elephant, but it's not by the door, and it's not by the plant.

"Where's the statue?"

"Statue?" the man says.

"The stone elephant?"

The man shakes his head. I step outside.

Outside, the pond is quiet, the surface still. Across the water, a bird with dark feathers and a question mark for a neck fishes the shallows on legs thin as matchsticks. The alligators, which seem to surface only at dusk, are nowhere to be seen.

I pull my phone from my pocket and call our realtor, but I only get her voicemail.

"Sheila, it's me. Just hoping for some good news. Call me."

I follow the pond around the back of the building, then cut up an alley to the parking lot. The lot's empty, mostly, a few beat-up cars in the spaces closest to the front entrance.

In the parking lot, though, is the elephant, the elephant and the boy. Freddy's running circles around it, a blue plastic guitar slung over his back, a green strap across his chest.

Rob's on the curb. He wears sweats and a shirt with the local university's Pegasus logo. He sucks a cigarette down to the butt, flicks it, pulls a pack from his pants and lights another. He pats the concrete beside him, and I sit.

"How's things?" he says.

"Fine," I say.

"How's the wife?"

By the light of morning, it's clear he's half my age. Acne dapples his forehead, and his goatee is patchy and thin. I can almost see the follicles straining underneath.

"She's going to be fine," I say. It might be a lie. I can't see the future, but I can hope.

"He yours?" I ask, and Rob nods.

In the parking lot, Freddy's doing handstands, lifting himself up and walking forward a few feet on his palms before falling over. One fall, he grabs his knee and looks at Rob as if he might cry.

"Don't start," Rob says. He turns to me, cocks his head, confidential-like. "Kid's a wuss. Trying to toughen him up."

If there's an order to the universe, I can't see it, can't fathom why, after a year of trying, after months of tests and more months of Lori on Clomid, he gets a son and we get a bowl full of blood, why this fucker has Freddy and I have a wife who won't get out of bed.

Rob draws on his cigarette, lets out a big cloud of smoke. There's a breeze, and some of the smoke blows back on us.

I'm feeling mean, and I'm feeling sorry for myself, and I'm thinking of Lori, of her refusal to tolerate stupidity and her disappointment in me when I do. Or maybe I'm not thinking at all, because next thing I know, I've ripped the cigarette from Rob's mouth and I'm standing over him, grinding the butt into the pavement with my sandal's soft rubber heel.

Rob's too surprised to do anything, then he regains his composure. Then he stands. My eyes come up to his chin, and my head is the size of just one of his biceps. All this because I can't seem to keep my mouth shut without uncrossing my arms.

It's like those monkeys, Mizaru, Kikazaru, and Iwazaru. *See no evil, hear no evil, speak no evil.* I did a report on them in high school and how in America we lost one. The one we lost is Shizaru: *Do no evil.* In Japanese pictures, he's there with the others, arms crossed. Used to be, I thought the message was to take the teachings and follow all four, except that there's a monkey for each and only so much room on a man's back.

As for evil, what is it, and how do we know when we do it? It's not the same as charting the distance between right and wrong. Those beg context, circumstance. *Evil*—the very idea's bound up in something bigger—an absolute—like Eden or one of those animals out back, slit-eyed and ready to strike. Say it exists, how could you possibly stand up to evil without courting the thing itself?

The arm goes back, and I'm ready for the punch. But Rob's eyes cut to the boy, and the fist drops. Then Freddy is calling, Rob and I turning.

"*Mira!*" he says. He pulls the guitar over his head and slings it by the strap. The toy hits the ground and skids a few feet before coming to a stop. And then Freddy is running. He runs at the elephant like he means to plow through it, leave a little Freddy-shaped hole in the statue like Wile E. Coyote through a rock. At the last second, he weaves, misses the thing, but keeps going. He circles back, and, this time, when he charges, I know that he means it.

"Look!" he calls, and he's running, reaching, mouth open and the sun in his teeth. Then he's up, soaring, arms like wings, the elephant underneath, and I know that he'll clear it, legs already windmilling, ready to land.

BETHANY PRAY
The Boss Who Fired Me During the Recession

Describing her, I say, she's a Modigliani face-wise
but when she walks in her custom-size narrow boots
she minces, or half-dances like a pony,

the sort of pony who is dear and a little silly
and wears a hat with a ribbon.
A little of this and a little of that—lacking a territorial integrity,

she slides vertiginously from apprehension to sourness to glee.
She told me she had a wandering eye as a child,
but in fact, she still does.

To think she doesn't know how the one eye floats out
to the right, or that resulting air
of being wholly lost.

Frankly, Cubism is painful, as much for the viewed
as for the viewer: the girlish gewgaws
and the monkish face above

and the fixed, unaligned eye.
She looked out at us with the other eye.
To her we were as paper, without dimension,

viewed as the Cyclops viewed Ulysses
and his men in the cave—
foreign, and a scourge.

NICOLE SEALEY
Even the Gods

Even the gods misuse the unfolding blue. Even the gods misread the windflower's nod toward sunlight as consent to consume. Flesh of their flesh, bone of their bone. Still, you envy the horse that draws their chariot. The wilting mash of air alone keeps you from scaling Olympus with gifts of dead or dying things dangling from your mouth—your breath, like the sea, inching away. It is rumored that gods grow where the blood of a hanged man drips. You insist on being this man: willing trial by ordeal, the ordeal of blood. The gods abuse your grace. Still, you'd rather live among the clear, cloudless white, enjoying what is left of their ambrosia. Who should be happy this time? Who brings cake to whom? Pray the gods do not misquote your covetous pulse for chaos, the black into which they were conceived. Even the eyes of gods must adjust to light.   Even the gods have gods.

MAUREEN SEATON
The Visions of Sane Persons

> *I shall speak of the tendency among sane and healthy persons to see images flash unaccountably into existence.*
> —Francis Galton

This is a tale not of science but of blue.

Some say this heat is the worst in history, but history is huge and I doubt it has never been hotter across the Northern peninsula.

Still, the bears are unhappy in their photo ops and video clips.

I'm not sure how I should approach the subject of sanity or if it is technically or even nontechnically correct to call what a person sees a vision.

We will need to contend with bears and wild cats if we plan to hike the forest to the dunes on the rim of the mood-ring lake.

Sane persons see forms in their heads automatically and involuntarily.

Some see colors when they listen to music.

Every once in a while a shot rings out and I hold my breath.

My friend Pam is the only living person I know who sees colors attached to numbers.

Turning to the bear as he walks beside me, I see death (white) and resurrection (rosy), but not always, and not always in that order.

Is it fair to assume that the essence of the problem of sanity and metaphor is that sanity lacks the author that metaphor possesses?

A bullet once killed a boy a mile away from the man who held the rifle.

The bear (magenta) follows the river (rainbow) to the dunes (khaki) and plunges into the Great (gold) Lake, where he drinks deeply until he is once again alive and (blue).

LISA SEWELL
Grusamericana *(Whooper)*

Marked by Apollo with a red coin on the forehead,
this one still waits, solitary, uncoupled

on extraordinary legs, not gull-like or chicken-like,
not tree-clinging or perching. He dreams

a wet return to the sand flats and shallows
of the Blackjack Peninsula, of flying *over lands*

with mutual wing easing their flight as in *Paradise Lost.*
Plate Eleven in my *Audubon* guide also shows the acid

yellow eye, black wing feathers secreted
beneath lush white plumage: that seven-foot span

and black wing tip flag flown only to conjure fear
or desire, or to flap in a needful migratory ride.

At age six, Ramakrishna fainted with rapture at the sight
as ancient as the Pleistocene, their heyday,

when the longed-for whooper calls echoed across wetlands
from California to New Jersey, bugle cry that begins

and builds in the twisting loops and coils of the long
esophagus carved invisible within the snowy

feathered sternum. For what is to be done: leap high
in the air, and make a half-turn before landing?

Toss back the head, then bend a willow neck,
bowing low and throwing sticks? Here is a philosophy

of wariness that sleeps while standing on one leg
but if I crane my neck, or use a crane to lift

my sorrows, or fold one thousand cranes with hope to mime
Sadako's agile fingers, will I stop the radiating sickness?

Will each beaked and folded sheet at the dark feet
of the monument bring good luck and good fortune

to the dead in Hiroshima? If he astonishes the air,
bounding up and over her arched preening shape, his crest

redder than usual, his plumage full, will she dance in answer?
We know they mate for life and are so long-legged,

long-billed, and long-lived, we imagine their love
is truer than ours. Of two eggs, only one survives

and sometimes I miss the *ker-lee-oo* and rusty mottled feathers.
In South Carolina, the sadness discernable in the salt marshes

arises perhaps from having once harbored
that light boned trumpet blast, that dancing whooper logic.

JOHN WARNER SMITH
Zydeco on Dog Hill

Before they put Cousin Gladys
inside the ground in a cornrow
of fair-skinned Creole men, I sat
in her funeral mass imagining
two shadows dancing in the swish
of a swift moving blade
that slit her dreams in half
and sent her father strolling
across the cane field
like a land-bending river, turning
a page she could never turn back:
news that a man had been killed,
her husband had been jailed.
I heard spoons scratching
a washboard, and a zydeco
accordion pump a groove
through a sweat-dripping rumble
of fast-shuffling feet. I felt
the wooden floor turn to water
and tasted the salty wave
as Jo Jo, her lover, swung out,
flaunting his gabardine
in two tones, his wide brim
fedora suddenly seen
whirling in a herd of flamingos
and a pool of whiskey-warm blood.

TRACY K. SMITH
Logos

for Linda Gregg

Safe in the light along the bank
Being in believing
No name   Only being

On the bank radiant and blank
Safe watching and seeing   On the brink
Of the light   Blank   No blame in being

Waiting then breathing in being   Seeing
Singing   Let my voice   Let my voice cease
Being   On the banks along that brink

After the blaze of knowing
That singing

ANNA SOLOMON

Alan at the Kirschbergs'

Alan Zimmer had been staying at the Kirschbergs' for a week when he saw their daughter in the elevator at Brigham and Women's. She was in a wheelchair. Alan, behind her, recognized the yellow kinks of her hair, and the dark roots that cleaved to her part.

He stepped forward. "Jenna! What are you doing here?"

She turned slowly, as if his voice had arrived from a great distance, and appraised him coldly, staring at his slippered feet and working her way up: the thin gown he knew made him look slightly pregnant; the clutch of wires he gripped in his right hand, connecting like flight routes to the nodes on his head.

"Hello, Alan." Jenna's eyes were cupped by purple crescents. He'd met her only twice—since she turned seventeen, her parents joked, Jenna rarely made public appearances—and he couldn't remember seeing her eyes, buried as they'd been behind her mass of curls. But now those curls were tied back and she stared at Alan as though he were naked. He noticed the nurse behind her chair, saw the reproachful, twitching jaw, then, pinned to one ungainly breast, the Women's Care Clinic badge. He understood that he should not have said the girl's name.

"I'm here for my test!" he cried, his voice treble to bury the silence. He pointed at his head, then at the doctors beside him, then swirled a little nutso circle around his ear. "For my tingling! My problem! You know!"

Jenna didn't blink. He looked at her feet, in crepe-paper slippers that matched his own. He wondered if her toes were cold. Once, when Alan pressed one of his girlfriends, Sybil, to try the rhythm method, she'd told him about her own abortion. She was thirty at the time, didn't know who the father was, could barely pay her rent, yet what she remembered most clearly were the socks she'd worn to the operation— blue ankle socks, stained blackish by a pair of cheap shoes—and how, when the nurse told her to undress—*everything, dear*—she refused to take them off. *I thought I would die,* Sybil said, *without those socks.*

The girl shifted her slippers on the wheelchair footrests; he was gawking. He thought of the Kirschbergs, cocooned in their ex-urban life up on the North Shore, trusting that their daughter was in school today. He pointed at his own feet. "Fancy duds they got here, huh?"

The elevator stopped, jolting him a little. He brought his face down near her ear. "I won't tell," he started to say—but then the door opened and Jenna was wheeled out into the bleached hospital glare. Cool air drifted up Alan's gown. He straightened and coughed and was grateful for the wires in his hand, for something to hold, though he suspected that this was what the doctors wanted him to feel, that they'd offered him the wires like people let children hold keys until there's something real to unlock or drive. It didn't matter. Soon these men would hook his wires up to their machines and press a button and then, as if from heaven—if one believed in heaven—he would hear their voices boom: "Ah-ha. Ah-haaaaaaaaaaaaaaaaaaaaaaaaaaaa." And then he wouldn't be crazy and he wouldn't be afraid and he would know. He would feel like a man again.

He'd met Ruth and Paul Kirschberg the summer before, at "Jewish Camp," which was what returnees like the Kirschbergs called the New Age, HinJew, JuBu retreat center set into the folds of a valley in the Berkshires. Julia had asked him to go with her, and because they'd so recently met, Alan understood that it was less a question than a test. Julia was olive-dark from summer then; with her fall of black hair, she looked like a Persian princess. The clinching factor for Alan was her claim that such an experience would improve the quality of their sex, which wasn't bad to begin with. So he ate the macrobiotic food. He sat through hours of silent group meditation only to discover that chanting group meditation was even worse. He contorted his body through morning yoga sessions, Julia deep breathing like a hurricane next to him. In Triangle, he pulled a waist muscle.

On the third night, they were introduced to the Kirschbergs, Paul dark and bearded, Ruth in a pea-colored toga-style dress. Mid-fifties, Alan guessed—just a few years older than he was, but they were the couple who parented everyone and everything, and in their presence, he felt as young as Julia. Every night after that, he steered toward them, and by the end of the week, he and Julia had secured an open invitation to visit the Kirschbergs' home in Gloucester. And though Alan guessed they'd extended the same offer to half the Jewish campers, and though he didn't intend for his relationship with Julia to become the sort of exclusive thing that required regular visits with other couples, he'd kept the scrap of paper with their address and phone number.

It was Ruth who answered. Alan hadn't planned to say anything about the tingling yet—he didn't want her to arrange for a healing ceremony or fast—but hearing her deep voice again, the way it seemed to contain space, invite you in, he wanted, suddenly, to cry. He'd been holding his terror like saliva in his throat, telling Sybil and Julia little bits of what was happening, but Julia's cooing only made him feel more frail, and Sybil was more concerned with what wasn't happening between his legs. He'd made it into a joke with both of them. Now he told Ruth everything, how the tingling started, two months ago, at home in Vermont, concentrating in his hands and feet before crawling into his chest, how once it claimed his face, curled over his ears, circled his head like a wreath of needles, how another time his eyeballs started to ache, as if his brain were squeezing them out from behind.

By then, he was prepared for this sensation; he'd already gone to the Rutland library and looked on the web, where he found nine neurological diseases involving tingling: one of these, Multiple Sclerosis, often presented itself in the eyes before moving on to induce weakness, lack of bladder and bowel control, and twitching. He told his internist, "MS," but the man barely seemed to hear him. At the hospital in Burlington, they slid him into the curved glacial cave of a Magnetic Resonance Imaging tube, where, inches above his face, a tilted mirror offered a view, out the back, of the door to Dunkin Donuts. The machine roared and clicked. Alan held himself so still that his left foot cramped and flew into spasm. Through the machine's guts, the technician spoke: "Mr. Zimmer, sir. Can you hang in there five more minutes?" He could. He did. Then they made him sign release forms and tapped his spine for fluidlike sap from a tree but this was water-clear, its benevolence shocking. They taped wires to his limbs and digits and shot him through with electric pulses. They sat him down and told him everything was normal. Normal! Even after he'd told them about his sudden loss of vision one day, which he'd read about, which belonged to at least three of the diseases! He said they were wrong. They got insulted. They referred him to a neurologist in Boston, which was an embarrassment. He'd grown up in the city. When he moved north to live "closer to the land," etc., and open his own cabinetry shop, when his city friends expressed skepticism about the services in such a place—schools, restaurants, *hospitals*—Alan had called them snobs and moved. He couldn't ask them for favors now. And he couldn't afford a hotel. And his parents had died, of general inactivity it seemed; their apartment was long gone. He needed a place to stay for who knew how long; the treatment might be difficult, prolonged…

"Of course," Ruth said. "You'll stay as long as you need to. I'm so sorry. Of course. You'll be part of the family."

Which might have terrified Alan if he hadn't believed that Ruth would say this sort of thing to anybody.

Alan and his doctors got off on the fourth floor. One was tall and beak-nosed, the other young and dark with long womanish lashes—Indian, Alan guessed—and as he followed them down a series of hallways, he liked the asymmetry of their pairing. It was like cross-pollination, or layering oak with pine. Together, they'd do good work.

In a small, dim room, they attached his wires to the machine. The tall doctor talked as he worked, explaining the examination—"An electro-encephalogram," he said, as if he'd learned the word before "mama"— and Alan sensed a great competence and vigor in the man's long limbs. The other doctor nodded, adjusted dials. Alan realized that his tingling was gone. This happened sometimes, for brief periods, and usually it was blissful—he'd never imagined what a pleasure it could be to feel nothing at all—but now it seemed problematic, possibly dangerous.

"My symptoms," he said. "If I'm not feeling them right now, will that affect the test?"

The Indian doctor looked up from the machine. He paused to let his lashes blink. "No, sir. This test is for central nervous system."

The white doctor said, "The nerve conduction velocity test you already had? That might be altered by immediate sensation, but this test is much deeper, so to speak." He leaned over Alan and pressed the nodes tight. "You'll feel a slight pressure, but that should be it. If it hurts, tell us. If you can't speak, raise your hand."

Alan closed his eyes. He felt optimistic for the first time in weeks. A rush of blood flowed into his scalp, then his left foot started tingling and he was grateful: he trusted the doctors, but still, wasn't it better to be consistent? Wasn't that what scientific "control" was all about? At the edges of his skull he felt a mild squeezing. He heard feet shuffling and tried to forget it, heard a pen scribbling and tried to let it go; he wanted to focus, to make it easy for the wires to pick up what they were after—

"Well then." The tall doctor's voice. "That's it. You can open your eyes."

The Indian was removing the nodes from Alan's head.

"That's all?"

The men nodded.

"What did you find?"

"Results will take a few days, at least. We need to send our findings to the lab, then they'll analyze them in conjunction with your spinal fluid samples."

"What if something happens in the next few days?"

"What sort of thing do you have in mind?"

Alan ignored the tall doctor's half-smile. They were all the same in the end, mocking, trying to placate. "Weakness," he said. "Or paralysis. I could go blind." He didn't mention MS; he'd learned by now that they didn't like patients who knew too much.

The man thumbed through Alan's chart. "It's been over a month, I see, since you began experiencing your symptoms. You seem to be in fine health now, yes? I think the chances of a sudden progression are very slim."

"But still possible. That's what you're saying. It could happen tomorrow."

The doctor closed Alan's chart. "I'm not a fortune-teller, it's true."

"If it's a comfort—" the Indian doctor stood slightly behind his counterpart, having removed the last node from Alan's head. "If it would make you more comfortable, I can perform a clinical examination. Check balance, vision, memory, these sorts of basic indicators."

"Is this where you make me walk on my heels and follow your finger with my eyes and remember silly phrases?"

A flush of rust bloomed on the man's face. "These are several of the components, yes."

"The other doctors did that," said Alan.

"Are you under the impression that we're paid to be original?" The white doctor began to unplug the machine.

Alan focused on the Indian. Perhaps he would find something the other one hadn't. Maybe some problem that had been subtle before was further advanced now, and detectable.

"Go ahead," he said.

The Indian smiled. He took out a safety pin and pricked Alan's toes. He gave Alan three things to remember: state of Arizona; blue fork; yellow ball. He took out a silver thing and clapped it against his hand, then stuck its cold flesh against Alan's arm and told him to nod when it stopped vibrating. He made Alan close his eyes and balance on his toes. He touched Alan's arm and asked how many fingers he felt. At the end, he asked Alan to repeat the three things. Then he said, "Good. All perfectly normal." And everything, even this final excruciating declaration, was the same as it had been in Vermont, except that the state had been Mississippi and the ball orange.

Alan let his forehead vibrate against the window of the train as North Station gave way to rail yards, then to cattails and marsh. He wanted the hill behind Julia's cabin, or the lane outside Sybil's house, crowded with saltboxes and old sheds and clotheslines. He wanted to be there with an erection. For a month now, he couldn't make it happen— as though a man in his condition did not deserve to perform an act that was designed to lead to procreation. He thought of the women who'd wanted babies—his babies—and some part of him wished he'd caved while he was still healthy.

He tried to comfort himself by thinking about how quickly they suffocated him. Just last week, he'd had to leave Julia's without any warning; he'd simply stood and dressed and left. She hadn't fought him; she knew he'd go to Sybil's anyway. But Sybil wasn't home. Alan had forgotten she had a date, a recently emigrated New York retiree looking for someone young to spend his money on—a man, Sybil added when Alan sneered, who wasn't much older than Alan. If he was rich enough, she said, who knew, maybe she'd rethink her uncommittment policy.

Alan felt ashamed now, on the train, surrounded by the waxy commuter faces, thinking about how he'd stood on Sybil's stoop, the house silent as stone, as the tingling spread up his leg and into his groin, then pushed up his stomach and into his chest. His breathing had gone shallow, his palms wet. Finally he'd gotten back in his truck and driven the twenty miles back over the pass to Julia's. Then he'd seen her shape through the kitchen window and thought, she'll think she's got me now. He backed out of the drive and headed aimlessly up the mountain, letting the engine's rumble mask his tingling, thinking of another woman, a third woman, who did not exist but who once would have been available, a woman who was mending a dress perhaps, under a table lamp. Self-sufficient yet soft. She would solve everything. She would barely look up as he entered, yet she would know him, and want him simply, needles glinting in her mouth.

The entire right side of Alan's body was numb as he entered the front hallway. He heard the Kirschbergs singing: a wordless, cloying chant. In the dining room, the table was set for Shabbat. Paul was sweeping while Ruth polished a pair of brass candlestick holders. Alan nearly laughed when he saw their gentle, diligent work, their trusting faces as they looked up. A desperate act, he thought, turning routine into ritual. Pretending against the boredom of domesticity.

"How did it go?" Paul asked. "Learn anything new?"

Alan shrugged. "It'll take a few days for the results. I should probably go home…"

Ruth's hand was on his shoulder. "That's the worst. Having to wait." She dropped her cloth and embraced him, surrounding Alan with the high, heady scent of the polish, and he couldn't help but relax into her hold. He was sorry for his uncharitable thoughts. The Kirschbergs were good, good people, better than Alan, surely—and there was Paul, looking at him, if not with love, then something close to it. When Ruth released him, he felt suddenly guilty for not telling them about Jenna. On the way out of the hospital, he'd found himself hoping to spot her hair—but then he'd forgotten all about her.

"Really, I could go," he offered. "At least until they call with the results."

"Absolutely not," said Ruth. "We'll show you some long walks, a bunch of cafés in town. See it as a little vacation, a place to rest." She handed him the Kiddush cup. "There's Manischewitz in the cupboard above the stove."

When Alan returned with the wine, Ruth was preparing to light the candles.

"Are we starting without Jenna?" he asked.

"She's at her boyfriend's house," Paul said. He rolled his eyes, and Ruth laughed.

Alan coughed lamely, covering his mouth. He pitied them, the way he pitied most parents—their obvious intoxication, their gaudy adoration. They'd been duped, made feeble. He watched as Ruth struck the match, lifted a leaning candle, and held the flame to its base until wax began to drip.

*

Alan took the walks they showed him. He went to the cafés and drank hot beverages out of chunky homemade mugs. As long as he had the time, he thought he might as well experiment, see if he could isolate some dietary element and correlate it with his tingling. He set himself a trial course: green tea one day, Chai the next, decaf coffee after that, then herbal tea, and finally espresso. By espresso, the doctors would call.

As for Jenna, he hadn't seen her since the hospital, had only heard a car returning her late the next night, water running in the bathroom across the hall, her bedroom door whining closed. He was still awake when Paul and Ruth achieved simultaneous orgasm in the third bedroom, Paul's grunts surprisingly bass, Ruth letting out an ascendant trilling sigh. A gentle murmuring, then more water. Alan felt bad for himself, but worse for Jenna: here was her mother, most likely postmenopausal, fucking without a care in the world.

He phoned Sybil on Sunday afternoon, when he knew she'd be sitting at her kitchen table, mildly depressed, hands kneading her face as she read the *Times* front to back.

"Alan. How are *you*?" She sounded unusually upbeat. "How's the tingling show?"

"Fine." This was what he'd called it himself.

"Guess who's here?"

"No idea." Though the coyness in her voice told him.

"New York man. He's in the shower. He's much nicer than I expected."

"Nicer than me, I'm sure."

"Well. But I miss you."

"Well, aren't you nice too." Nicer than normal, Alan thought; she was speaking out of pity, not desire. "So much niceness I can't take it."

"I'm serious," she said. "When are you coming back?"

"New York man can get it up, I bet."

"So can you, when you're not wigged out. Do you miss me back?"

"I miss your body."

"And I love talking to you too. Do you miss Julia?"

"Not really." Though he missed her body too—fleshy where Sybil's was lithe. He missed all the women. Their waists and their assurances and their anger and their thighs, so many hefts and textures of thigh. For a period of Alan's life, it had seemed that he lived in a great forest of thighs.

He called Julia the next day.

"Alan. I've been thinking about you."

He could taste the smoked flavor of her lips, her clothes, the woodstove breath in her cabin.

"Are you OK? Have you gotten any results?"

"I'm fine," he said, then blurted, "I miss the hill behind your place." The truth was, he missed all the hills, and the valleys too. From the Kirschbergs' house, all he had to look at was marsh. He wondered if Jenna found it as uninspiring as he did, if she wished her parents had raised her in the city like normal Jews—if there, she wouldn't have gotten pregnant. He thought of girls he'd dated growing up: Leah Fishman, Pam Cohn, Cynthia Miller. They'd been polished in a way Jenna wasn't, their hair blown straight, their faces made up to look simpler; they seemed so well contained it was hard to imagine that their insides weren't just as spotless.

"It'll be here when you get back," Julia said.

She wouldn't ask when that was, of course, not outright, and for a moment Alan was sorry—she hadn't been a skittish woman when they met. Then he felt the familiar irritation: she made him feel, sometimes, as if he'd swallowed her.

"Everything all right on your end?" he asked.

"Great. Just great." She was walking now, he could hear her slippers scuff along her floor. Then the scrape of the ladle she kept in the water bucket. Water pouring into a Mason jar. She took a gulp, then said, "How are Ruth and Paul?"

"Fine." Alan wanted to tell her about Jenna. *The poor thing,* he wanted to say, as he imagined a father might say to a wife about a child. But Julia had ideas about people. Expectations. As in the Kirschbergs were The World's Most Open and Loving Couple, not people whose daughter kept a life behind their backs. She took things personally. Besides, she would have advice, which he wouldn't want to take, which would hurt her.

He said, "I'm picturing your mouth. Your lips on the jar, your neck when you swallow."

He felt her wanting to ask, again, was he OK, but she said nothing. Whereas Sybil would laugh, Sybil would ask if he was trying to initiate phone sex. But this was part of what he loved about Julia: her earnestness, her heart. He did love her. He wanted to kiss her. He said, "I miss your mouth."

*

Alan's beverage experiment yielded nothing. His tingling came and went just as randomly as before, sometimes spiking as if his nerves were being cracked, at others settling into a barely present hum. On the afternoon of the herbal day, it was in his chest again. Both legs, both arms, and his chest. He felt like he'd been filled with fire. He paced the Kirschbergs' rooms, but the decor filled him with confusion: South American tapestries next to nudes painted by artist-friends next to postmodern sculptures next to Judaica. He tried listening to music but couldn't pay attention. Finally, he walked outside and started down the path through the trees that led to the marsh. He'd discovered a cluster of rocks the day before, piled black and damp below the high tide line like a last-ditch effort by the glacier to break up the monotony of the grass.

Jenna sat on the tallest rock. She saw him before he could shrink back into the trees. Alan didn't want her to feel caught by him again—she was supposed to be in school—but he couldn't help feeling relief at the sight of her.

She blew smoke rings as he walked toward her.

"How goes it?" he asked, stepping onto the rock below hers.

She nodded, sucking hard on the cigarette, her halo of curls shaking with the effort. It was the sort of hair a grown woman could wear beautifully, turning it into a Medusa-evoking advantage, but Jenna looked engulfed by it. Alan had to squint against the sky.

"I haven't told them," he said. "Just so you know. And I won't."

"Yeah." She blew out. "I figured that."

She trusted him. Or she was teasing, it was hard to tell, the way her gaze kept wandering past him, out over the marsh.

"Do you want me to thank you?" she asked.

"What?"

"You're looking at me like you want me to say something else."

"No, no." Was he? Did he? "I just want you to know I'm not thinking about it. I've forgotten it. Woosh. Gone."

"Right."

"But if you want, you know, to talk—feel free."

She took another drag and let rings spill out. Not as well-formed as Sybil's, but then Sybil had seventeen years of smoking on her. Alan's fingers were cold. "My own situation?" he said. "It's pending now.

I'm waiting for the results of that test."

Jenna tossed her cigarette into a tidepool by Alan's feet. "You're still tingling?" She looked at him sideways.

"I know it sounds funny, but sometimes it's numb too, and lately, I think it makes me weak." He felt this as he said it, his left calf muscle fatigued.

"If—" Jenna lit another cigarette, inhaled, blew it out her nose "—if you could have the results of your tests be anything, what would they be? What's your fantasy?"

He laughed weakly. "It's not a fantasy."

"Pretend it is. What would the doctor say to you? He'd walk in with the results and look at you and say what?"

"Anything. Something. Anything except for nothing."

"Just give me some possibilities here. What sorts of diseases do you imagine you might have?"

"I don't imagine, I know. I've done research."

"OK. What?"

"MS, for starters. That's the most likely scenario—"

"And what would happen to you then?"

"They can't know. I could just tingle for the rest of my life, or I could be in a wheelchair next year. I might be unable to control my facial expressions, my bowels."

Jenna looked unimpressed. "What else?"

"Besides MS, there's a whole range of autoimmune disorders. Lupus. Rheumatoid arthritis. I don't have HIV. But I could have cancer—"

"Cancer causes tingling?"

"A tumor can swell and pinch nerves."

"But they haven't found any tumors?"

"No."

"And they don't think it's any of those other things?"

"They haven't said so, no. But for most of these diseases, there isn't one decisive test. It's not like strep throat, or pregnancy."

Jenna slid down off her rock. She stood close enough he could smell something like patchouli, and under it, the stale smoke in her clothes. Her parents knew she smoked—they talked about it like someone might talk about a child's pet frog, an obsession that would run its course—but he wondered if they'd seen her in action, the ease with which she maneuvered the cigarette, the confidence. He wondered what it would take to rattle them.

"I wish you luck, then," she said. "I certainly hope you get some good, conclusive results. I'm sure it would be a great relief to know that you have cancer."

Her cigarette hissed as it dropped into the tide pool, then she took off walking toward the path. Her hair was brighter than anything, even the oppressive marsh grass, even the fingernails of green just budding on the trees, all of it mocking him with its radiance. Cancer. She was only teasing, but still, he couldn't shake her tone. It was Ruth's assuredness, yes, but something else—an honesty that only children possessed.

Alan squatted down next to the tide pool. His fingers shook as Jenna's bobbing butts dodged his grasp. He wanted to stop, but he couldn't; he was certain, suddenly, that his fingers were failing. On he went, trying to undo her damage, to save the tide pool from the butts, or the butts from the tide pool, or whatever other purpose might be his, yet he caught nothing. His hand plunged, emerging draped with algae. When he looked up, she wasn't gone, as he'd dreaded. She was watching him from the trees, like a witch.

At dinner that night, Ruth and Paul asked how Alan was feeling, but when he started to tell them, "Not so good"—to tell how earlier in the day the tingles had seemed to clutch even the hairs on his chest—they didn't appear to be listening. Paul passed Ruth a dish of roasted beets. Ruth forked spinach onto Alan's plate.

He said, "You think I'm dying."

They chewed. Paul took a swig of wine. "What makes you say that?" He looked sincere, but it wouldn't be hard, not with that beard.

"You think I have cancer."

"Don't be silly," Paul said.

"A tumor."

"What are you talking about?"

"You haven't been honest."

"How have we not been honest?"

"What do you think is *wrong* with me?"

Ruth said, "Nothing, Alan." She was always saying his name, as if it would make him feel special.

"I want to know," he said. "You think you're holy people, truth seekers—tell me the truth."

"Alan."

"Ruth."

He watched her eyes tighten.

"Ruth just tried to tell you," said Paul. "We've talked with a couple doctor friends who think your problem is psychological as much as it is physical. But we knew that would make you angry, and only make it worse. We figured better to get the tests—better to let the tests reassure you."

"Reassure me of what? That I'm crazy?" Alan heard his voice dint off the Kirschbergs' dining-room light fixture, a triangular job made of slate—probably cut out of a ledge in Vermont. His voice rose. "Do you have any idea what this is like?"

"You're not crazy." Paul's voice was maddeningly calm. "Psychosomatic doesn't mean you're imagining things. The tingling is really happening—but its source is your brain, not some underlying disease."

"Oh—ho! So I *am* crazy, see? Why shouldn't I have cancer, at least? Everyone has cancer!"

Paul chuckled. "They've done scans. Blood tests. They haven't found any tumors."

"That's what Jenna said!"

"Then there you have it!" Paul paused, glass halfway to his mouth. "Jenna?"

"Down at the marsh today."

Paul looked at Ruth, who raised an eyebrow.

"She skipped school," Alan said.

"This is becoming a pattern," Ruth said.

"Are you blaming *me* for that?"

"No, Alan."

"Are you sure?"

"I don't see how it has anything to do with you."

"What do you think it has to do with?" he asked. "The boyfriend?"

No answer.

"Hormones?"

"GOD?"

Ruth stared at him. She held her plate with both hands, her fingers visibly trembling. Alan thought of Julia. He hoped they wouldn't associate her with him when she arrived one day, husband and infant in tow, expecting kindness.

"Excuse me," he said, and stood.

Paul laid his napkin on the table. He folded it into a triangle, folded it again, then worked it into a little tent and pitched it next to his wine glass. When he finally spoke, all he said was, "Maybe you should get a dog."

Alan started to pack. He would drive into the city, park near the hospital, and sleep in his car until the doctors arrived in the morning. They couldn't ignore him if he was standing there. He wouldn't leave until he got an answer. Then there would be a plan, a necessary course of treatment. Perhaps side effects too—nausea, hair loss—but these he could bear if he knew what needed doing. He got down on the floor next to his suitcase. The tingling flooded his hands. If he knew what needed doing, he thought, if the doctors would help him, keep him, he could bear anything: Jenna's hostility and the Kirschbergs' not liking him and dying and a million other indignities.

Feet, on the stairs. Paul and Ruth were coming, he guessed, to tell him he had to leave. They would discover him on his knees like this, hunched over his fingers as he crossed and uncrossed them. No, they hadn't found any tumors. But not all cancers were tumorous. He'd read about one, soft-tissue something, that grew not round but creeping, in the crevices between organs and veins. He needed to finish packing. His fingers were functioning, his motor skills were still intact. The doctors needed to see this, before it was too late.

Still, the door didn't open. Were his ears failing him too? Or were the Kirschbergs waiting outside, hands tunneled around their own perfect, undiseased ears?

He stepped toward the door and turned the knob. He would yank it back, let them fall into his room. Of course he was leaving. They didn't need to tell him.

But when he flung open the door, there was only a slow bass beat coming from Jenna's room across the hallway.

He knocked.

"What."

"Jenna? It's Alan—"

Her door opened. She didn't look surprised to find him there, only annoyed and scolding. Where she'd come home from, he didn't know, but she'd already changed into pajamas, printed with red cabooses. A child's pajamas, her wrists and ankles jutting.

"What," she said again.

What had he imagined saying?

"I'm leaving. I just thought I'd say goodbye."

"Goodbye."

"Do you—I need to ask—do you really think I have cancer?"

Jenna raised a dark eyebrow. "Did I say that?"

"Not exactly."

"Jesus, you really are a freak."

Alan felt a stab in his sternum. "Can I ask you," he said slowly, carefully, the idea arriving as he spoke, "can I ask you what it was like, being, you know…pregnant? Did you feel trapped? Or did you feel necessary?"

Jenna folded her arms. "Please leave."

"But Jenna."

"I'm serious."

Alan wanted to hug her. He wanted to feel the flannel of her pajamas and the wooliness of her hair. He opened his arms and stepped forward and there she was against his chest, wriggling but warm.

"Let go!" she cried. "Get away from me!"

He held her tight.

"Get off!"

He felt her jabbing elbows, her small breasts, the small electric fury she'd become, jumping and twisting in his arms.

"Alan!" Paul shouted from behind him.

Alan tried to let go, but couldn't. She was so sad, and he, it turned out, was so strong still, his arms huge around her shoulders.

Outside, the moon was full. Alan was sweating. He pulled off his sweater, threw his bag in the trunk, and stood in his T-shirt facing the house. After Paul pulled him off Jenna, she'd started to cry, and Ruth and Paul embraced her. They'd come to ask about her truancy but the talk would turn, he knew, to her abortion. There would be confession, shock, shame, reckoning. There would be no mention of Alan.

He wondered if it would be the same with Sybil and Julia some day, not the shock but the sudden intimacy, the squeezing out—if in some way they loved each other more than they loved him.

Or maybe before that could happen, he would die, and they would hold hands at his funeral and bond over his impotence.

The automatic yard light switched off.

Alan could go to each of them now, and ask their forgiveness. He would like to confess. He would like to be shouted at and to reckon too. But he'd kept no secrets. He'd made no promises.

He held his hands in front of his face, trying to see them in the dark. They weren't tingling. It had abandoned him again, taken away its static, soothing agony. Or—if you believed Paul—he'd abandoned it. Did it matter? The doctors would never believe him now.

Alan could smell the marsh, like a woman's underarms.

Upstairs, the light in Jenna's bedroom went out. Alan's hands came visible to him now, glowing a pale, fish blue, and beyond them he saw that the moon had lit the marsh grass too, an orange-gray flush that seemed to move toward him as he watched. It was impossible, Alan knew, to see color by the moon, just as it was impossible to see individual tongues of grass from such a distance, yet he saw both these things. Then he saw long black shadows striping the marsh. He'd dismissed the marsh as nearly Midwestern in its dullness, but now he saw that it was broken all over by these shadows—gulleys—and it struck him that he'd been here before. Not this particular spot but a marsh somewhere near here, in Ipswich maybe, on a day trip with his parents when he was eight, or maybe ten. His parents! They didn't know that the marshes were not for tourists. They'd let him run out a hundred yards, then farther; then he'd glanced back to find that they were talking, not watching him, and he slipped down into one of the gulleys. His sneakers sank in the mud. There was nothing but mud, and mussel shells, and a small skull by his feet, a raccoon's maybe, or a skunk's. He let out a cry when he saw the skull. He wondered where its body had gone, and whether touching it would make him sick. He wondered how long it would take his parents to see that he was gone, or if they would forget him altogether, if maybe they already had. But if he climbed out now, he would lose the game. He waited, staring at the skull, listening to his heart.

"Alan?" It was his mother's voice.

Then again: "Alan!"

He heard grass swishing, her voice shrill with panic.

"Alan!!! Alan!!!"

His mother, who never ran, was running, dodging stones, hurtling grass like an Olympian. Like Paul had come for Jenna, tearing Alan away, his force astounding. It was their fear that made them alive.

PIMONE TRIPLETT
Because There Is No Ending

we are not asked to see, the ridged folds
of the black walnuts, fallen, come veined
as any mind split from its skull, leaching
what little parades as peace. Rot
and wet. My right instep, sneaker's
underneath, crushes a once greener skin
gone brackish at the cap. Looking up,
the branches meet in an arch you can
walk under, pass through. And down
the road, when I hear the patient father
calling to his child stay away from the stick,
I know he means street because of the cars
and the highway in his head
that's been riddled for months now
with the tumors. The girl is seven.
She's putting some of the still unbroken
nuts in her plastic bag for her collage
because the seeds inside are small
and hard. I bring food to their porch,
I say you are in my thoughts. A week ago
when the wife asked, what's my name,
he said, you are the woman. She says,
It started with a pounding in the temple.
Then the years' cells brewing fault,
breaking bole from bark, furrows from solid
trunk making inroads. So we're standing
quiet at the door when a cardinal unseen
in the leaves spits its double spondees into air
because it is his season to do so.
Reap kernel. Make more of the blunt
limits, semifleshy. The branches
meet. Everyone loves hard as they can,
like it helps.

PIMONE TRIPLETT
My Dear Ego, Be

Clear, please, as a glass house.
Ladled in plates, liquid
form, silica, sand, dolomite, lime.

Then be tempered, shaped, craned
till you stand fastened to the forest
floor, reflecting.

And if a sudden garden struts
up, rising
in ribboned slope of pine and pin oak,

laurel or fleabane, you can draw markers
for their names, it's all yours, isn't it, the bits
to talisman or tame? Please,

quit that stupid trembling.
Why not be the wild
turkey last season who slammed the glass

again and again, all
gobble and snood, scrimmage of spit,
wattles on fire at first seeing

itself? Be the crack
that comes after crash. Or shard
that hangs for its moment,

see-through guillotine,
over the broken world
called choice.

KIMBERLY SWAYZE
Church

Because he could not afford to bury her, Wilson was still living with his mother. On the whole, though, his luck was holding. It was winter. The power company had shut off the electricity, removing any temptation he might have had to turn on the heat. He slept, or tried to sleep, in the corduroy chair, bundled in variegated layers of wool. The coffee wasn't helping. He was averaging six or seven cups a night.

After inertia, his biggest problem was ice: how to get enough and get it regularly; how to transport it; how to avoid notice. Ice, in its various permutations, was always on his mind. Like the cold, it was a constant, and also a shape shifter. It was capable of transubstantiation. It found him, discovered the chinks, the crevices, the subtlest crenulations. During his microscopic interims of sleep, he dreamed of snow.

Now, just after 3 a.m., the traffic noise was at its ebb. In the rivers of slush, it was barely a trickle. Really, what was the point of living in the past? No matter how many times he reworked the last three weeks, retread his every misstep, in the end, here he was in the corduroy chair, and another hour had gone by. Soon he'd have to leave for work. Continue his quest for ice. That was the future. He would have to deal with this other thing eventually. He knew this. He did know it. Not today, though, and probably not tomorrow.

An hour and several shots of bourbon later, he used the toilet and combed his hair, placed his palm against the tarp in the bathtub to check the temperature. He would shower at work when he was cleaning one of the rooms. He looked in the mirror. Blinked. Everything looked familiar but not the same. The towels. The shower curtain rod. By candlelight, the bathroom was haloed with inscrutable meaning. He had seen stroke victims on television describe the way the world felt different, smelled different. Burnt toast. Music. When he breathed in through his nose, he caught a faint but unmistakable whiff of sulfur deep in his sinus cavities. He hadn't been able to find the flashlight, but had come up with a box of utility candles. Candles. How romantic.

There just wasn't any way to explain it. He had gone over and over it at work as he made beds, wiped countertops, hung fresh towels.

So far, no one had asked. Wilson and his mother lived alone. Other people were tenuous and sporadic. Neighbors were invisible. On those rare occasions when he shared the elevator, the other tenant followed the rules, stared at the display as the elevator creaked from floor to floor. It helped, too, not having a phone.

Wilson took his break, then went back to work, moving on to the next room, habitually saving his favorite parts for last: the folded comment card and foil-wrapped chocolates on the desk, the small bottles of shampoo and conditioner with the hotel's logo, the washcloth folded like a fan. The finishing touches. Wilson undertook these tasks with pleasure. He was an undertaker. This thought fired every neuron. He couldn't work. He couldn't think. He folded towels.

In the precarious balance of luck and mischance, his job at the hotel was another piece of providence: though part-time, it provided Tuesday-through-Saturday access to ice. The people at the twelve-step meetings he attended, if, in some parallel universe, he decided to tell them about it, would call this an example of a Higher Power at work in his life. Wilson had no very decided ideas about what this meant. Sometimes, as he listened to the group offer these testimonials, he was visited by an image of a white kite in a blue sky, impossibly blue, impossibly high and out of reach. At the end of his shift, he filled the fifty-gallon cans on his trolley with empty garbage bags, wheeled it around to the ice machines in the corner alcoves on the sixth and seventh floors, then took the service elevator down to the loading dock. One of these days, he'd get caught. Not today, though, and probably not tomorrow. And by then, who could say? Wilson had heard about this: it was called Magical Thinking.

For the past three weeks, Wilson had bivouacked his mother in the bathtub in an ice-filled tent constructed on the inverse igloo principle. There was certainly nothing magical about that. He realized now that it was a mistake, a terrible error that grew exponentially more terrible every day. He should have run down and called someone three weeks ago. A paramedic. A priest. He didn't know any priests, had no idea where priests could be found. At the time, it had seemed better to wait, until he could figure out the arrangements. He wasn't sure what *the arrangements* entailed, but he knew they would cost money, probably a lot of money. She had been a small person. When he'd laid her gently in the bathtub, she had looked, in her baggy sweater, almost unrecognizably tiny.

Who did you call when your mother died in her sleep? It wasn't an emergency. But it wasn't a nonemergency either. It was confusing. And then you had to go to work. Maybe you would call from the payphone in the lobby after your shift. But then you didn't. This was always the way with Wilson, and he knew it. But he also knew that he was Powerless. Twelve-step meetings had persuaded him of this, if of nothing else. The Next Step, though, was to find this Higher Power. This was the sticking point. This was the part that Wilson's mother had called "a bunch of happy horseshit." Wilson had once seen a headline on the cover of *Time* magazine that announced the discovery of a "God" gene. He suspected he didn't have it. "If you want to drink, drink," his mother had said. "If you don't want to drink, then don't. But don't try to hand me this crap about God."

Wilson was not a joiner. He attended these meetings to comply with a court order. He complied, but he did not join. He sat in the back. He found groups where they left you alone, didn't call on you to speak up or urge you to tell your story. He tried not to fidget in the folding chairs, drank endless cups of burnt coffee from percolating urns, waited for them to pass the basket back around, when the crumpled dollar bills had been replaced by signed court slips. He fished around in the basket for his own, folded it up, tried to leave in a hurry. He listened, however.

Some people droned on for what seemed like hours, revealing horrible, uncomfortable details with vivisecting precision and, sometimes, with an off-kilter bravery, a peculiar pride. They seemed to need this pillory, its exhilarating flush of shame perhaps a substitute for alcohol. Wilson wouldn't know. He hadn't quit drinking, and he didn't plan to do so now. Certainly not now. Some of the stories he heard filled him with dread. There were boyfriends out there looking for some of the women, vowing to drag them home, sometimes to kill them. A husband who died in a fire caused by a cigarette. The worst part, according to the wife, the part that haunted her, was not knowing whose had been the cigarette. His? Hers? Wilson wasn't sure why this was the important distinction. Other people had lived under bridges, been homeless for years.

Wilson's own situation did not represent the worst predicament. Not by a long shot. Suffering was ubiquitous, was everywhere, often self-created but sometimes of its own making. Raw selves in narrative form hovered slightly above their heads, groundless, indeterminate, helplessly flawed. At the end, everyone held hands in a circle and intoned prayers. They were short prayers, but Wilson still didn't know the words. He moved his lips, chiming in loudly here and there to make up for his lapses. The prayers didn't end with "Amen" the way they did on TV. They ended with "It Works!" Whatever that meant, these people were earnest. They were very earnest. Some of them.

Twelve-step groups usually met in churches. Wilson, in fact, had never been in a church for any other reason. The meetings took place in an annex, most often in the basement, in a place called a Fellowship Hall, a kind of modified cafeteria, with a kitchenette and sometimes a little side room with a few recliners or a ping-pong table. Wilson thought about this. He had never been in the upstairs part of a church, though he had seen it on television and in movies. The Sanctuary. A place of respite, where you could go if you'd done something awful but were sorry. Where you'd be sheltered, shielded. Where someone else would take the problem off your hands. Relieve you of it, like a headache or a bad debt. Was there such a place? Wilson doubted it.

During meetings, everyone was free to get up and wander into the kitchenette to refill their Styrofoam cups of coffee or use the bathroom. Wilson used these excuses often. He was restless. Then he would sit back down and let his eyes drift out of focus. If you did this long enough, the fluorescent lights blended together in a fuzzy firmament. Your periphery became a tunnel through which your thoughts wandered, out of focus, toward the light. There was usually an ice machine in the kitchen. Wilson would hear a periodic clunk, the birth of an ice cube. It would startle him out of these moments of distraction. Halfway through, there was a break so that people could smoke. Outside, they set up empty coffee cans and urged everybody to respect church property. Everybody had to do this: everybody smoked.

A week ago he'd stood on the sidewalk in front of the church with a girl named Darlene. It was not completely anonymous. Not really. She had detained him on the way out for the loan of a cigarette. A loan. That's what she'd called it. He tried to be polite. He could keep still only by shifting from one foot to the other. "Some meeting," she commented. He nodded. It seemed like a safe response. "I didn't grow up here," she said, without any connection. People talked this way, he'd noticed, when thrown together out of context, when the lack of context was all they had in common. Some people wanted to be here, but most people didn't. She smiled at Wilson. "I really hate this fucked-up town."

She was attractive, and Wilson noticed that he automatically gave her an obscure benefit of the doubt. He wondered why that was. Because she was pretty, in her tall, furry boots and shiny ponytail, he wanted her to be nice, smart, interesting. Really, what possible difference could it make?

"That last guy," she said, "Larry. He made a lot of sense, you know?" He nodded again, though he couldn't remember who Larry was, or what had been said. She shivered. "And his wife. Jenny. It's so, I don't know, kind of sweet, isn't it? Both of them? Sort of. Not really, I guess. Not much. I guess it's a lot of bullshit. Jesus, it's cold." Then, of course, the inevitable "Do you have a car? Can I get a ride home?" In these groups, you were obliged to help. You were not supposed to refuse a request from someone in need. But they all seemed to need everything, all the time. Wilson was used to going it alone. And he wasn't supposed to be driving.

Darlene had climbed into the car, bouncing a little on the bench seat. "This car smells like booze," she said. She sat up straight and started looking around. "Jesus, what a night," she said, fiddling with the latch on the glove box, "I could use a drink if you've got it." Wilson fished under his seat for the pint, passed it over without looking at her. She took several noisy swigs and swung the bottle back at him, nudging it against his elbow. Wilson took it and started to slide it back underneath the seat. "No," she said, "leave it," patting the seat between them. She fished around in her shapeless, fuzzy bag and came up with some chewing gum. She didn't offer him any. While Wilson piloted the car, turning where she said to turn, she chewed the gum, plucking it out of her mouth occasionally to take another drink and then popping it back in.

"This is it," she said finally, pointing him to a rundown motel, the kind where you rented by the week, by the month. "This is me." She got out of the car, bending down to peer inside before shutting the door. "Thanks," she said. Her gaze swept over him, fixed upon the pint still lying on the seat. She held onto the door for a while. "You have to slam it," Wilson said, "or it won't latch." As he pulled out of the parking lot, he saw her in the rearview mirror fumbling with the foil on a fresh piece of gum, looking up now and then at one of the motel's windows. After he dropped her off, he drove around for a while with the Buick's heater on full blast. It would only make it worse when he got home, but the heat was like nothing else in his life: it was radiant, was like a blessing.

Wilson stopped at the Cherry Mart on the way home for a pint. He paid the clerk for two bags of ice and took six from the freezer outside. Most nights he didn't bother with a candle. He sat in the dark. Without the television, he'd been left to his own devices. His own voice in his head, not talking to him. He had to be careful what he said. Watch his step. It was uncomfortable, like having company all the time. He was never alone. Most of the thoughts were not good thoughts. Some were whip cracks, the snap of high tension wires, a frenzy of electric eels that could jazz his nerves in an instant. Fear was like coffee. You drank cup after cup after cup.

Like electricity, television already belonged to the past. It was what he'd done with his mother. Laugh tracks, ads for paint, the weather, teenage pregnancy. He'd get up from time to time and go to the kitchen to get snacks, refill their glasses with ice. Come back to the cackle and rasp as his mother choked on one of her coughs. Sometimes one of those cop shows. Pointing at the TV. "You believe that?" Wilson's mother had done most of the talking. She had a lot of opinions, about the people on the shows, about pet videos, celebrities, about politicians who cheated on their wives. Wilson did not agree or disagree. Really, it was nothing to do with him.

He turned on the TV sometimes at work when he cleaned the rooms, but didn't listen, didn't watch. He picked up wet towels, sometimes things worse than wet towels, vacuumed. Disembodied voices droned in the background. Once in a while guests came back to the room to look for something left behind. They never found it. That threw Wilson off his game for the rest of the shift. He didn't like to think about the people who'd been in the rooms he was cleaning. The rooms. That was the thing. Putting the rooms to rights. Opening the drapes and closing the sheers behind the drapes. Making sure the count came up true on the minibar.

At home, there was no defined work. The place was always a mess, really. Neither Wilson nor his mother had been big on housework. Their empties piled up. They didn't open the blinds. Sometimes he hauled a duffle to the basement and did laundry. Not often. He pretty much had to be down to his last sock. Work provided racks of clean uniforms to change into at the start of the shift. Wilson's mother wore the same thing every day, a nightgown, a shapeless sweater. They ate food you didn't have to cook or use dishes for. Wilson went out for groceries, booze, cigarettes. He took out the trash. Once in a while his mother asked for something special. Fried chicken. Sometimes Taco Bell. This made him happy. He whistled on the way down to the car. Wilson liked the tidy rooms at the hotel. Their identical perfection. Their vacancy. He couldn't imagine living there. It was like TV.

Soon, something would have to be done. Lack of sleep was making him cry, sometimes even at work. Not cry, really, but tears. Tears leaking out the corners. He wiped them away with the back of his hand. They returned. As quickly as his mind could seize possible solutions, it tossed them aside, like a person rooting through the hamper looking for something left in a pocket. It was never there. Tears reminded him of childhood, but Wilson's childhood was remote. He could remember his mother, then, the way she was. Humming. Sometimes rolling her hair onto pink foam curlers before she went to bed. Cursing at the dog. They had had a dog once. A long time ago.

He did realize it was probably too late. Whatever happened, he was probably going to jail. None of this would look good. Wilson didn't have words. He couldn't make anyone understand. People in twelve-step had gone to jail. A lot of them, actually. Whenever they talked about their experiences, Wilson felt sick. That and the coffee. His stomach was sour. He fought his gag reflex. He'd go out to his car during smoke breaks, force down an enormous swig from the pint under the seat and chew up a Life Saver. That gave him an hour.

What Wilson would like would be to bury his mother in the country. It seemed like a nice idea. But where was the country? He didn't know. He'd never been there, though he'd seen it on television, heard about it, read about it. Ducks, ponds. A nice setting, with fields. Country lanes. If the country was a real place, that actually existed, shouldn't he be able to find it on a map? In Wilson's experience, there was the city, and outside the city, beside the freeway, a sort of wasteland, with stretches of median and fenced-off scrubby areas leading to urban sprawl, then suburban sprawl. Miles of industrial district. There was nowhere quiet, or private, or secluded. Either there were people or there were fences and government signs. County sheriffs. State patrol. Rest areas. On the outskirts of this, rifle ranges, saw mills, crazy rural vigilantes.

The country. That was stupid. She would think it was stupid too. But he would figure something out. He and his mother had coped with things as they came up, but they were ungainsayably impractical people. They did not plan for the future. They lived day to day. Really, they had never had much choice in the matter. Now he had to be practical. If he could just hold on for another week, if his mother could hold on, her social security check would arrive and he could pay the rent. This would give him time to think. Leisure to think.

Leisure. It sounded like vacation. Wilson had never been on vacation. He could be found at the opposite end of the spectrum. Waiting to cash in on your mother's social security made you feel like a cheap hood. It wasn't like that, though, with him and his mother. She sent him down to cash the checks, pay the rent. He worked part time at the hotel, bought the groceries, paid the utility bills. It was how they had always done things. It was different this time, though. He knew that. He did know the difference between right and wrong. It seemed as if the world contained a lot more of the latter. Much of it, though, might come from failing to act, from not knowing what to do. Like the people in those meetings, the boundaries between the rights and the wrongs were off-kilter, but it was hard to pinpoint exactly where the problem was.

The immediate problem at hand was ice, slowly but most assuredly melting, a constant trickling down the bathtub drain. Sundays and Mondays were difficult days. Wilson drove around, buying as many bags of Polar Bear Ice as he thought he could afford, stealing the rest from motels without security doors, from the unlocked, empty Fellowship Halls, from 7-Elevens. He was an ice burglar now, and there was no way to make it stop. The laws of physics aside, in the real world, you expended weeks of furiously concentrated energy making up for short periods of inertia. A slogan from meetings came back to him: *We are only as sick as our secrets.* Wilson was sick. He figured he was very sick. But he was not the sickest person he knew.

The sickest person he knew was a guy named Stew, who apparently had no secrets. Whatever meeting Wilson showed up to, Stew was there. He smelled bad. His arms and his goitered neck were scribbled with prison tattoos. He always started out with God and gratitude, but what he really wanted to talk about were his crimes, and there were a lot of them, mostly to do with sex. Things he'd done to women. Children. He claimed, swore, over and over again, to be sorry. He blamed himself, but he blamed alcohol more. Sometimes he cried and put his head down. He lingered over the crimes themselves in terrible particulars. You could feel him. The ghost of him, rubbing its hands. He was a born narrator.

The details were vivid. They stuck in your mind, which was the last place you wanted them to stick. Stew snuffled and blew his nose. Usually, when someone wept, others would rub the person's back or shoulder, say consolatory things, things full of hope or absolution. No one ever did that with Stew. At most, someone would murmur, a sound halfway between the clearing of a throat and a hum. This lack of response didn't appear to bother Stew. That wasn't what he came for. His displays of remorse were the price of his admission, the ticket stubs that forced the group to let him inside, let him keep telling his horrible tales.

Maybe Wilson should call a funeral home. He had only a vague idea of what that was, and no idea what it would cost. A thousand dollars? Two thousand? It was all the same, really. Maybe they would make a payment plan. Or would have. Wilson wasn't kidding himself. He didn't have options. At most, what he had left were the illusions of options. The ghosts of options. He worked part time and lived in a place with no heat. Soon he would probably live nowhere, would have no address. Options were cash. Cash, too, was a ghost.

Wilson had never stolen anything other than, recently, a lot of ice. He thought about this. Perhaps the ice was a gateway crime, a rehearsal for something much, much worse. If you did it for your mother, maybe it was OK. He could rob a store, take care of the situation and then leave town. Things to think about were security cameras, fingerprints, and the absolutely vast and unpredictable array of things that could go wrong. But everything was already wrong. The bathtub was at the hub of a wrong universe. He sat in the driver's seat outside the church, sweating, freezing.

What if, tomorrow, he went upstairs? To the Sanctuary. Not at night, but in the morning, when there would be someone there. It was something to think about. Maybe the pastor would have advice. Help. Probably not help. Maybe advice. Wilson figured he would hang around outside, but in the end, he wouldn't go in. Really, he had no right to be there, no right to ask. He wasn't a member. He wasn't a member of anything. He didn't belong. In this sense, he was more anonymous than anyone else.

Someone banged hard on the passenger's side window and Wilson jumped, crashing against the steering wheel, arms vibrating crazily. Darlene jerked the door open and hurled herself into the seat beside him. Wilson covered his face with his hands. He was quaking, gasping for air. Darlene did not notice. She sobbed, her hair sticking to her face, fists clenched, her jaws working soundlessly as if in some convulsive prayer. Wilson fought to restore his respiration. "Goddamn it, Jesus, fuck," she yelled, slapping the dash. She twisted in the seat and clutched Wilson's arm. "The son of a bitch kicked me out," she gulped, "I've been looking for you. I've been freezing my ass off out here." She swallowed hard. "I've got to have a place to stay. Just for one night. Please."

Wilson's mind fled in a hundred panicked directions. "No," he said, "no, you can't. My mother. I live with my mother." He could see she was struggling to make sense of what he'd said. "No, really," she said, "this is like, an emergency. You have to help me. You've just got to!" She yanked on his arm. "I promise, just one night." Wilson could feel the blood beating in his neck. "I'll take you to a shelter," he offered. "I'll take you somewhere." His brain was racing. "No, no, no!" She was frantic. He wrenched his arm back, held up his hands. "I can't. My mother and I, we can't." Darlene's eyes narrowed. "You've just got to talk to her, then. You've just got to explain that I need this. One night, for Christ's sake. It won't kill her." That was for sure. "I'll clear out in the morning. In the morning, I'll be gone." Wilson shook his head from side to side, his heart thundering. "No," he said, "You have to listen to me. There must be someone else, someone you know." He looked around wildly. Everyone else had already left. The parking lot was deserted.

The girl would not let go. She gripped his arm, pulling, pulling. Under her breath, she kept murmuring *please, please, please,* maybe to Wilson, maybe to God. She rocked back and forth in the seat. Wilson felt sick. He did not want her touching him. She drew closer, pushed her face against his shoulder. He could feel the warmth of her body. He edged away, as far as he could go. Darlene slid closer, trapping him against the door. She put her hand on his thigh. She began to stroke, using her palm, her fingernails. Wilson's stomach roiled, his mouth filled with brine. He knew what would happen next. Wilson clenched his jaws together, choking as his mouth filled up. He made a desperate attempt to shove her away in time but he wasn't fast enough. She shrieked, leapt aside, snatched her purse away from the stream of vomit. Her jacket, her furry boots, were splattered. "Mother fuck!" she screamed. She jumped out of the car, cursing, staggering, examining her clothes.

Wilson tore out of the parking lot. He rolled down the windows. He drove around and around, shivering. He drove mindlessly until he'd lost all sense of direction. In an unfamiliar neighborhood, he found a liquor mart open late, its neon flashing, the rest of the buildings around it dark and empty. This could be it. Things were bad, bad. This couldn't really make it worse. He tumbled inside and stood there, panting, quaking. The fat guy at the register scowled at Wilson, at his puke-stained pants. "What do you want?" he asked, surly, sliding one hand beneath the counter. "Bourbon," Wilson said. He wandered away, scanning all the shelves once, then circling around again. He browsed aimlessly in slow motion, thinking. His scalp prickled. He eyed the clerk in his periphery. You didn't have to have a gun. You could pretend. "Look, asshole," the guy said, "what do you want?" Wilson pulled his hand out of his pocket. "Nothing," he said. "I don't want anything. Sorry." He left the store.

Tuesday morning he'd be back at the hotel. Work was almost always the best place to be. He knew what to do and he did it methodically, without hurry. He could usually get through an entire shift without talking. Even the hotel elevators were soothing, smooth and noiseless, not like the elevator in his building, which threatened to jerk to a halt between floors, to trap him inside with his enormous bags of ice. The air in the hotel was not fresh air. It was healthier than that, like cake and clean sheets and gift shop flowers. On the top floor, it smelled faintly of chlorine from the pool. When he passed a guest in the hallway, he ducked his head. Out of respect. Sometimes they said "good morning" or asked him where to find something. Once, a lady had asked him the way to the chapel. The hotel had a chapel. He had never been inside. He had seen it listed in the directory of Guest Services.

Wilson could leave town. He could do that. That was what people sometimes did when things went bad. He had no ideas, though, about where he could go. Or where he could stay. There were bound to be missions. The YMCA. Even if he could find work right away, it would be a few weeks before he'd see a paycheck. It had taken three months to find this job. He tried to picture himself somewhere else and failed. He couldn't even picture any somewhere elses. When Wilson was in school, his teachers had said he suffered from a lack of imagination. He was suffering now. This was where he and his mother had always lived. It would be terrible to leave her behind, especially after these recent weeks of maintenance and anxiety. And they would be bound to find him. His social security number. His license plate. When they found her, they would come looking for him.

The thought kept returning: there had to be someone he could tell. It might be best to tell a cop, though the mere thought sent him shuddering. Maybe if he turned himself in, they'd let him go. Or put him in a hospital for the criminally insane. Criminally insane. There was a happy thought. Maybe he could write the cops a letter, not reveal until the very end where to find him. They'd have to read the whole thing first, know the whole story, before they said, "All right, Mac, that's it," clapped the cuffs on, sprang into action, called an ambulance, the six o'clock news. They might go easy on him if they could understand how it really happened. But how to explain? No one would understand. He knew one thing: there was no chance he was going to "open up" at one of those meetings.

He knew how it would be. There would be sympathy, some of it genuine, and there would be a gleam in a few people's eyes revealing their pleasure in another confirmation that everybody was as nasty as everybody else. This was not the part that would bother him, though. If he was going to tell someone, he wanted that person to express shock, to have some kind of a normal reaction. He would settle for wary disbelief, outrage, consternation. These people were immune. They had heard everything. Or if they weren't immune, they had trained themselves never to betray it. Whatever awful thing they heard, they said, "It's not your fault. It happens to everyone." Wilson knew that some things were your fault. And some things definitely did not happen to everyone.

After the usual routine of ice, and bourbon to counteract the evening's coffee, Wilson sat. He looked out the window at the windows of the apartment building across the street. Some were dark, and others were lit, like a patchwork, but irregular. He could see people moving around, in their kitchens, at dinette tables, on sofas. Sometimes the person in one apartment was only a few feet away from the person in the next apartment, but they didn't know it. Only Wilson knew it. It made him feel a little like a god. A Higher Power. If God existed, he was probably like that. He couldn't really do anything, but he could watch. His power came from being far enough away. He could watch everyone at once.

Wilson went into his room and lay down on the bed. It was the first time he'd lain down since his mother died and he'd become paralyzed, a fixture in the corduroy chair. He knew he wouldn't sleep. Maybe he could clear his head. Make a real plan. Something straightforward and methodical, like work. Something step by step where the steps made sense and led somewhere conceivable. A clear course he could actually follow, like a map to the country with straight roads and well-marked turnings. The window in his room had a heavy drape. That made it quiet inside.

His place was a little like a church. An old building. Dark. Still. Over the years, a lot of people had lived there, had lain down where he lay, in the same room. Had slept their sleeps, had thought their thoughts. Like a church, it was chilly, as if no one lived there full time. Now, with the candles, the resemblance was heightened. If you knew what you were listening for, you could hear presences, absences. The things that came and the things that went, that had begun and that had ended. You could hear your own pulse, and from across the hallway, another sound. The faint trickling. The holy waters.

ANNE PIERSON WIESE
Middle Distance

In the church, midweek at noon,
there is a middle distance
between the piercing blue
window of pure belief
and the bone vault housing
my heart's disbelief, a dim
yielding distance related
to my prayer: another day's
delay before you are nowhere—
for death fixes all distances
                like a new nail.

BRUCE WILLARD
The Calling

Sometimes at dusk when the earth gives its sweet breath to the trees,
I think how I have taken a stranger's life and whispered not
so much as his name to the asphalt sky.

How each year, on my mother's birthday, I hear the warbled rasp
of his breathing and it pushes and draws me like a blues harp
soaked in whiskey from which the bent yawl of reeds
becomes the song I have to play.

Biking that night, decades ago, I felt the desert wind coming over
    the ridge
meeting the November valley air, spermy smell of fennel and
    ceanothus,
past the oak and manzanita, past the cereus and chaparral grass,
past the cornering lanes, past the houses I mistook for home,
past the church at Mt. Carmel with its weathered perfection.

If I was drawn to him, no line was visible. There were no lines.
Just a mountain road, uphill tick of my pedaling,
and his downhill whir of speed, the sound of his nylon jacket flapping,
then click of handlebars, crush of steel and skull.

Beside the road where we lay, an owl called. Listen,
I thought. And I heard how its voice survives each question,
how each question survives the shadow of clouds.
And I called to my stranger in the voice of the owl,
knowing not even his name. I called to him and he became
to me like wind on a flagpole or in a tree; something moving
that cannot be moved.

JAKE ADAM YORK
Letter Written in Black Water and Pearl

To Yusef Komunyakaa

When I rise from the bank
the water's slow as shadow
in my steps, thick as blood.
The whole river's secretive,
still, dark as roux
cooled in the skillet, as rank,
as sweet, ancient as catfish,
ancienter. The moon's
sifted light clouds rumor
to lilies or daffodils,
an egret on the farther shore,
a hunger, a stare, a patience
I could recite. We have
waited all night, nights,
like a bridge for something
to rise, like water
for something to fall.
*

I know what Bogalusa means,
that tea of deadheads
and late-fallen leaves
no one left can read,
snuff-black pools that bathe
grandmothers' gums.
So many words one has
to know not to say.
So many names. The young,
unconvicted hand. The bricklayer.
The deputy. Names
of flowers and warblers and stars.

Last breaths of the disappeared.
I keep my hands folded,
my map blank
as next week's papers,
my ears, clams
with mouths full of sand.

*

So many songs I can't sing
with my one poor tongue.
I need a jukebox for a throat
so the midnight's moan
translates what a wolf
once said to a girl in the trees,
so their branches confess
what the fog told them not
to see. I need the lisp
of a horn valved to spit
which is the sound of a shadow
forgetting what hanged it
in the dark. How do I explain
the way it slips the steam
like a shirt, how it slides
beneath the glass and does not
rise again, how the half-light
fingers the rails of the bridge,
how many things
no one's done?

*

Birds the color of history
talk in our sleep. Our salts
can't forget what water
told them, what stars
once telegraphed to the river
the trees have written
in themselves, what they say
to the wind, to the sawmill's
blades, to flame,
to bromine and mercury,

what they burn in the air.
Dreams walk us back
to the shore, pull the shirttail
from the milkweed, the cattail
from the reed, fold
the kerchiefs into herons,
questions for the shoals.

*

Night slips again
into its last, locked groove.
Mockingbirds stutter
the rasp of broken reeds.
I lean from the eaves
of moss and cypress,
the vestibules of the tung.
Cormorant, coelacanth, snake,
the world below is molten.
Dark iridescence,
the muscle gives back the bone.
The spine's fleer, the orbits'
gape, the ghost of a face
waking beneath my own.
Here, I bent so close
breath didn't know
which mouth to fill.

JAVIER ZAMORA
Dancing in Buses

Pretend a boom box blasts
over your shoulder. Raise
your hands in the air. Twist them
as if picking mangoes. Look
to the right as if crossing
streets. Look to the left,
slowly as if balancing orange
baskets. Bend as if picking
cotton. Do the rump. Straighten
up as if dropping firewood. Rake,
do the rake. Sweep,
do the sweep. Do the Pupusa-
Clap: finger dough clumps. Clap.
Do the Horchata-Scoop:
your hand's a ladle, scoop.
Reach and scoop. Now,
duck. They're shooting. Duck
under the seat. Stiffen.
Deceive. Don't breathe.

"¡Hands behind your head!
 ¡Drop down!
 ¡Look at the ground!
 ¡Don't look up!
 ¡Roll over!
 ¡Face the scope's mouth!
 ¡Do the opened-mouth!
 ¡Flinch!
 ¡Do the protect-face-with-hand!
 ¡Don't scream!"

ABOUT MAJOR JACKSON
A Profile by Gregory Pardlo

If, in the 1980s, you had been a resident of one of those communities associated with the term, "urban renewal" might occur to you as double-edged with its bureaucratic optimism, and the implied whitewashing—easy as calling a do-over—of recent history. And if parts of your community were within the expansion radius of an ambitious university, you might be ambivalent toward the opportunities offered by that advancing institution as well.

As a poet, Major Jackson was shaped by this period of his native North Philadelphia's burgeoning gentrification, when Temple University began to broaden its vision to include, along with inquiry, a spirit of acquisition. Like many from historically black urban communities, Jackson understood early on, as he writes in the poem, "Hoops," that "If the slum's our dungeon, / school's our Bethlehem." Jackson's worldview contains both the community and the institution, as he identifies with the acquired and acquiring on both sides.

School looms metaphorically in Jackson's life and work. It refers to brick and mortar, but also to a life of the mind. It refers to a life in the arts, and specifically literature. And the changing nature of that life from sequestered intellectualism to social engagement gives Jackson's poetry a sense of wistful benevolence. We find the poet balancing his esteem for tradition with the weight of his concern for the world around him.

As Jackson admits, "my path in poetry has been extremely unconventional." Indeed, there is something Hollywood about it: his good fortune in having been delivered to the right mentors at the right moments, his having the talent, temperament, and commitment to take advantage of their guidance, and his uncanny ability to navigate a welter of contradictions without any irritable reaching for resolution. His life is a screenplay waiting to be made. Let's make the opening scene a tracking shot:

At Temple University in the late 1980s, we find the future poet touring the campus with a group of fellow incoming first-year students. Picture the group's guide, shirted in the school's iconic cherry red, and walking backwards as he narrates features of the academic landscape. One of the incoming students asks the guide's advice for getting around the

community at large. Jackson needs no such advice. This is where he grew up, shaped early by the studious asceticism of a Catholic primary school, and later, the pride of the Philadelphia public school system, Central High School. Given this pedigree, Jackson is used to bridging social gaps. He has developed a cosmopolitan sensibility as a result of too often being the guy with cultural knowledge others lack. He is patient with people who are unfamiliar with communities like his. He is solicitous with familiars who don't have access to the academy. All this in preparation for his mission to cut a path through the undergrowth of the American literary mind to make way for others to share their stories.

 Casting his mind's eye (in a filmic dissolve) to the surrounding neighborhood, Jackson surveys the topography of memory. These streets will be the setting for many of his poems. Amid the jagged lots' "lush epitaph of dandelions / & weed brush," he will note, "A corner lot of broken TVs empties / and spills from a suitcase of hurt." The boarded-up row houses north of the avenue named after the famed Civil Rights attorney, Cecil B. Moore, and west of arterial Broad St.—amid the real and imaginary devastation we associate with crack-ravaged urban spaces—bookend the homes and businesses of those who will soon directly and indirectly populate Jackson's poetry. The barbershop where Mr. Pate, who, by virtue of Jackson's loving artistry, will forever "cherish [the] tiny little heads" that have become casualties of street violence. There is his neighbor, a police officer, who for years greeted the young Jackson with questions, like *where is Mozambique,* in lieu of hello. *Where is Poland,* or *where is Algiers? How many boroughs in New York City?* And he would slip Jackson three dollars for every A on his report card. There is Sun Ra, the sensational and eccentric jazz musician, who lived only a few blocks away in Major's neighborhood of Germantown and held New Year's Eve concerts each year at the Painted Bride Art Center, a popular meeting place for musicians and artists. And this is the one area, as we return to the original scene, that the campus guide admonishes students to avoid at all costs. For "out there," the guide says gravely, "those people are dangerous."

Jackson cites this interaction with the campus guide as one of the more formative of many "double consciousness" moments of his life. The reference is to W. E. B. Du Bois' analysis of African American subjectivity as paradoxical, in which one is always conscious of unflattering (to say the least) cultural assumptions without, while maintaining a sense of pride and self-love within. In many ways, Jackson's evolving response to this paradox, which appears in many guises, will animate his work for years to come. The ever-changing dynamics of race and class in America, for example; and the enfolding of the mysterious and marginal "town" into the pleats of the university's corporate "gown"; the sometimes conflicting pursuit of life in the ivory tower leveraged against one's care for the roots of community.

Jackson seems little interested in choosing sides or engaging in a Pollyannaish soft-pedaling of these discrepancies. He wears them like mismatched socks (although, I must say, I've been shopping with the man and he would never wear mismatched socks). His instinct is to serve as witness rather than to judge or wag a disapproving finger. This is another distinguishing characteristic of his work. As if for Jackson, artistry were the *only* rational response one could have to the contradictions of urban life.

Major Jackson's poetry is grounded in his sense of the ethical obligation we have to the communities we claim. Noting that "our communities widen and constrict" with time and context, the tenor of his poems is as evocative of Whitman as it is of the late Black Arts milieu out of which it finds some of its most potent influences. Of note is the literary relationship he developed at Temple University with his first creative-writing professor and doyenne of the Black Arts Movement, Sonia Sanchez, whom Jackson is quick to praise as singularly responsible for his embrace of poetry. That embrace has now grown to encompass three poetry collections: *Leaving Saturn* (U. of Georgia Press, 2002), winner of the Cave Canem First Book Prize and Finalist for the National Book Critics Circle Award; *Hoops* (2007) and *Holding Company* (2012), both from W. W. Norton; and scores of awards and fellowships, including a Pew Fellowship, a Whiting Writers' Award, two nominations for the NAACP Image Award, a Witter Bynner Fellowship from the Library of Congress, and an artist fellowship from the Radcliffe Institute for Advanced Study at Harvard University.

For all the expansiveness of Jackson's poetic vision, the note he strikes most consistently is that of praise. It is "this notion of praise in poetry," he says, that affected him most deeply in the work of the earlier generation of African American poets. He points to, for example, Sanchez's invocations of the ancestors, those hypnotic roll calls that affirm our sense of belonging as much as they honor those who have come before us, and the dedication to honor our history that we find in the work of Robert Hayden. "[Jackson's] lyric tongue," Afaa Michael Weaver, another important, early mentor figure, writes in a 2002 review of *Leaving Saturn* in these pages, "rises out of the emblems of urban despair and chaos to make love his language."

I met Major in the mid '90s. Our paths first crossed sometime around 1994, when I asked the Philly poet Lamont Steptoe to organize a reading series for me at the jazz club my grandfather had opened, and which I was managing, in New Jersey, a few minutes across the river from Philadelphia. Among the poets Steptoe featured that I can easily recall were Martín Espada, the South African poet Dennis Brutus, and Major Jackson. I thought the reading series was fun. Indulgent. It certainly didn't make any money. In other words, at the time, I had no idea what a stellar lineup Steptoe had produced. But this suggests the esteem in which Major was held in the Philly literary scene very early in his writing life.

After I left the bar business, I met Major formally in a circle of metal folding chairs as we sat together beneath banks of fluorescent lights. The International Ladies' Garment Workers' Union let the *Painted Bride Quarterly* use vacant space once a week in its downtown office building to hold editorial meetings. I had been recommended to the editorial board on the basis of my enthusiasm alone, and I remember being thoroughly confused as to how this man sitting before me could refer so confidently to work by poets whose names seemed distant and mythical to me—Yusef Komunyakaa, Sharon Olds, Philip Levine, Nikki Giovanni, Gerald Stern, and even Gwendolyn Brooks—as if he had met them personally. Of course, in addition to being a hungry student of poetry, Major *had* met all of these poets, and many more. After college, where his undergraduate degree was, counterintuitively, in accounting, Major served as Curator of Literary Arts at the Painted Bride Arts Center. This was a job he cultivated out of an internship in bookkeeping at the arts center. "This was where I found myself as a writer and an artist," he says.

"What does it all come down to?" I ask him. In addition to being the Richard Dennis Green and Gold Professor at University of Vermont, a core faculty member of the Bennington Writing Seminars, a member of the Creative Writing Program faculty at New York University, and Poetry Editor of the *Harvard Review,* Jackson maintains a dizzying schedule of visiting and guest positions leading workshops on and off campuses across the country. What is the point of this peripatetic life?

"I want to be a lightning rod for someone who wants to write and sing his or her particular life," he says. That comment might send us scrambling back to the streets of North Philly in search of some Rosebud-like symbol of motivation if it weren't for Jackson's 2011 tour of the slums of Kibera, an impoverished community that borders the Royal Nairobi Golf Club in Nairobi, Kenya. This was one leg of the tour sponsored by the International Writing Program at the University of Iowa, which exposed Jackson to people bravely enduring conditions grievous far beyond any we might find in North Philly. Like North Philly, however, those conditions are, unconscionably, man-made. If neglect and indifference produced the slums of his youth, Jackson observed, here the forces are more venal. "The corruption is phenomenal," he says. But at the root of things "we find a similar class struggle."

Jackson's mission in Kenya was to engage with local writers and expand the literary conversation between our two nations. During one workshop, he shared with participants the poem, "Listen Children," by Lucille Clifton:

listen children
keep this in the place
you have for keeping
always
keep it all ways

we have never hated black

listen
we have been ashamed
hopeless   tired   mad
but always
all ways
we loved us

we have always loved each other
children   all ways

pass it on

    Between the tears the poem elicited from participants, some of them remarked their surprise at the sentiment the poem conveys. "They said they thought African Americans did not love themselves," Jackson said, having trouble even repeating the words.

    I can't help but read this as a kind of a revision of the earlier double-consciousness moment he experienced on the campus of Temple University. The stakes are higher now, and the circumstances are even more complex, if that is possible. I imagine Jackson's sense of community is expanding and contracting in ways that can only produce a further exacting poetic vision. His most recent book, *Holding Company*, is evidence of his capacity for reinvention. While he explored and expanded the conventions of the lyric narrative in his first two books, *Holding Company* is more lyric, less narrative. Or rather, the narratives are more attenuated, more angular in their progress. The book hints at Jackson's willingness to strike out for new territory.

Jackson recently edited *The Collected Poems of Countee Cullen,* which will be published by the Library of Congress this year. Bringing renewed attention to this important poet of the Harlem Renaissance is a service to American letters and individual readers alike. Because of this kind of work, along with his own consistently enterprising poems, we may one day evaluate Major Jackson as an institution unto himself.

Gregory Pardlo's book Totem *won the American Poetry Review/Honickman First Book Prize in 2007. His poems have appeared in American Poetry Review, Boston Review, Callaloo, Gulf Coast, Harvard Review, The Nation, and The Best American Poetry. A finalist for the Essence Magazine Literary Award in poetry, he is recipient of a New York Foundation for the Arts Fellowship and a translation grant from the National Endowment for the Arts. His second book,* Digest, *is forthcoming from Four Way Books.*

THE GREAT DREAM
A Plan B Essay by Floyd Skloot

In the Plan B essay series, writers discuss their contingency plans, extraliterary passions, and the roads not traveled.

For my family, Plan B wasn't the fallback plan for when life went awry. Life was already awry, and they'd already seen their hopes and ambitions compromised. So Plan B—what they would do if they didn't do what they were doing—was The Great Dream, their private idea of themselves. Moving through their days like miscast actors in a play they didn't like, they devoted their most creative energies to imagining and refining their true calling, the life they weren't leading.

My father was a butcher. He owned a poultry market in Brooklyn's Red Hook neighborhood, leasing the building at regularly increasing cost from his mother and older brother, paying protection money to the Mafia, watching business dwindle as supermarkets began to appear and the neighborhood became crisscrossed by new highways. Nearing fifty, he was tired of waking at 4:00 in the morning and getting home at 7:00 every night, six days a week. With forces coalescing against him, he resurrected an old dream: founding a line of clothing exclusively for short men. No shirts with horizontal stripes, nothing checkered or plaid, no slacks with inseams longer than twenty-nine inches, no fat ties, no three-button jackets. He talked about this over dinner, night after night, refining concepts, *V-neck shirts! No bulky sweaters!* while my mother said *Not this again.* I'm convinced that thinking about what he'd love to do kept him together during the stress of his market's inevitable failure. *Make a fortune dressing five-foot guys like Andrew Carnegie.* Though my father ended up managing the daily operation of his brother-in-law's dress factory until dying at fifty-three, he continued refining ideas for his imagined breakout. *Pants and shirts the same color so your shape looks longer!*

My mother was a housewife. This was not something to be spoken aloud. She was meant to be an aristocrat or member of the Manhattan *haut monde*, a famous artist, yet somehow was in Brooklyn with this chicken butcher, a man she couldn't imagine knowing. She never forgave him for marrying her. My mother's way of being a housewife involved hiring a full-time maid we couldn't afford, sleeping behind a closed bedroom door until early afternoon, refusing to entertain her in-laws in her own home, and cultivating an increasingly Zsa-Zsa-Gaborian accent to establish the fact that Lillian Skloot did not come from or belong anywhere around there. Since the life she was living didn't truly exist for her, Plan B had to be grand enough, expansive enough, and bold enough to cover both her quotidian and fantasy worlds. That was hard work. She spent hours gluing buttons onto blank greeting card stock, drawing red lips on the buttons' rims, black dots for eyes within the buttonholes, and topping them with chic, elaborate, lofty hats made of bits of feathers and silky cloth she'd collected. Then she would box up a dozen of these Noble Notes and offer them to friends as gifts. In restaurants, she folded linen napkins into the shape of women's faces topped by turbans, and drew on red lips and the longest eyelashes possible before handing these Princesses over to fellow diners. She drew red lips and long eyelashes on cardboard tubes of toilet paper rolls and designed fancy hats for them too, presenting these Elite Ladies as decorative items to slip over opened liquor bottles. She played and sang a repertoire of six songs on the piano in our living room, acted in community theater productions, and loved costume parties, any activity she could participate in as someone other than herself.

My brother, eight years my senior, was a traveling salesman—envelopes, then pressure-sensitive adhesives, then metal bolts—just waiting for the time when he could step out to become a playboy and card shark. Everything suave and smooth, that was the plan's underpinning. Hushed and loose where our home had been loud and tight. Life as a game of finesse, not a battle of force. He would fly from New York to Las Vegas or Reno to hone his skills. I have a photo of him diving into a Las Vegas swimming pool beside Pat Boone as four bikinied women on chaise longues watch, hands shielding their eyes from the glare. I have another photo of him, his cards fanned downward, a Kent dangling from his lips, smoke drifting up to conceal his expression. I kept those two photos together on the album's page, though they were taken several years apart, because I thought they represented my brother coming as close as he could to doing what he was meant to do.

But I was wrong. At fifty-seven, dying from complications of diabetes, blind, obese, needing dialysis every few days, he made a final trip to Reno. It was an astounding feat of preparation, arrangement, coordination, and sheer will, and though he had to cut the trip short, I think this was the moment he'd been waiting for. There's a photo of him there, wheelchair snug against the card table, wearing the wraparound shades he needed to protect his damaged eyes, smiling James-Bondly, debonair, and I see exactly what living the dream, even for a brief moment, looked like for him.

In late 1973, at the age of twenty-six, I was living in miserable accord with my family's template. The Great Dream, my private idea of myself, had been lost. I was out of touch with what I knew I was called to do, who I knew myself to be. Silent as a writer for two years, I was working as a program analyst for the Illinois Bureau of the Budget, something for which I had neither training nor passion. I'd gained fifty pounds, and to accommodate my expanding body, I wore cast-off, speckled, polyester, sans-a-belt suits sent by my seventy-one-year-old Uncle Saul when he was through with them. Literally and figuratively, it was painful to look in the mirror.

Yet it hadn't been long since I'd understood, with fullness of heart and mind, that I was meant to be a writer. Not just that I wanted to write, but needed to write every day. Until the age of twenty-one I didn't know what I wanted to do with my life. All so-called plans were clichéd and detached from my actual talents: I would be *a professional baseball player*, despite lack of size or sufficient skill; I would be a *romantic actor*, despite what I looked and sounded like, which was suited only to comedy; I would be *a singer*, despite a tendency to change key, drift out of pitch, and be overwhelmed by tremolo; I would be *a physical therapist*, despite poor academic performance in science and math, and a lack of interest in the profession. Stumped, I began writing my thoughts in a notebook, trying to work out what I truly wanted. Almost at once, the writing shifted away from rational thoughts toward feelings, memories of childhood, fractured images that caught the emerging emotions. This felt like something central to my being. I enrolled in a poetry class. Writing in earnest, reading contemporary poets, I felt as if I had found home, my Place. I went to graduate school at Southern Illinois University to study with the poet Thomas Kinsella, whose work I loved, and began publishing. I knew I would devote myself to writing for the rest of my life, no matter what else I had to do to pay the bills.

Yet here I was, four years later, unrecognizable to myself. I was my father imagining shirts with short cuffs. I was my mother with her fake accents, with less to show for myself as an artist than her toilet-paper-tube bottle toppers. I was my brother losing six months of savings at a pai gow poker table in Reno.

One night in 1973, I dreamt of my grandparents in their Manhattan apartment, Rosie squeezed into her tiny kitchen cooking flanken as Max stood in the doorway kibitzing, unable to fit in the space with her. When I awoke, and before dressing for work, I went into the living room, sat at the rickety roll-top desk where I normally paid bills, and wrote a poem before the images and sounds of my grandparents could fade. That night, I set my alarm for an hour earlier than usual and in the morning went to my roll-top desk.

There would be no Plan B. No fallback into a fantasy of what I was meant to do. My parents and brother had taught me well the consequences of letting life get in the way of their dreams. Over the next sixteen years, writing early in the morning or late at night, writing over lunch hours or on weekends while working full-time in the field of public policy, I managed to complete a book of poems, two novels, a few short stories, and to lose sixty pounds. The writing output was small, and some of it now seems to me rushed, but the practice remained in place.

And when, in 1988, at the age of forty-one, a viral illness targeted my brain, left me permanently disabled, and seemed intent on silencing me, I was saved over time by the long habit of making sense of my world through daily writing.

Floyd Skloot is the author of seventeen books, most recently the poetry collection The Snow's Music *(LSU Press, 2008), the memoir* The Wink of the Zenith: The Shaping of a Writer's Life *(U of Nebraska Press, 2008/2011), which was named by Poets & Writers as one of seventy-nine essential books for creative writers, and the short-story collection* Cream of Kohlrabi *(Tupelo Press, 2011). Skloot has won three Pushcart Prizes, and his work has been included twice each in* The Best American Essays, Best American Science Writing, Best Spiritual Writing, *and* Best Food Writing *annual anthologies.*

PATRON SAINT OF QUIET LIVES
A Look2 Essay on Barbara Pym by Raina Lipsitz

> *The Look2 essay series, which replaces our print book reviews, takes a closer look at the careers of accomplished authors who have yet to receive the full appreciation that their work deserves. Reviews of new books can still be found on our blog at http://blog.pshares.org/*

I.

In her 1977 novel, *Quartet in Autumn,* Barbara Pym wrote of her heroine Letty: "She had always been an unashamed reader of novels, but if she hoped to find one which reflected her own sort of life she had come to realise that the position of an unmarried, unattached, ageing woman is of no interest whatever to the writer of modern fiction." Letty was giving voice to her creator's fervent wish to see her "own sort of life"— one without a husband or children, which revolved around work— reflected in the fiction of her time. With a handful of exceptions, it was not, and Pym wrote twelve novels in part to compensate for this lack. Like Pym herself, her heroines are memorable for their humor, wit, and resignation to disappointments great and small.

Pym has been accused by critics of writing the same novel over and over again. Since she is no longer around to defend herself, others have done it for her: "That there is a sameness to Pym's work is by no means a disparagement; like Austen, and so many other British greats—E. F. Benson, Angela Thirkell, Nancy Mitford, and Agatha Christie in her Marple mode—she worked with a small brush on a small canvas," writes Michael Adams in *Open Letters Monthly: An Arts and Literature Review.* Pym's was a narrow patch of soil, expertly tilled.

A critic for The Guardian once remarked that Pym's books were "delightfully amusing, but no more to be described than a delicious taste or smell." This type of dismissal was common early in her career; Pym was considered capable and entertaining, but lacking in scope and gravitas. Although her novels were well-received and regularly published from 1950 to 1963, and although she continued to produce high-quality work at a steady pace between 1963 and 1977, Pym was devastated by her inability to publish at all throughout the latter period. Her friends, family, and former publisher assured her that her work was rejected during this period not because its quality had declined, but because its subject matter was out of step with the times—the world of her novels was insulated from the sex, drugs, and social revolution then capturing the public's imagination. "I get moments of gloom and pessimism when it seems as if nobody could ever like my kind of writing again," she wrote in 1970. Two years later she noted in her diary, "The position of the unmarried woman—unless, of course, she is somebody's mistress, is of no interest whatsoever to the readers of modern fiction" (a sentiment she would later attribute to *Quartet in Autumn*'s Letty, substituting "writer" for "readers").

Pym was rediscovered and her career briefly revived in 1977—fourteen long years after she had last been published and only three years before she died. That was the year in which Philip Larkin and Lord David Cecil characterized her, in the January 21st issue of *The Times Literary Supplement,* as the most underrated writer of the last seventy-five years. (Pym was the only writer then living who was so characterized by two different respondents to the *TLS* poll.) "The six novels of Barbara Pym published between 1950 and 1961...give an unrivaled picture of a small section of middle-class post-war England," wrote Larkin. "She has a unique eye and ear for the small poignancies and comedies of everyday life." According to Lord Cecil David, Pym's "unpretentious, subtle, accomplished novels, especially *Excellent Women* and *A Glass of Blessings,* are for me the finest examples of high comedy to have appeared in England during the past seventy-five years."

Publication of Pym's novels resumed immediately following these endorsements, beginning with *Quartet in Autumn,* which was nominated for the Booker Prize, and continuing with *The Sweet Dove Died,* which, although previously rejected by a number of publishers, was published to critical acclaim in 1978. Pym died of breast cancer two years later, at the age of 66. Several previously unpublished works were published after her death. More than thirty years after this long overdue renaissance, at a time when literary success is even more closely tied to marketability than it was in the 1960s, Pym—modest, female, and without a contemporary champion—has again faded into obscurity.

II.

Born in a little village in Shropshire in June 1913, Pym shared a home with her younger sister, Hilary, for most of her life. Her mother Irena's position as assistant organist in the Pyms' parish church exposed Pym to many colorful clergy members and other local figures who would later populate her novels. Hilary Pym was briefly married, but Barbara, despite having a number of male friends, admirers, and lovers, never married or had children.

She began writing her first published novel, *Some Tame Gazelle*, very shortly after taking a degree in English literature at Oxford, and finished it in 1935, when she was only twenty-two years old. The book, which is eerily prescient, features two fifty-something unmarried sisters, Harriet and Belinda Bede, who share a cottage in a small town in the English countryside. "It was never our particular intention," wrote Hilary, several years after her older sister's death, "in spite of the prophetic circumstances of *Some Tame Gazelle*...to live together, but it somehow turned out that from about 1938 right up until the time of her death in 1980 we were never apart for more than a year or so at a time."

Pym graduated from Oxford in 1934 and briefly returned to Shropshire before traveling throughout Germany and central Europe. In 1938, she went to live with Hilary in London. Hilary was taking a secretarial course in hopes of working for the BBC; Barbara spent her days working on a novel and writing long letters to friends. When World War II broke out, she returned to her native village. Later she enlisted in the Women's Royal Naval Service (WRNS) and served in Naples until the end of the war, after which she was hired as an assistant editor at the International African Institute in London. She worked at the Institute until her retirement, and the petty intrigues of the academics and office workers she encountered there provided rich material for her later novels. When she retired in 1974, she moved to Barn Cottage, a country home she and Hilary had bought in Oxfordshire. The sisters were active in their village's community life, which revolved around the church. They lived at Barn Cottage until Barbara's death in 1980.

The unusual circumstance of sharing a household with her sister for most of her adult life lent Pym's depictions of intimate but nonsexual ties between women a depth rarely encountered outside of Jane Austen.

While Pym was an admirer of Austen's and in many ways her heir, she was not merely an updated version of the earlier writer. They are often compared due to the specificity of their social worlds and their rural, isolated settings, as well as the limited scope of their narratives and the neatness of their plot structures. The ordinary (and, for some readers, maddeningly trivial) concerns of Pym's characters—food, parties, clothing, romance—are also reminiscent of Austen; other aspects of her novels, most notably their endings, are decidedly not. Austen is famous for marrying off her heroines at a novel's end; Pym prefers to finish on a note of bittersweet wistfulness.

As John Updike noted in the February 26, 1979, edition of *The New Yorker*, "Miss Pym has been compared to Jane Austen, yet there is a virile country health in the Austen novels, and some vivid marital prospects for her blooming heroines." Though Pym often allows her heroines a rather tentative optimism ("it seemed as if I might be going to have what Helena called 'a full life' after all," thinks Mildred Lathbury at the end of *Excellent Women*), none of her characters can be described as living happily ever after.

Perhaps this difference can be attributed to Pym's physical surroundings and the temperament that grew out of them. Her childhood home of Shropshire is one of England's most rural and sparsely populated counties; it is also landlocked, and significantly colder in wintertime than other parts of the country. During the spring and summer, it's verdant, bucolic, and breathtakingly lovely; a place uniquely suited to meandering, solitary strolls, and quiet, meditative evenings. Though hardly a recluse, Pym was not a woman who craved society. Educated and well-traveled yet unworldly, Pym won friends easily. She relished the company of a small inner circle of friends and family but was essentially indrawn, pensive, and shy. Hers was a world of limits: comfortable and familiar and staid.

She did take risks in her work, though not until later in life. *An Academic Question,* which was published posthumously, represents a rare attempt on Pym's part to assume the perspective of a woman whose circumstances were markedly different from her own; the novel's narrator, Caroline Grimstone, is not only married but a mother as well. Pym gains perspective on her subject by bringing "Two women who had just retired from jobs in London" into the mix in Chapter 15:

> They were rather nice, spinster sisters, one in her late fifties and the other just sixty. Their lives were busy in an admirable way, full of interest and the pleasure of having time to do the things they had always wanted to do. I regarded them with envy as they described alterations they were making to their garden and the motoring holiday in Shropshire they had planned for later in the year. They were still good-looking and one of them, I felt sure, had once been beautiful. They must have loved in their time, perhaps loved and lost and come through it unscathed.

This is a neat summary of Pym's apparent ambivalence about the married life she could only imagine. As lonely and wistful as her single heroines occasionally are, married Caroline hardly fares better: her husband is dull, fussy, and unfaithful; her life as a professor's wife is tedious, stultifying, and intellectually barren. She loves her daughter but feels unfulfilled by motherhood. She envies the unmarried sisters' freedom and their apparently happy and productive lives. At the same time, she recognizes the social advantages of being married. In Pym's work, there are often advantages to being on the other side of the marital divide.

Contemporary retellings of Austen novels abound, but Pym has considerably less hope than her predecessor of being repackaged for a new generation. She wrote much oftener of unrequited love than of mutual romantic passion, and she doesn't traffic in unequivocally happy endings. Yet she was a writer of uncommon delicacy, humor, and compassion whose work deserves a wider audience than it has.

III.

Pym's novels stand out as carefully constructed comic gems, inviting the reader to bask in the warmth of their comfortingly familiar, self-contained worlds (generally a remote village in the sparsely populated English countryside). She returned again and again to the same set of themes: relationships between men and women, relationships between two women, and the experience of being an unmarried woman of a certain age. Loneliness haunts Pym's work, but her heroines are much more than lonely spinsters.

Pym's description of Letty's life in *Quartet in Autumn* applies in some ways to her own: "It was a comfortable enough life, if a little sterile, perhaps even deprived. But deprivation implied once having had something to be deprived of...and Letty had never really had anything much." Pym was comfortable, but not wealthy; she worked in an office to earn money, and made enough to buy a pleasant country cottage with her sister. Unlike Letty, however, she enjoyed the constant companionship of a cherished sister. In *Quartet in Autumn,* Letty wonders, "might not the experience of 'not having' be regarded as something with its own validity?" The question echoes throughout Pym's work; she answers it with a resounding affirmative.

In her 1955 novel, *Less Than Angels,* a pair of sisters, Mabel and Rhoda —one widowed, one never married—share a house and a contented life, devoid of sex but enriched by the easy companionship and minor irritations common to most long-term marriages. The same novel features another pair of women, the Misses Clovis and Lydgate, who live together but are not related; they are academics, the sort of mannish, pragmatic women who don't mind living untidily and eating most of their meals "out of tins" (one senses authorial judgment in the description of their shared flat, or perhaps merely bafflement, at the idea that two women could bear, let alone thrive in, such circumstances; Pym herself was a fastidious housekeeper and an accomplished cook).

Less Than Angels' Rhoda Wellcome is a fussbudget: she worries about her sister Mabel's inefficiency in the kitchen, insists that they do the washing-up immediately after dinner and lay the table for the next morning's breakfast before they go to sleep, and sneaks downstairs after Mabel has gone to bed to correct her sister's placement of the silverware. Her harmlessly neurotic presence provides comic relief. And yet even Rhoda is granted a dignity so often absent in contemporary novelistic portrayals of unmarried, middle-aged women: she is allowed feelings, desires, and tiny moments of pathos that transcend her touchingly scrupulous attention to domestic detail. Pym is careful to show us that Rhoda, while occasionally, in some cosmic way, disappointed, is far from unhappy in her everyday life. On coming to live with her sister Mabel after the death of Mabel's husband, Gregory, we learn that:

> *It was a very satisfactory arrangement and Rhoda was not in the least envious of her sister's fuller life, for now that they were both in their fifties there seemed to be very little difference between them.*

She would perhaps have liked what she called 'the experience of marriage,' a vague phrase which seemed to cover all those aspects which one didn't talk about, but she would not have liked to have had it with poor Gregory Swan. She was still sometimes faintly interested in men, as she was now in Alaric Lydgate, but in what way she hardly knew. She certainly did not think of marriage anymore.

In Pym's world, women in their fifties tend not to "think of marriage," but they do not cease to think of men. They are not sexless automata, endlessly performing their household duties (although Pym's heroines are often seen tidying up); they are complex human beings with rich inner lives. At one point in *Less Than Angels,* Rhoda's beloved niece, the callow 19-year-old Deirdre, thinks of her aunt: "How silly Rhoda is…almost as if she were interested in Father Tulliver in a flirtatious way." But Pym doesn't allow Deirdre's naïve perspective to stand unchallenged: "She was as yet too young to have learned that women of her aunt's age could still be interested in men; she would have many years to go before the rather dreadful suspicion came to her that one probably never does cease to be interested."

What makes Pym's work so appealing is her enormous compassion for her characters. This is particularly evident in *Less Than Angels,* in which Pym employs a technique similar to Virginia Woolf's in *Mrs. Dalloway.* Like Woolf before her, Pym weaves in and out of various characters' consciousnesses, so that her reader is exposed to, among others, the perspectives of a 19-year-old girl and her slightly older, vastly more experienced lover. Pym's deepest, most enduring portraits were of women like her: unmarried, childless, educated, and comfortable. But, particularly in *Less Than Angels,* she attempted to show us everyone: male and female, young and old, virginal and experienced, married and unmarried, maternal and childless. And her portraits are universally just, generous, and, at times, almost shockingly sympathetic; *Less Than Angels'* Tom Mallow—fickle, caddish, chillily detached—manages to retain the love of three different women, even after he serially abandons and betrays them. Selfish, amoral Deirdre is deemed worthy of sympathy and friendship by Catherine, the woman from whom Deirdre steals Tom. Pym's characters are never entirely good or entirely bad; they are merely people. She eschewed the Victorian morality of the previous century: in her world, as in life, people are complicated, virtue often goes unrewarded, and conniving and cruelty often go unpunished.

Even the man-stealing Deirdre is originally presented as a figure of pity. We first encounter her deeply uncomfortable at a party: "At nineteen she was still young and sensitive enough to be conscious that she was standing alone and had nothing to drink and to mind about it." It is not until later in the novel that she is courted by a man, and then almost accidentally: "Tom had never had to make much effort with women, who took a natural and immediate liking to him, so he did not lay himself out to be particularly interesting to Deirdre or to ask her anything about herself...[he] was certainly not aware of Deirdre as anything much more than a satisfactory audience..."

Deirdre is banal and rather pathetic (in Tom's eyes, she was "rather sweet, really, like a puppy or a colt"). Even with the considerable advantages of youth, attractiveness to men, and marriageability, she does not inspire envy. It is funny, odd-looking, unmarriageable Catherine Oliphant ("not the kind of girl to attract a man," in Rhoda's view) whom one wishes to be. Catherine earns a living from writing fiction, maintains a cozy bohemian flat, is under no illusions about men, and does exactly as she pleases. (Shortly before stealing the older woman's boyfriend, Deirdre wishes she *were* Catherine: "If only I lived by myself in a flat like Catherine's, thought Deirdre...then I shouldn't have to worry about family peace and hurting people's feelings.")

Catherine, of course, pays for her enviable independence with occasional loneliness—much as her creator paid for her own, real-life independence. Pym's letters and diaries reveal a woman whose overall happiness was complicated by periods of intense romantic longing and ordinary human loneliness. Of herself and a female friend, Pym wrote quite cheerfully in 1943, "Of course we're both pretty splendid. We both want the same kind of things. And fancy people not getting married and having children when they are able to...if all else fails we can always start a teashop." A month later, her tone darkened: "When I got out of the train at Paddington in the twilight full of dim hurrying figures I felt about the most lonely person there. Oh, to be cherished and comforted at a journey's end." Yet at supper on the same evening of her lonely arrival in Paddington, Pym met a young Canadian officer who offered her a cigarette: "We got talking and he finished by paying for my meal."

Pym's most keenly unhappy moments—nearly always brought on by loneliness or rejection—were often assuaged or wholly reversed a week, a day, or even an hour later. As well as painful romantic disappointment, she experienced thrills, pleasure, and "heavenly" joy in the company of men. Hers was not a pitiable life—nor was it sexless, despite her sororal living arrangement. She embarked on several love affairs while a student at Oxford, including a tortured attachment to a man named Henry Harvey, the love of her life and the model for *Some Tame Gazelle*'s Henry Hoccleve. Pym herself was not always as proper as her characters; in her diary she wrote of Henry's roommate catching her in bed with Henry, "reading 'Samson Agonistes'...with nothing on." As then 21-year-old Barbara jauntily noted, it was "Really rather funny. I stayed to supper."

Of a character in the posthumously published novel *An Academic Question*, Pym writes, "Dolly had remained single, though she had always given me to understand that her life had not been without love. But now, in her sixties, she had grown away from human beings and only kept in touch with her former lovers for practical and material advantages; she was more moved by the sight of a hedgehog's little leg raised to scratch itself than by any memory of a past love." The degree to which these sentences reflected Pym's feelings about her own station in life is not entirely clear, but it is clear that they were at least partially inspired by her own experiences. It is doubtful that Pym kept in touch with Henry only for "practical and material advantages," but it is not unlikely that, as her life drew to a close, she was more moved by wildlife than by memories of past loves.

By *Less Than Angels*' end, the reader has the distinct impression that Catherine's free and independent life—lonely as it may sometimes be—is richer and more rewarding than Deirdre's life of devotion to a series of unworthy men. Pym seemed to view her own life in similar terms: "Pleasure and pain in an agreeable mixture. That's what I feel when I think of Oxford and my days at St. Hilda's," she wrote in her diary in 1935. The sentiment held sway throughout the rest of her life as well.

Like so many writers, Pym coped with her most difficult emotions by writing them down. She was self-aware to an often painful degree, but she also took comfort in self-mockery. When Henry Harvey married a Finnish woman named Elsie, Barbara was, in the words of her close friend and biographer Hazel Holt, "badly hurt." But rather than discontinuing her longstanding correspondence with Henry, she began sending the couple long, satirical letters—occasionally going so far as to send separate letters to the new Mrs. Harvey, whom she addressed as "My darling sister Elsie." In these letters she often adopted the persona of a lovelorn spinster.

While she sometimes truly felt like a lovelorn spinster, she was also conscious of the extent to which she enjoyed exaggerating such feelings for comic and dramatic effect. "What a depressing letter I write to my dear sister!" she declared in a 1938 letter to Elsie. "She will say, 'Oh, this Barbara, she is always weeping and ill-treated and suffering, *nicht wahr?*' Whereas in reality, she is smoking, eating, drinking, using much lipstick, making new clothes, writing letters to dear friends, thinking out a new novel, reading nice poems by Mr. John Betjeman, making plans for visiting a foreign country, and dreaming at night of somebody she loves very much." (The "somebody" was not Henry, but another lover.)

Pym's daily life was one of extraordinary richness and fulfillment. She was a firm believer in drawing emotional, as well as physical, sustenance from the small daily pleasures of food and drink. "Life's problems are often eased by hot milky drinks," thinks the heroine of *No Fond Return of Love* as she drifts off to sleep at the end of the novel's first chapter.

Such statements are easy to caricature. But Pym was not a trivial person; if she occasionally transformed her feelings into punch lines or prescribed—tongue half in cheek—strong tea or a cup of Ovaltine to ease emotional pain, it was because she felt too deeply, rather than not deeply enough. "Life is first boredom, then fear / Whether or not we use it, it goes, / And leaves what something hidden from us chose, / And age, and then the only end of age," wrote Pym's friend Philip Larkin in his poem "Dockery and Son." Though the two had overlapping senses of humor, Pym was not nearly as cynical as Larkin.

IV.

Pym's was a world of muted emotions, populated by women with the emotional resilience and resourcefulness required to live alone (or to take care of themselves while living with others). When their worlds are upended—when, for example, Catherine Oliphant's live-in lover in *Less Than Angels* abandons her for a 19-year-old graduate student—they do not fall apart. Instead, they fix a cup of good, strong tea and pull themselves together. They are either "excellent women" ("excellent" being shorthand for proper, well-behaved, and virtuous) or trying very hard to be. They are full of the virtue admired by John Updike in *The New Yorker* in 1979: "*Excellent Women*, arriving on these shores in a heyday of sexual hype, is a startling reminder that solitude may be chosen, and that a lively, full novel can be constructed entirely within the precincts of that regressive virtue, feminine patience."

The most exciting event in Pym's world was the occasional arrival in town of a handsome new vicar. An unmarried woman over the age of thirty had little hope of finding someone to marry, and opportunities to flirt were confined to offering to do a man's laundry or type up his notes or have him over for a nice Sunday roast. Many found the constraints of this lifestyle uncongenial and even oppressive. But for a certain type of woman—the type who shared Barbara Pym's passion for literature, church, cooking, housekeeping, and quiet country living—village life was more comfort than trap.

Some Tame Gazelle's Bede sisters are quite content within the confines of this life, and not at all pathetic or repressed (despite Belinda's occasional fears that others view them as such). Harriet and Belinda lead happy, full, and comfortable lives. Pym's characters are not above or beyond romance, but we see them engaging in other pursuits as well, including reading, thinking, discussing literature, going to church, preparing meals. The women of Pym's novels have interests and concerns outside of themselves. They devote the largest share of their energy, passion, and intellect to being upstanding members of their communities.

Pym's heroines have male love interests, and, even in middle age, suitors, but they live independently of these men, whom they consider a bit more than mere diversions and a bit less than central figures. Men make life more interesting, but they're hardly necessary to one's existence (in fact, for the Bede sisters, male suitors are threatening and disruptive). Ultimately the women choose each other over marriage to men.

A scene in which Belinda visits her old lover Henry's house for a few hours while his wife is out of town and allows him to read to her as he used to do in their college days has a powerful yet subtle eroticism;

as one reviewer wrote in a 1983 edition of *The New York Times Book Review*, "restraint is the point."

Like all of Pym's novels, *Some Tame Gazelle* is built on this sense of restraint, which breeds intense emotional responses to relatively little action. Nothing much happens in this book: old friends come to visit; the sisters attend several social events at their village church; Henry's wife takes a trip. Yet such events take on the significance of high drama for the reader who comes to care about its protagonists.

We care about Belinda because she is the kind of heroine whose heroism comes from quietly accepting life's little indignities and sparing herself and her neighbors the pain and embarrassment acting on her desires would surely bring. We wish the best for her precisely because she does not scheme, manipulate, or even advocate on her own behalf; we feel protective of a woman whose disappointments are so keenly felt and whose desires, so touchingly modest in their scope, are nevertheless destined to remain unfulfilled.

The notable tenderness with which Pym treats characters like Belinda is laced with usually gentle mockery. Because she wrote her characters with herself and her loved ones in mind, her capacity for sympathy is profound, yet she is unflinching and exacting when it comes to honing in on their flaws. Her humor is incisive without being unkind; she knows just where to slip in the knife and how to do it without leaving a scar. In *Quartet in Autumn*, Janice Brabner, a local do-gooder, decides to go around the neighborhood visiting the elderly who live alone. Attempting to invite Marcia to a charitable get-together, Janice begins, "Some of us at the Centre have been worrying about the lonely ones."

The next lines are classic Pym, simultaneously acid and forgiving of the woman's tactlessness, and always insisting on her characters' dignity: "Could she really have prepared that sentence, for this was what came out. Marcia gave her no encouragement."

V.

Pym was diagnosed with breast cancer in 1971 and began treatment in London. The cancer went into remission, but she then suffered a minor stroke which resulted in a form of dyslexia that caused her to misspell most of her words when writing. The cancer returned several years after her retirement and it became clear that this time, she was dying. Just after Christmas 1979 she entered Sobell House, an Oxfordshire hospice, and died there a short time later, on the morning of January 11, 1980.

"Throughout her [final] illness she had maintained a cheerful stoicism, very down-to-earth and practical, never self-pitying," writes Hazel Holt. "She was sustained, certainly, by her strong faith and still able, as she had been throughout her life, to draw comfort from small pleasures and ironies...this is, perhaps, the greatest gift she has bequeathed to all who read her." Pym's stoicism was decidedly British in flavor. Americans tend to believe that one can and must always strive to improve one's circumstances, while Pym exhibited a paradoxically optimistic brand of resignation that was less like giving up and more like acclimating, with grace and good humor, to whatever life brought her.

Pym made the lives of socially marginal women like herself matter, in spite and even because of their mundanity. She imbued their lives with grace, dignity, relevance—even a sort of quiet heroism. In 1943, when Pym was serving in the Women's Royal Naval Service, she wrote in her diary, "On Friday evening I was having supper when Marion Booth, a very attractive looking MT driver came and sat by me and we talked about German and Rilke and the necessity of hanging on to the things that matter—painting for her, writing and literature for me and music, of course. This is important, otherwise you will lose yourself completely... 'it is much more important to be oneself than anything else.'"

Throughout her life, Pym was determined to be herself: to keep writing despite fourteen years of rejection, to keep falling in love though never marrying, to keep up her spirits while dying of cancer. "Still struggling on—perhaps a little better!" she wrote in a 1979 Christmas card to Philip Larkin, several weeks before her death. "The stoicism, courage and endurance that she gave to her heroines were qualities that she herself had in abundance. She also shared their vulnerability (to the end her eyes were those of an anxious girl), together with their ability to make the best of things..." wrote Hazel Holt.

Despite their limited scope, Pym's novels possess qualities of universality and timelessness that transcend gender, class, and geographic location. Everyone experiences love, loss, rejection, loneliness, and sorrow, and everyone can appreciate the simple beauty of life's most ordinary comforts: the first melty bite of macaroni and cheese; the hot milky drink before bed. "The small things of life were often so much bigger than the great things," thinks *Less Than Angels*' Catherine, "the trivial pleasures like cooking, one's home, little poems especially sad ones, solitary walks, funny things seen and overheard." As Alexander McCall Smith wrote in *The Guardian* in 2008, "although Pym's novels are about as far away as possible from engagement with the great political and social issues, they are powerful reminders that one of the great and proper concerns of literature is that motley cluster of small concerns that makes up our day-to-day lives."

Pym's heroines defined themselves by what they had rather than what they did not. Pym reminds us that one needn't have children to count—nor go to war, run a business, or hold public office, for that matter. It is the small, ordinary experiences that lend most lives their meaning.

On the last page of *Quartet in Autumn*, a novel about four aging office workers nearing retirement which was published only three years before she died, Pym wrote, "it made one realise that life still held infinite possibilities for change." These words sum up their author's unquenchable optimism. Even when faced with obscurity, illness, and death, she never lost the ability to marvel at life's potential.

Raina Lipsitz writes and edits short stories about herself and others at imaginarymoney.com. Her writing has appeared in The Atlantic, The Brooklyn Rail, Buffalo Spree, Free Inquiry, Kirkus Reviews, McSweeney's, Nerve.com, *and* The Yale Review of Books. *She holds a Master's degree in creative nonfiction from Columbia University and is a staff writer at* Catalyst, *a nonprofit seeking to advance women in business.*

SARAH EHRICH
A Conversation with Gail Mazur

This interview about the Blacksmith House Poetry Series, which will celebrate its fortieth anniversary in 2013, was edited and condensed from a tape recording made as part of the Cambridge Historical Society's oral history initiative.

Gail Mazur is the author of six books of poetry, including *They Can't Take That Away from Me,* a finalist for the 2001 National Book Award; *Zeppo's First Wife: New and Selected Poems,* winner of the Massachusetts Book Award and finalist for the Los Angeles Times Book Prize and Paterson Poetry Prize; and *Figures in a Landscape,* published in spring 2011 by University of Chicago Press. She has long played an active role in the Cambridge and Boston poetry communities, as Distinguished Writer-in-Residence at Emerson College and as the founding director of the Blacksmith House Poetry Series. Sarah Ehrich, a student of Gail Mazur, received her MFA in poetry from Emerson College in May 2012 and was awarded the Academy of American Poets Prize.

Sarah Ehrich: Could you begin by telling me some of the basics about the Blacksmith House and how the Blacksmith House Poetry Series began?

Gail Mazur: The Blacksmith House was the home and workshop of the village smithy in Longfellow's poem. We now know that it also became the home of a former runaway slave, Mary Walker. During World War II, it was the Window Shop, which was begun as a Viennese restaurant to help support people who were escaping Nazi Germany. A lot of German Jewish women in Cambridge had started this restaurant as a way to give employment to refugees and survivors from the Holocaust.

At a certain point, in the late '60s or early '70s, The Cambridge Center for Adult Education bought the building. For a while, the bakery of the Window Shop, which was a great bakery, famous for its Sacher torte, was continued, but the upstairs rooms were classrooms.

In 1973, I had been part of a group that met weekly to talk about the future problems of Cambridge. Gordon Cairnie, the owner of the Grolier Poetry Book Shop, had just died and I thought, there's not going to be any central, physical focus for poetry here; the Grolier had meant so much to me because it was not inside a university. So I went to the director of the Cambridge Center for Adult Education, Alida O'Loughlin, who also met with this group at the Unitarian Church every Thursday, and I said, "Can I have a space for poetry?" I don't know what I was thinking of, a poetry room or something. Alida said, "Well I can give you the Blacksmith House one night a week. On Monday nights." And I said OK. And I thought, I'll do this for a couple of weeks.

SE: What were you doing in Cambridge at the time?

GM: I was writing poetry and hanging out at the Grolier and raising my family. I mean, I didn't have a job. I had taken a couple of courses in filmmaking and thought I would be a filmmaker, but I was really too shy for the entrepreneurial business.

SE: How did you discover the Grolier?

GM: My oldest friend is a photographer, named Elsa Dorfman, who had worked at Grove Press and was very close to Allen Ginsberg, Robert Creeley, and Denise Levertov, and that whole group of poets. She had discovered the Grolier because of Ginsberg. And when I moved here, she brought me there. It just seemed like heaven to me. There was Gordon Cairnie, this old man who immediately liked me and who sat on the couch all day by the window, and there was all kinds of stuff between the cushions. There was a letter from Ezra Pound's son, Omar Pound. It was pretty raffish. Gordon had photographs of some poets on the wall, but it was very haphazard. There was a black ribbon around William Carlos Williams' photograph and he had probably died four years before. I thought, this is all really alive here.

I met everyone at the Grolier. One day, Robert Lowell came in and I was breathless. Gordon, who was crotchety, said, "Cal"—that was Lowell's nickname—"Cal, this is Gail Mazur, she's a poet too." And I thought, I never in a million years would have said I'm a poet. I thought, you know, there's got to be a long apprenticeship before you can say that, and you've got to be past even that. I don't remember the conversation. All I remember is that Gordon was tongue-tied around Lowell, and when he left, Gordon said, "Poor Cal, I can never think of a thing to say to him." [Laughter.]

After Elsa brought me there, I went to the Grolier every day. I was just addicted to it really. My kids were in day camp and I would go there. At four o'clock I would fall into a bar with some other regulars, and at five o'clock I'd be home making supper. Because I had gotten married when I was an undergraduate, it was almost like a second childhood. Something like the way I would have imagined living if I hadn't gotten married. For those few hours every day. And I thought I was on my way to becoming a street person because I hung out all the time. But in fact, I was a Jewish mother. And a Jewish daughter. [Laughter.]

My children were born twenty months apart, so they were very close, and I was very involved with them. Life was pretty engaging. But I think that running the series, I couldn't have predicted that it was going to put me at such ease in the poetry world. You know, if the Grolier was going to close, I really wanted there to be something in its place, because I had found where I really wanted to be.

SE: What were the first few weeks like at the Blacksmith House?

GM: I had my first reading with Fanny Howe and William Corbett, both poets whom I knew. There were tables and chairs, and the only obvious place where we could see and hear a poet was at a table that faced the bathrooms. So that's what we did.

That first night, there wasn't room for all the people who wanted to come. I always say they were hanging from the rafters. It was an incredible success. So I thought, well, I'll do it again next week. And after that, I thought, this is really great, people really want this. And it became a weekly reading series.

I remember the first week I stood up and said, "Fanny Howe," and sat down. And then I stood up and said, "Bill Corbett," and sat down. [Laughter.] It kind of went on like that until I got so I could say, "Please welcome..." Or pretty soon, I could say something about them. But for a lot of poets, it was their first reading. And a lot of people whose work you would know now gave their first readings there. Which is a testament to the community of poets here. There was a community building, and that was very gratifying to me. And that became clearer and clearer every year. Frank Bidart once said to me at the Blacksmith House, "This is my home, this is my poetry home." Which to me was wonderful. And the great thing about those first five years, before they redid the building, was that people came in, and since it was crowded, they had to sit at tables with other people, whether they knew them or not.

I felt really a mission to have people get comfortable with poetry. To have this storefront, rather than a university, where you could come. Not only poets, but people's friends who weren't poets. There were often people who would say to me when they were leaving that it was the first poetry reading they'd ever been to. That pleased me as much as having a glittering audience of people you were almost terrified to read to because you admired their work so much.

SE: How did you spread the word about the series and who came?

GM: Well, I wasn't very organized, since I was doing it week by week the first year. Really. [Laughter.] It was always breathtakingly last minute. It was a continuation of my college career of doing everything later than last minute. It seemed like I needed to keep myself scared. I made posters and I put them up on lampposts and telephone poles all over Cambridge. That was the publicity. And now I think, how did people know to come?

The first few weeks, it attracted a lot of people who came every week for several years. They were people who took poetry courses at the Adult Ed. They were poets who lived around here. A lot of them lived in one building. There was rent control then, and there was a building on the corner of Linnaean Street right on Mass Avenue where the super was a fiction writer. There was a huge waiting list for the rent-controlled apartments in there, but writers always moved to the top of the waiting list. So it was like a little beehive. Marie Howe lived there, Stuart Dischell, Askold Melnyczuk. Steve Cramer. It was amazing.

Before a reading, I would walk down Church Street. There was a bookstore, Reading International, on the corner of Church and Brattle, and their literary magazine section was in the window right at the corner. And sometimes you'd look in there and see Robert Lowell browsing before he came to the Blacksmith House, or other poets browsing, and I would say, "Oh, it's going to be a good crowd," and I'd run to arrange the tables.

I have somewhere a photograph of Frank sitting with Elizabeth Bishop and Octavio Paz at one of the little tables.

SE: I'm curious to know more about the logistics.

GM: While I was running it, the series was about thirty readings a year. As time went on, people started asking me for readings and would say so-and-so was coming to read at the University of New Hampshire, can she come read for you first? So it got to be pretty much a national thing. I see that in the anthology I published from the readings in 1974, there were very few people who weren't from the Boston area. Then that changed to be more balanced. And it was exciting. It was exciting and people knew about it all over the country.

But I didn't have a budget! I passed the hat. If you realize that in those years the plane from New York was sixteen dollars, I could ask anybody. By the first and second years, poets like Mark Strand and Alan Dugan were coming to read. Just practically everyone said yes because nobody was getting money. And you know, after I passed the hat, sometimes they would get enough for their transportation and twenty or thirty dollars.

The hat was actually a basket with a handle that my aunt had sent filled with fruit and jellies one Christmas. [Laughter.] I still have it. And I would go around to the tables after the reading, weaving in and out, and people would put a dollar in. Every once in a while, a real grown-up who wasn't a poet would put a five or ten in. That was really enough for those first few years.

When Reagan became president, the cost of everything went up. He deregulated the airlines, so that was the end of that ease of travel for me to invite people without being embarrassed that I didn't have real money. And I think that's probably when I started having a budget and raising money.

There were other ingredients to the situation that were historical. The Vietnam War was winding down. A lot of us had moved from global activism to local activism. I did a lot of political stuff at the Blacksmith too. Also, in the Johnson era, the National Endowment for the Arts had really developed, so Alice James books started around that time and *Ploughshares* had started right before then.

SE: What was the connection between *Ploughshares* and the Blacksmith Series?

GM: There were, for me, real parallels between them. I think because DeWitt [Henry] and I worked on things together. When DeWitt and Peter O'Malley started *Ploughshares*, it had a collective aspect. DeWitt was very much a community-oriented person and was wide open to everything really. *Ploughshares* had more women writers in its contents than any other magazine at the time. It had more African Americans. He had African American and women guest editors before other established little magazines did.

SE: What was the Blacksmith House's role in being politically active at this time?

GM: We had an antinuclear reading. I had AIDS readings. The third week of the series, I had a reading to protest the imprisonment of three women in Portugal, called the Three Marias, who had the nerve to publish a book on feminism and had been imprisoned. It was just a natural part of what I was interested in. I tried to have and did have an open attitude toward what kinds of poetry we would have, so there was a sort of wild range of poets reading. All of that was important to me. And is important to me.

SE: Maybe you could think back to some of the most memorable readings?

GM: One of my favorite readings in terms of introducing a poet was Eavan Boland's reading. We didn't know her work. *I* didn't even know her work. But Seamus Heaney had suggested that she contact me and I was delighted. Her presentation of self was just beautiful. She's a strong woman and she was writing beautiful lyric poems, and there was a sense of something really happening there that night. It was this incredibly unselfconscious presentation of the poetry—confident, unapologetic. And a few years ago, I had Major Jackson introduce a terrific group of young poets from Cave Canem.

Another poet who was an absolute American original was Alan Dugan. He read for me two or three times. I remember he insisted there be a six-pack of beer on the podium and that was sort of disconcerting for me the first time. [Laughter.] But he read his poetry like nobody else. "This is a job," he would say at the beginning of a reading, "I am going to work for an hour." That is exactly what he would do. One hour, six bottles of beer. And Dugan was through.

I think it was the first season that Dugan and Mark Strand had a sort of face-off about whose basket was fuller of money. One of them, and I'm not going to say which, took home sixty dollars and the other took home thirty-eight. And the one with sixty made sure the one with thirty-eight knew it.

Probably the most memorable for me were the readings of the work of dead poets. I loved introducing Pessoa to an audience and introducing Thom Gunn. Thom Gunn wasn't that familiar here, but there were people in Boston who had worked with him or studied with him and who loved his work. We had a fantastic Frank O'Hara reading—Robert Pinsky, Frank Bidart, Lloyd Schwartz, Eileen Myles, Maureen McLane, and Bill Corbett read—and O'Hara's sister and nephew came. I remember also a beautiful Akhmatova reading with a huge audience that included many Russians. Those readings were memorials and a way again to make us feel the sense of community and that the community wasn't only geographical, it was a community of poetry. Just a few years ago, I organized a reading combining Norman Mailer's *Armies of the Night* with Lowell's antiwar poems and "For the Union Dead." And of course, this past fall, Andrea Cohen opened the season with an Adrienne Rich tribute, and those of us who read were pleased that one of Adrienne's sons came.

SE: What influence did the Blacksmith House community have on your poetry?

GM: Doing the Blacksmith House made it so much easier for me to love reading aloud, to love it as part of the process. I felt more at ease up there.

One of the great things that happened to me because of the Blacksmith House was I met my friend Lloyd Schwartz, who called to ask me for a reading the first season. After we talked for an hour—he's just an incredibly warm, lovely man—he said, "Would you like to go to Lowell's office hours?" I don't know if you know about Lowell's office hours. Every week at ten in the morning on a Tuesday or Wednesday, you could go to this seminar room in the basement of Quincy House at Harvard (where he had an apartment) and talk. It wasn't like a seminar exactly, it was almost like a salon. Except it was totally unpretentious. I mean, there was no hierarchy except Lowell was it. One day, after John Berryman's suicide—they were such close friends—he brought in the brand new copy of Berryman's posthumous book, *Henry's Fate*, with the suicide poems and he read them. But another time, we talked about Broadway musicals. It was just amazing. The associative leaps of his mind were an education, an education about thinking like a poet.

So all those things fed into my work. But one of the ways it fed into my work was I made friends who were invested, generous critics. We were invested, generous critics of each other's work. There are certain friends who aren't competitive and really are invested in you getting your poem to be the best it can be. And that's what you hope for.

It's so hard for me to imagine what would have happened if Mike and I hadn't gone to those Cambridge Now meetings and met Alida. In fact, I was so shy that Mike had to come with me to meet her to ask if I could have a space for poetry.

I feel lucky to have found what I wanted to do in an atmosphere in which I can do it. And not in a careerist way, but for me personally as a poet, everything grew out of the Blacksmith House and the environment. Because I think to write good poems, you have to have some kind of crazy confidence.

SE: It sounds like running the Blacksmith House Series, you were able to develop that confidence.

GM: Yeah. And I don't know how to put this, because I don't mean to be immodest. I had a stage presence, which was completely natural after a while. That it was just me. I was as at ease as I could possibly be. As I am now, talking to you. And the fact that people could rely on me to be witty in a situation where they might be overawed, contributed to the informality. And you know, just seeing people you recognize at readings is great. I love that sense of community, so I feel lucky to have landed in it. And tried to keep it going.

I didn't grow up knowing there was such a thing as poetry readings. I don't think I grew up knowing there was such a thing as living poets. Most people don't. But as Frank O'Hara says at the end of "Autobiographia Literaria," *And here I am, the center of all beauty. Imagine!* I love that. And I have felt that.

Sarah Ehrich earned her MFA in poetry from Emerson College in 2012. She is a writing instructor at Emerson College and Boston College and coordinates emersonWRITES, a free creative writing program for Boston Public School teenagers. She lives in Cambridge, Massachusetts.

POSTSCRIPTS
Alice Hoffman Prize for Fiction · Spring 2013

The Alice Hoffman Prize for Fiction *Ploughshares* is pleased to present Karl Taro Greenfeld with the second annual Alice Hoffman Prize for Fiction for his short story, "Strawberries," which appeared in the Winter 2012-2013 issue of *Ploughshares,* edited by Ladette Randolph and John Skoyles. The $1,000 award, given by acclaimed writer and *Ploughshares* advisory editor Alice Hoffman, honors the best piece of fiction published in the journal during the previous year.

About Karl Taro Greenfeld

Karl Taro Greenfeld is the author of six books, most recently the novel *Triburbia* (Harper), published in 2012. His fiction has appeared in *Harper's, The Paris Review, One Story, The Best American Short Stories,* and *PEN/O. Henry Prize Stories.*

About "Strawberries," Greenfeld writes, "I start stories with an image or feeling in mind—in this case, the dishes with swastikas on the bottom and the strange bar in Liège—and then start writing and see if I get anywhere. Sometimes I do and sometimes I don't, and very often I can't tell which is which. I wrote this story a couple years ago and then put it away because I didn't think it worked. I took it out after two years and looked at it again and thought it was pretty good, so I sent it out. Then something happened that never happens: a few very good journals all said they wanted it. I have always wanted to publish a story in *Ploughshares,* so here it ended up."

EDITORS' SHELF
Book Recommendations from Our Advisory Editors

Fanny Howe recommends *Summer of Hate* by Chris Kraus: "The book, like her others, is an enlivened series of memories that take place on the Southwest border, and examine the prison system and real estate. Pretty stunning and very original." (semiotext(e), August 2012)

Philip Levine recommends *A Larger Country* by Tomas Q. Morin: "What a pleasure to open a first book of poems & find a world, one somewhat like my own, but different in marvelous ways yet always a world that is true to its own laws of causality & fate, reward & punishment. This world is, of course, the invention of Tomas Q. Morin, a young poet who writes with startling intelligence & resourcefulness. In poem after poem the writing takes unexpected turns, yet somehow through his artistry he makes these surprises feel necessary. Morin is also a space & time traveler, for his memory is a catalog of who we are & what we've done, & he loves to enter the minds of others & render them for inspection, damnation, & sometimes love. Even in his dreamlike poems, the voice is steady, unrelenting, & at times hilarious yet always calm. I will call the voice of this poet a "common" voice, a voice that can speak for anyone, better still, an adult voice, one that is never clever, that never strains for attention or to be different, a voice a poet could take into an entire lifetime of memorable writing." (American Poetry Review, November 2012)

Joyce Peseroff recommends *Clangings* by Steven Cramer: "This book-length collection invents, from the pretzel logic and language of manics and schizophrenics, a way of seeing the world that's hilarious, heartbreaking, and utterly unique." (Sarabande, October 2012)

David St. John recommends *Quick Draw: Poems From a Soldier's Wife* by Abby E. Murray: "This remarkable chapbook is searing and heartbreaking, yet absolutely clear-eyed and fiercely present at every moment, as the poet records and reveals the intimacies of a husband and wife against the backdrop of war." (Finishing Line Press, 2012)

David St. John also recommends *That Said: New and Selected Poems* by Jane Shore: "This gorgeous collection of more than thirty-five years of Jane Shore's poetry feels long overdue. Her exquisite and formally poised poems reflect upon the passages of both the individual and the family. These poems, sometimes deceptively dressed in the reflective calm of Elizabeth Bishop, reveal a passionate mind always excavating the pressures of time." (Houghton Mifflin Harcourt, April 2012)

EDITORS' CORNER
New Works by Our Advisory Editors

Nick Flynn, *The Reenactments: A Memoir* (W. W. Norton, January 2013)

Paul Muldoon, *The Word on the Street: Rock Lyrics* (Farrar, Straus and Giroux, February 2013)

Jay Neugeboren, *The American Sun & Wind Moving Picture Company* (Texas Tech University Press, February 2013)

Jean Valentine, translator (with Ilya Kaminsky), *Dark Elderberry Branch: Poems of Marina Tsvetaeva* (Alice James Books, December 2012)

Kevin Young, ed. (with Michael S. Glaser), *The Collected Poems of Lucille Clifton 1965-2010* (BOA Editions, August 2012)

CONTRIBUTORS' NOTES
Spring 2013

Peter Balakian's recent books of poems include *Ziggurat* (University of Chicago Press, 2010) and *June-tree: New and Selected Poems 1974-2000* (HarperCollins, 2001); *Black Dog of Fate* (Basic Books, 1997) won the PEN/Martha Albrand Award for memoir and was recently issued in a tenth-anniversary edition. He directs creative writing at Colgate.

Sandra Beasley is the author of *I Was the Jukebox* (W. W. Norton & Co., 2010), winner of the Barnard Women Poets Prize; and *Theories of Falling* (New Issues, 2008). Other honors for her work include positions as the 2013 Visiting Writer at Lenoir-Rhyne University and the 2010 University of Mississippi Summer Poet in Residence, a DCCAH Artist Fellowship, and the Friends of Literature Prize from the Poetry Foundation. Her latest book is *Don't Kill the Birthday Girl: Tales from an Allergic Life* (Crown, 2011), a memoir and cultural history of food allergy.

Erin Belieu is the author of four poetry collections, all from Copper Canyon Press. Her forthcoming, *Le Deluge*, will be out in 2014. Belieu teaches writing at Florida State University and is the codirector of VIDA: Women in Literary Arts.

Emily Bernard's personal essays have been reprinted in *The Best American Essays, Best African American Essays,* and *The Best Creative Nonfiction.* She teaches African American literature at the University of Vermont. Her most recent book, *Carl Vechten and the Harlem Renaissance: A Portrait in Black and White,* was published by Yale University Press in February 2012.

Traci Brimhall is the author of *Our Lady of the Ruins* (W. W. Norton & Co., 2012), winner of the Barnard Women Poets Prize; and *Rookery* (SIU Press, 2010), winner of the Crab Orchard Series First Book Award. Her poems have appeared in *The Kenyon Review, Slate, The Virginia Quarterly Review, New England Review,* and elsewhere. She's received fellowships from the Wisconsin Institute for Creative Writing, the King/Chávez/Parks Foundation, and the National Endowment for the Arts.

Jericho Brown worked as the speechwriter for the Mayor of New Orleans before receiving his PhD in creative writing and literature from the University of Houston. The recipient of the Whiting Writers'

Award and of fellowships from the National Endowment for the Arts and the Radcliffe Institute at Harvard University, Brown is an assistant professor at Emory University. His poems have appeared in journals and anthologies, including *The American Poetry Review, The Believer, jubilat, Oxford American, Ploughshares, A Public Space, Tin House,* and *100 Best African American Poems.* His first book, *Pease* (New Issues, 2008), won the American Book Award.

Stephen Browning lives in Menlo Park, California, with his beloved wife, Patricia. For many years he has courted the muses of poetry, painting, and printmaking. A collection of his botanical poems, *Hunger for Light* (Daniel & Daniel Publishers, 2006), is available in print and as an e-book.

Maggie Dietz is the former director of the Favorite Poem Project and author of *Perennial Fall* (University of Chicago Press, 2006). She teaches at the University of Massachusetts Lowell.

Mark Doty is the author of eight books of poems, including Fire to Fire: *New and Selected Poems* (Harper Perennial, 2008), which was awarded The National Book Award in 2008. This spring Prestel Publishing will publish his collaboration with the painter Darren Waterston, *A Swarm, a Flock, a Host: Mark Doty and Darren Waterston's Compendium of Creatures.* He is also at work on a new collection of poems, *Deep Lane,* and a prose study of Walt Whitman titled *What Is the Grass;* both will be published by W. W. Norton & Co. He teaches at Rutgers and lives in New York City.

Jaclyn Dwyer is pursuing a PhD in creative writing at Florida State University, where she was awarded a Kingsbury Fellowship. Her work is forthcoming or has appeared in a number of literary magazines, including *Witness, Prairie Schooner,* and *New Ohio Review.* Jaclyn lives in Tallahassee and is at work on a novel. www.jaclyndwyer.com

Martín Espada is the author of more than fifteen books. His latest collection of poems, *The Trouble Ball* (W. W. Norton & Co., 2011), received the Milt Kessler Award, an International Latino Book Award, and a Massachusetts Book Award. His previous collection, *The Republic of Poetry* (W. W. Norton & Co., 2006), was a finalist for the Pulitzer Prize. His book of essays, *Zapata's Disciple* (South End Press, 1998), has been banned in Tucson as part of the outlawed Mexican American Studies Program. The recipient of a Guggenheim Fellowship, Espada teaches at the University of Massachusetts-Amherst.

Didi Gibbs' poems have appeared in *Passages North, Poetry South,* and *Sierra Nevada Review,* among other publications. She divides her time between Vermont and Florida, and currently teaches humanities at the University of Central Florida.

Nathalie Handal's most recent books include *Poet in Andalucía* (University of Pittsburgh Press, 2012), which Alice Walker praises as "poems of depth and weight and the sorrowing song of longing and resolve"; and *Love and Strange Horses* (University of Pittsburgh Press, 2010), winner of the Gold Medal Independent Publisher Book Award. *The New York Times* says it's "a book that trembles with belonging (and longing)." She is a Lannan Foundation Fellow, winner of the Alejo Zuloaga Order in Literature, and Honored Finalist for the Gift of Freedom Award, among other honors.

Tony Hoagland's books of poems include *What Narcissism Means to Me* (Graywolf Press, 2003) and *Donkey Gospel* (Graywolf Press, 1998). He teaches at the University of Houston. Recently, he has founded The Five Powers of Poetry (fivepowerspoetry.com), a program for coaching high-school teachers in the teaching of poetry in the classroom.

David Huddle holds the 2012-2013 Roy Acuff Chair of Excellence in the Creative Arts at Austin Peay State University in Clarksville, Tennessee. He's the author of six volumes of short fiction, seven collections of poetry, four novels, and a book of essays on writing. Recent titles are *Nothing Can Make Me Do This* (Tupelo Press, 2011) and *Blacksnake at the Family Reunion* (Louisiana State University Press, 2012). He teaches at the Bread Loaf School of English and the Rainier Writing Workshop.

Elise Juska's short stories have appeared in *The Gettysburg Review, The Hudson Review, Salmagundi, Black Warrior Review, Harvard Review, The Missouri Review,* and elsewhere. Her new book, a novel told in stories, is forthcoming from Grand Central Publishing in 2014. She lives in Philadelphia, where she teaches fiction writing at the University of the Arts.

Laura Kasischke's most recent collection of poems, *Space, in Chains* (Copper Canyon Press, 2011), received the National Book Critics Circle Award. She lives in Chelsea, Michigan, and teaches at the University of Michigan.

Joanna Klink's most recent book is *Raptus* (Penguin Books, 2010). She is currently the Tin House Writer-in-Residence at Portland State University.

Rebecca Lehmann is the author of *Between the Crackups* (Salt Publishing, 2011), winner of the Crashaw Prize. Her poems have been published in journals including *Tin House, The Iowa Review,* and *Narrative* magazine. She currently lives in North Texas.

Alex Lemon is the author of *Happy: A Memoir* (Scribner, 2009) and three collections of poetry: *Mosquito* (Tin House, 2006), *Hallelujah Blackout* (Milkweed Editions, 2008), and *Fancy Beasts* (Milkweed Editions, 2010). A fourth collection is forthcoming from Milkweed Editions. He lives in Fort Worth, Texas, and teaches at Texas Christian University.

Jamaal May is the author of *Hum* (Alice James Books, 2013), winner of the Beatrice Hawley Award. His poems appear widely with his most recent work found in *New England Review, Indiana Review, Gulf Coast,*

The Kenyon Review, and *The Believer.* A Detroiter and graduate of Warren Wilson's MFA program, Jamaal has received fellowships and scholarships from Bread Loaf Writers Conference, Cave Canem, Callaloo Workshop, and Bucknell University, where he was named the 2011-2013 Stadler Fellow. He has served as associate editor of *West Branch* and is currently the series editor and graphic designer for the Organic Weapon Arts Chapbook Series.

Jeffrey McDaniel's fifth book, *Chapel of Inadvertent Joy,* is coming out in fall 2013 from Pitt Press. He teaches at Sarah Lawrence College.

Erika Meitner is the author, most recently, of *Makeshift Instructions for Vigilant Girls* (Anhinga Press, 2011), and *Ideal Cities* (HarperCollins, 2010), which was a 2009 National Poetry Series winner. Her poems have been published in journals including *The New Republic, The Virginia Quarterly Review, The Southern Review,* and *Tin House.* She is currently an associate professor of English at Virginia Tech, where she teaches in the MFA program.

Szidónia Molnár is a freelance writer. She lives in Washington, D.C., with her husband and children.

Fred Moten is the Helen L. Bevington Professor of Modern Poetry at Duke University. He is author of *In the Break: The Aesthetics of the Black Radical Tradition* (University of Minnesota Press, 2003), *Hughson's Tavern* (Leon Works, 2008), *B. Jenkins* (Duke University Press, 2010), and two forthcoming books: *The Feel Trio* (Letter Machine Editions, 2013) and *consent not to be a single being* (Duke University Press).

Harryette Mullen is the author of several poetry collections, including *Recyclopedia* (Graywolf Press, 2006), winner of a PEN Beyond Margins Award; and *Sleeping with the Dictionary* (University of California Press, 2002), a finalist for a National Book Award, National Book Critics Circle Award, and Los Angeles Times Book Prize. She teaches American poetry, African American literature, and creative writing at UCLA. A collection of her essays and interviews, *The Cracks Between What We Are and What We Are Supposed to Be,* was published by University of Alabama Press in 2012. Her *Tanka Diary* is forthcoming from Graywolf Press in 2013.

Vi Khi Nao is pursuing an MFA at Brown University and living in Providence, Rhode Island. Her work has appeared in *NOON, Alice Blue Review,* and *elimae.*

Jay Nebel's poems have appeared in *American Poetry Review, Narrative, Tin House,* and other publications. He lives in Portland, Oregon, with his wife and their two children.

Sharon Olds lives in New Hampshire and New York City. She teaches in the graduate program in creative writing at New York University, where she has been involved in outreach writing workshops—one at Goldwater Hospital (twenty-seven years) and one for veterans of Iraq and Afghanistan (three years).

Her most recent book, *Stag's Leap* (Knopf, 2012), has been shortlisted for the T. S. Eliot Prize.

Yaddyra Peralta is a poet. Her work has appeared in or is forthcoming in *Jai-Alai, Abe's Penny, Tigertail, Hinchas de Poesia,* the Miami Poetry Collective's *Cent Journal* series, and *Lies and Truth,* the poetry supplement to the Tabloid series accompanying Miami Art Museum's 2010 New Work Miami exhibition. She received her MFA in creative writing from Florida International University.

Carl Phillips is the author of twelve books of poems, most recently, from Farrar, Straus and Giroux, *Silverchest* (2013) and *Double Shadow* (2011), which won the Los Angeles Times Book Prize. He teaches at Washington University in St. Louis.

Sherri Phillips was born and raised in Georgia and now resides in New York City. She completed her MFA at The New School and has a BS in mathematics. Her short fiction has appeared in the magazine *Killing the Angel,* and she currently is writing a novel that she hopes to complete by the summer of 2013.

Catherine Pierce is the author of *The Girls of Peculiar* (Saturnalia, 2012) and *Famous Last Words* (Saturnalia, 2008). Her poems have appeared in *The Best American Poetry, Boston Review, Slate, Ploughshares, FIELD,* and elsewhere. She codirects the creative writing program at Mississippi State University.

David James Poissant is the author of *Lizard Man,* winner of the 2011 RopeWalk Fiction Chapbook Prize. Other stories appear or will soon appear in *The Atlantic, Playboy, One Story, Glimmer Train, The Southern Review, New Stories from the South,* and *Best New American Voices.* He lives in Orlando with his wife and daughters and teaches in the MFA Program at the University of Central Florida. His first story collection will be published by Simon & Schuster in 2014 to be followed by a novel in 2015.

Bethany Pray is a poverty law attorney specializing in child neglect and, more recently, public housing law. Her poetry has appeared in publications including *The Virginia Quarterly Review, Pequod,* and *The Four Way Reader.* She graduated many years ago from the Warren Wilson College MFA Program for Writers, and recently moved to Colorado.

Nicole Sealey is a Cave Canem graduate fellow whose work was selected for inclusion in *Best New Poets 2011.* She is winner of the 2012 Poetry International Prize and finalist for the 2011 Third Coast Poetry Prize, and her poems have appeared in or are forthcoming in *Callaloo, Harvard Review, Ploughshares, Poetry International,* and *Third Coast,* among other literary online and print journals.

Maureen Seaton is the author of fifteen poetry collections, including *Stealth,* with Samuel Ace (Chax Press, 2011), and *Sinéad O'Connor and Her Coat of a Thousand Bluebirds,* winner of the Sentence Book

Award (Firewheel, 2011), with Neil de la Flor. Carnegie Mellon University Press will publish *Fibonacci Batman: New and Selected Poems* in 2013. Seaton's awards include the Iowa Prize, Lambda Literary Award, the NEA, and the Pushcart. She teaches poetry at the University of Miami. www.maureenseaton.com

Lisa Sewell is the author of several books of poetry, most recently *Long Corridor,* which won the 2009 Keystone Chapbook Award. She is also coeditor with Claudia Rankine of *American Poets in the 21st Century: The New Poetics* (Wesleyan, 2007) and *Eleven More American Women Poets in the 21st Century: Poetics Across North America* (Wesleyan, 2012). She is currently working on a series of poems focusing on endangered species. She lives in Philadelphia and teaches at Villanova University.

John Warner Smith earned his MFA in creative writing at the University of New Orleans. He is a second-year fellow in the Cave Canem Retreat. He has published poems in *Callaloo* and will be published in a forthcoming issue of *African American Review.* Smith's play, *Sugar,* will debut in a presentation by the Grambling State University Department of Theatre Arts in 2013. Smith resides in Baton Rouge, Louisiana, where he directs a statewide organization dedicated to improving public education.

Tracy K. Smith is the author of three poetry collections, most recently *Life on Mars* (Graywolf Press, 2011), which won the 2012 Pulitzer Prize.

Anna Solomon is the author of the novel, *The Little Bride* (Riverhead Trade, 2011). Her stories and essays have appeared in *One Story, The Georgia Review, Harvard Review, The New York Times Magazine, MORE,* and elsewhere. The recipient of two Pushcart Prizes, The Missouri Review Editor's Prize, and fellowships from MacDowell, Yaddo, and Bread Loaf, Anna holds an MFA from the Iowa Writers' Workshop. She lives in Providence, Rhode Island, with her husband and two kids.

Kimberly Swayze holds an MFA and a BA in English from the University of Washington. Her poetry has appeared in *Poetry Northwest* and *The Seattle Review.* "Church" is her first work of fiction.

Pimone Triplett's most recent collection of poems is *Rumor* (Triquarterly, 2009). She teaches in the MFA Program of the University of Washington.

Anne Pierson Wiese received the Academy of American Poets Walt Whitman Award for her collection, *Floating City* (Louisiana State University Press, 2007). Her poems have appeared in *Ploughshares, The New England Review, The Hudson Review, Raritan, The Southern Review, The Antioch Review,* and *The Virginia Quarterly Review,* among other publications.

Bruce Willard's first collection of poems, *Holding Ground,* is due out from Four Way Books in March 2013. His poems have appeared in *African American Review, AGNI,*

Connotation Press, Harvard Review, Mead magazine, Salamander, 5 A.M., and other publications. He divides his time between Maine and California.

Jake Adam York was the author of three books of poems, including *A Murmuration of Starlings* (Southern Illinois University Press, 2008) and *Persons Unknown,* published in 2010 by Southern Illinois University Press in the Crab Orchard Series in Poetry. His work was recognized with fellowships from the National Endowment for the Arts, the Colorado Council on the Arts, and the University of Mississippi. An associate professor at the University of Colorado Denver, York also edited *Copper Nickel.* He passed away in December 2012, while this issue was being assembled.

Javier Zamora was born in San Luis La Herradura, La Paz, El Salvador. At the age of nine he immigrated to the "Yunaited Estais." His chapbook, *Nine Immigrant Years,* is the winner of the 2011 Organic Weapon Arts Contest. Zamora is a CantoMundo fellow and a Bread Loaf work-study scholarship recipient. He has received scholarships from Frost Place, Napa Valley, Squaw Valley, and VONA. His poems appear or are forthcoming in *Dirty Laundry Lit, Interrupture, NewBorder, The Poetry Show,* and elsewhere.

GUEST EDITOR POLICY

Ploughshares is published three times a year: mixed issues of poetry and prose in the spring and winter and a prose issue in the fall, with each guest-edited by a different writer of prominence. Guest editors are invited to solicit up to half of their issues, with the other half selected from unsolicited manuscripts screened for them by staff editors. This guest editor policy is designed to introduce readers to different literary circles and tastes, and to offer a fuller representation of the range and diversity of contemporary letters than would be possible with a single editorship. Yet, at the same time, we expect every issue to reflect our overall standards of literary excellence.

SUBMISSION POLICIES

We welcome unsolicited manuscripts from June 1 to January 15 (postmark dates). All submissions postmarked from January 16 to May 31 will be returned unread. Submit your work at any time during our reading period; if a manuscript is not timely for one issue, it will be considered for another. Our backlog is unpredictable, and staff editors ultimately have the responsibility of determining for which editor a work is most appropriate. We accept submissions online. Please see our website (www.pshares.org) for more information and guidelines. Unsolicited work sent directly to a guest editor's home or office will be ignored and discarded.

All mailed manuscripts and correspondence regarding submissions should be accompanied by a self-addressed, stamped envelope (s.a.s.e.). No replies will be given by e-mail (exceptions are made for international submissions). Expect three to five months for a decision. We now receive well over a thousand manuscripts a month.

For stories and essays that are significantly longer than 5,000 words, we are now accepting submissions for *Ploughshares Solos* (formerly *Pshares Singles*), which will be published as e-books. Pieces for this series, which can be either fiction or nonfiction, can stretch to novella length and range from 6,000 to 25,000 words. The series is edited by Ladette Randolph, *Ploughshares* editor-in-chief.

Simultaneous submissions are amenable as long as they are indicated as such and we are notified immediately upon acceptance elsewhere. We do not reprint previously published work. Translations are welcome if permission has been granted. We cannot be responsible for delay, loss, or damage. Payment is upon publication: $25/printed page, $50 minimum and $250 maximum per author, with two copies of the issue and a one-year subscription. For *Ploughshares Solos,* payment is $250 for long stories and $500 for work that is closer to a novella.

MILLER WILLIAMS ARKANSAS POETRY PRIZE

The Law of Falling Bodies
Poems by Elton Glaser
Winner: 2013 Miller Williams Poetry Prize
$16.00 paper
"Over the years Elton Glaser has, with a quiet fortitude and an exceptional lyric precision, fashioned a commendable body of work, and this new collection is his best thus far."
—David Wojahn

Praise Nothing
Poems by Joshua Robbins
Finalist: 2013 Miller Williams Poetry Prize
$16.00 paper
"It's difficult to believe this is a first book, but, remarkably, it is. What a debut!"
—Susan Wood

Chord Box
Poems by Elizabeth Lindsey Rogers
Finalist: 2013 Miller Williams Poetry Prize
$16.00 paper
"Both sensual and cerebral, *Chord Box* oscillates with gravitas and light: an indelible debut."
—Alice Fulton

The University of Arkansas Press Poetry Series' annual
$5,000 Miller Williams Arkansas Poetry Prize
For submissions in September and October of 2013
One winner and up to three finalists will be published in 2015
For more information: www.uapress.com

 800-626-0090 • www.uapress.com • facebook.com/uarkpress

NEW FROM
AUTUMN HOUSE PRESS

LITTLE RAW SOULS

stories by
STEVEN SCHWARTZ

"Steven Schwartz is a capacious writer; bucking the trend, a lot happens in these stories. He takes the time and has the skill and graciousness to give each of his stories a full world in which men and women wrestle with their conflicting codes, reaching for the right thing among all of the easy and delectable choices."

—Ron Carlson

"*Little Raw Souls* is a beautiful book—I loved watching these characters bumble and brave their way through compromise, integrity, and freedom from illusion."

—Joan Silber

"I love Steven Schwartz's characters for the way that, even as they work with such patience and fortitude in the face of radically diminished expectations, at holding up their end, as they understand it—or holding up more than their end—they feel so piercingly the full extent of their failures. *Little Raw Souls* is one of the most openhearted and emotionally intelligent story collections I've ever read."

—Jim Shepard

87 ½ Westwood St
Pittsburgh, PA 15211
(412) 381-4261
www.autumnhouse.org
ISBN: 978-1-932870-65-7
$17.95

ALL AH TITLES ARE AVAILABLE THROUGH AMAZON.COM,
YOUR LOCAL BOOKSTORE, OR DIRECTLY FROM THE PUBLISHER.

Dorothy Sargent Rosenberg Annual Poetry Prizes

Prize winners for the 2012 competition, announced February 5, 2013

$7,500

Leslie Elizabeth Adams, Michelle Y. Burke, Nina Riggs, Brittney Scott, Ali Shapiro, and Sam Taylor

$5,000

Josh Booton, Jenny George, Tess Jolly, Kerry Kwock, and Rebecca Macijeski

$2,500

Ameerah Arjanee, Ruth Awad, Michael Boccardo, Jodie Childers, Brieghan Gardner, Rochelle Hurt, Courtney Kampa, Tracey Knapp, Hannah Oberman-Breindel, and Matthew Thorburn

$1,000

Anders Carlson-Wee, Weston Cutter, Adam Fell, Dana Koster, and Brittany Perham

Honorable Mentions: $250

Quan Barry, Jeremy Bass, Brittany Cavallaro, C. Doyle, Rebecca Dunham, K.A. Hays, Emily Ruth Hazel, Bryana Johnson, Nate Liederbach, Debbie Lim, Sandra Lim, Crystal Simone Smith, and Tess Taylor

Thank you to everyone who entered and congratulations to our winners!

Look for further information for 2013 in the Fall issue of *Ploughshares* and also at

www.dorothyprizes.org

time	space	support
3 years	Austin	$27,500 per year

MFA IN WRITING

THE MICHENER CENTER FOR WRITERS
The University of Texas at Austin

www.utexas.edu/academic/mcw
512-471-1601

BENNINGTON WRITING SEMINARS

MFA in Writing and Literature
Two-Year Low-Residency Program

Read one hundred books.
Write one.

Annual Liam Rector Poetry Prize
*(Open to all current graduating
Writing Seminars poets)*

FICTION ♦ NONFICTION POETRY

Partial Scholarships Available
Bennington College Writing Seminars
One College Drive
Bennington, VT 05201
802-440-4452
www.bennington.edu/MFAWriting

FOUNDER • Liam Rector
DIRECTOR • Sven Birkerts

CORE FACULTY

FICTION
Shannon Cain
Martha Cooley
David Gates
Amy Hempel
Bret Anthony Johnston
Sheila Kohler
Alice Mattison
Jill McCorkle
Askold Melnyczuk
Brian Morton
Rachel Pastan
Lynne Sharon Schwartz
Paul Yoon

NONFICTION
Benjamin Anastas
Sven Birkerts
Susan Cheever
Bernard Cooper
J.C. Hallman
Dinah Lenney
Phillip Lopate

POETRY
April Bernard
David Daniel
Major Jackson
Ed Ochester
Brenda Shaughnessy
Mark Wunderlich

WRITERS-IN-RESIDENCE
Lyndall Gordon
Donald Hall
Rick Moody
Bob Shacochis

PAST FACULTY IN RESIDENCE
André Aciman
Douglas Bauer
Frank Bidart
Tom Bissell
Amy Bloom
Lucie Brock-Broido
Wesley Brown
Peter Campion
Henri Cole
Elizabeth Cox
Robert Creeley
Nicholas Delbanco
Stephen Dobyns
Mark Doty
Stephen Dunn
Thomas Sayers Ellis
Katie Ford
Lynn Freed
Mary Gaitskill
Amy Gerstler
Vivian Gornick
Barry Hannah
Jane Hirshfield
Jane Kenyon
Michael Krüger
David Lehman
Timothy Liu
Barry Lopez
Thomas Lynch
Valerie Martin
E. Ethelbert Miller
Sue Miller
Paul Muldoon
Howard Norman
George Packer
Carl Phillips
Jayne Anne Phillips
Robert Pinsky
Francine Prose
Lia Purpura
David Shields
Jason Shinder
Tree Swenson
Larissa Szporluk
Wells Tower
Rosanna Warren
James Wood

SANTA MONICA *Review*

spring 2013

available now

Fictions & Essays

Lisa Alvarez / Don Waters
Joseph O'Malley / Alice Stern
Michael Cadnum / Benjamin Solomon
A novella by Robley Wilson

Cover: Christopher Hutchinson

$7 copy / **$12** yr. subscription
SM Review / Santa Monica College
1900 Pico Blvd. / Santa Monica, CA 90405
www.smc.edu/sm_review

MA
Master of Arts
Publishing & Writing
- book
- magazine
- electronic

MFA
Master of Fine Arts
Creative Writing
- fiction
- nonfiction
- poetry

EMERSON COLLEGE
BOSTON MASSACHUSETTS

Home to Redivider and Ploughshares

www.emerson.edu • gradapp@emerson.edu • 617.824.8610

PLOUGHSHARES
Stories and poems for literary aficionados

Known for its compelling fiction and poetry, *Ploughshares* is widely regarded as one of America's most influential literary journals. Most issues are guest-edited by a different writer for a fresh, provocative slant—exploring personal visions, aesthetics, and literary circles—and contributors include both well-known and emerging writers. *Ploughshares* has become a premier proving ground for new talent, showcasing the early works of Sue Miller, Edward P. Jones, Tim O'Brien, and countless others. Past guest editors include Richard Ford, Raymond Carver, Derek Walcott, Tobias Wolff, Kathryn Harrison, and Lorrie Moore. This unique editorial format has made *Ploughshares* a dynamic anthology series—one that has established a tradition of quality and prescience. *Ploughshares* is published in April, August, and December, usually with a prose issue in the fall and mixed issues of poetry and fiction in the spring and winter. Inside each issue, you'll find not only great new stories, essays, and poems, but also a profile on the guest editor, book reviews, and miscellaneous notes about *Ploughshares*, its writers, and the literary world. Subscribe today.

Subscribe online at www.pshares.org.

☐ Send me a one-year subscription for $30.
  I save $12 off the cover price (3 issues).

☐ Send me a two-year subscription for $50.
  I save $34 off the cover price (6 issues).

Start with: ☐ Spring ☐ Fall ☐ Winter

Name _____

Address _____

_____

E-mail _____

Mail with check to: Ploughshares · Emerson College
                       120 Boylston St. · Boston, MA 02116

Add $30 per year for international postage ($10 for Canada).